SinceMegalopolis

Since**Megalopolis**

The Urban Writings of Jean Gottmann

Edited by
Jean Gottmann and
Robert A. Harper

The Johns Hopkins University Press
Baltimore and London

©1990 The Johns Hopkins University Press
All rights reserved
Printed in the United States of America

The Johns Hopkins University Press
701 West 40th Street
Baltimore, Maryland 21211
The Johns Hopkins Press Ltd., London

The paper used in this publication meets the
minimum requirements of American National
Standard for Information Sciences—
Permanence of Paper for Printed Library
Materials, ANSI Z39.48-1984.

Frontispiece: Jean Gottmann in 1983. Photograph courtesy of Dr. Rossotti, St. Anne's College, Oxford.

Frieze: Photograph courtesy of Professor
Christos Doumas, Director, Perá Collection,
National Museum of Greece, Athens.

Library of Congress Cataloging-in-Publication
Data will be found on the last page of this
book.

Contents

Preface

In the late 1950s a French geographer, Jean Gottmann, wrote a seminal study on the great metropolitan centers of the northeastern seaboard of the United States for the Twentieth Century Fund. He called his study *Megalopolis* and thereby redefined a term that has become not only a basic part of the language of urbanists throughout the world, but also a standard entry in dictionaries and reference works alike. The word's diffusion is evident by noting its appearance in the recent editions of the Larousse (French) and Japanese encyclopedias and in a forthcoming Italian book on history of the twentieth century. Though many limit Gottmann's contribution to his formulation of the idea of megalopolis, which the *Random House Dictionary* (1966) defines as "an urban region, especially one consisting of several large cities and suburbs that adjoin each other," it was far more than a name or word: megalopolis has formed a blueprint for urban study by Gottmann and urbanists generally.

In retrospect, there are three key reasons why *Megalopolis* became so seminal a work: (1) the timing of the book's publication, (2) Gottmann's decision to focus the study on the then largest metropolitan region in the

world, and (3) the insights of Gottmann's mind. Let's explore these
briefly.

The timing of the book. A new urban form had its beginnings in the
world around 1950. The new urban entity involved the outward sprawl of
the city into economically city-tied, but politically separate, suburbs.
The economy of the suburbs was based on the use of the automobile
and newly designed roads that permitted a shift in the urban employment base from an economy driven by manufacturing to the present service and information functions, particularly what Gottmann called the
quaternary functions: business management, finance, and related support services such as advertising, law, and marketing, among others.
These trends are easy to decipher today, but when Gottmann wrote
Megalopolis they were just developing. He identified them and wrote of
their workings and the rationale behind them. *Megalopolis,* in a significant way, created a new way of interpreting the changing urban scene.

The focus of the study. Gottmann's choice of the northeastern seaboard of the United States provided him with arguably the best location
at the time to examine the emerging trends in urbanization. This region
had long been the leading urban area in the United States, which
boasted the largest modern economy in the world; furthermore, the
region represented the most highly developed concentration of large
urban centers in the world. Here in the corridor from Boston to Washington the shift of the population to the suburbs and to a "white-collar" job
base emerged early, and it spread quickly to other large metropolitan
centers in other parts of the country and world.

The insights of Gottmann's mind. As a geographer, Gottmann approached the study from a holistic perspective of the discipline and with
an attention to the spatial dimensions of the developing patterns he
saw. But he brought far more to the study than would the usual geographer. As a Frenchman, he approached *Megalopolis* without the myopic
view of an American, and, with his classical European education, he uti-
lized his background in art history and architecture, classical history,
and political science to great effect.

For Gottmann *Megalopolis* became more than an end in itself. It was
the beginning of a new focus for the kind of thinking and scholarship
that has accounted for most of his writing ever since. (For a list of his
urban publications, please refer to the bibliography at the end of this
book.) Before *Megalopolis* Gottmann's reputation had been established
in political geography, regional geography, and resource management,
and he had taught these subjects at the Sorbonne in Paris and the
Johns Hopkins University in Baltimore. The major thrust of his writings
had, in fact, been in political geography and they centered on Europe,
the Middle East, and the Soviet Union. But in 1942 Gottmann com-

menced a long stay in the metropolitan northeastern United States that would last until 1965.

Gottmann's intrigue with the metropolitan northeastern seaboard began during World War II when he commuted regularly from Princeton University in New Jersey, where he was a member of the Institute of Advanced Studies, to Washington and to Boston. A position on the faculty of Johns Hopkins and then, in 1946 and 1947, with the United Nations in Lake Success outside New York City gave him the opportunity to view other dimensions of this region. It was within his continued association with the Institute of Advanced Studies, however, that his thinking about megalopolis developed. Abraham Flexner, founder of the institute, arranged for Gottmann to undertake the study, *Virginia at Mid-Century* (Henry Holt, 1955), which took him to the Washington–northern Virginia portion of Megalopolis. In 1950, Robert Oppenheimer, director of the institute, suggested the actual term "megalopolis" during discussion. The term was first used by Gottmann in a French article in the same year; it then appeared in the conclusion of the study of Virginia in 1955. It was Oppenheimer who arranged for the Twentieth Century Fund to underwrite the larger study and the publication of *Megalopolis*. From 1956 until 1960 Gottmann engaged in full-time study of the region.

Since the publication of *Megalopolis* in November 1961 Jean Gottmann has been recognized as one of the world's leading scholars of the urbanization process, and he is regularly invited to present his ideas to international urban conferences and scholarly symposia throughout the world. His work has attracted particular attention in Japan, where the world's largest metropolitan complex has developed between Tokyo and Hiroshima. He has visited the country several times at the invitation of the government and business leaders. In Italy, politicians and scholars have consulted him about their own version of a megalopolis in the plain of the Po River in the North.

Gottmann's writings since the book's publication deal with various dimensions of the large metropolitan centers of the world: the origins of their formation, the importance of urban centrality, the new dimensions of what is now called "the transactional city," and the lifestyle of modern city dwellers. In all he has produced more than eighty articles and papers, and his talks have been reproduced in various collections. Unlike *Megalopolis*, however, his more recent writings have been published in specialized urban journals, particularly *Ekistics*, a periodical developed by C. A. Doxiadis, the urban visionary who was a particular admirer of Gottmann's work. The only collection of Gottmann's urban writings is in a book, *La città Invincibile*, published in Italian in 1983 and reissued in a second edition in 1986.

The dimensions of Gottmann's thinking about modern urbanity have continued to expand in the years since *Megalopolis*. Unfortunately, none of his writings had been collected into one source in English, so the idea came to me to produce this volume. Though Jean and I have been close friends over the years and have continued to correspond about the changing urban scene, it seemed inappropriate for me to make the selections for this book. Thus, I suggested to him that he select from all his many publications those that he thought best expressed his views of urban forces and their results. He welcomed the opportunity, but also pointed out that both the hardcover edition of *Megalopolis* published by the Twentieth Century Fund and the paperback edition published by the MIT Press were out-of-print. This volume, therefore, contains excerpts from *Megalopolis* and Gottmann's personal selection of his urban writings. Gottmann's introduction, "The Opening of the Oyster Shell," is completely original and was prepared for this volume. It presents his current thinking on the subject.

The final selection of the chapters is Gottmann's, as I have stated. I suggested that they be grouped into the seven sections contained herein to reveal the various dimensions of his thinking, and I selected the excerpts from *Megalopolis* to provide his base line judgment on the subject. With the exception of part IV and part V, the chapters are presented in chronological order so the reader can appreciate the development of Gottmann's ideas over time. The chapters are reproduced as they originally appeared, without updating or further editing, except for the elimination of the few original illustrations, which were in too poor a condition to photoreproduce, and some minor changes to make the chapters consistent in style and format.

This book is the definitive statement of Jean Gottmann's views on the urban scene since World War II. It is not his last word, however. Though he is retired, his interest in the changing urban landscape is as active and progressive in outlook as ever, and he continues to write and lecture. It is to be hoped that the present volume will stand only as the first of a set of volumes that will contain new research and writing by this master of urban geography.

Robert A. Harper
Professor Emeritus
Department of Geography
University of Maryland
College Park

Acknowledgments

Jean Gottmann and Robert A. Harper express their gratitude to the publishers of those writings by Jean Gottmann which are reproduced here by the publishers' permission: The Twentieth Century Fund, New York City, New York, authorizes the reproduction of long excerpts from Gottmann's book, *Megalopolis: The Urbanized Northeastern Seaboard of the United States* (1961); the review, *Ekistics,* Athens, Greece, authorizes the republication of the papers and articles that have been published earlier therein; and *The Town Planning Review,* Liverpool, England, authorizes the republication of the papers, "Planning and Metamorphosis in Japan" and "Urbanization and Employment: Towards a General Theory." The other chapters in this book are at the disposal of Jean Gottmann, for reproduction and distribution. Specific credits for the chapters appear below:

Chapter 1, "Orbits: The Ancient Mediterranean Tradition of Urban Networks," was presented as the Twelfth J. L. Myres Memorial Lecture, Oxford University, Oxford, England, 2 May 1983.

Chapter 2, "Urban Centrality and the Interweaving of Quaternary Activities," originally appeared under the same title in *Ekistics,* May 1970, pages 322–31.

Chapter 3 combines two articles, "Capital Cities" which originally appeared in *Ekistics,* March/April 1983, pages 88–93, and "The Role of Capital Cities" which originally appeared in *Ekistics,* November 1977, pages 240–43.

Chapter 4, "The Study of Former Capitals," originally appeared under the same title in *Ekistics,* September/October–November/December 1985, pages 541–46.

Chapter 5, "Economics, Esthetics, and Ethics in Modern Urbanization," originally published by the Twentieth Century Fund, appeared in *Ekistics,* April 1963, pages 197–204.

Chapter 6, "The Growing City as a Social and Political Process," originally appeared under the same title in *Transactions of the Bartlett Society,* 1968, pages 11–46.

Chapter 7, "How Large Can Cities Grow?" originally appeared under the same title in *Revista da Universidad de Coimbra,* 1978, pages 3–14.

Chapter 8, "Megalopolitan Systems around the World," originally appeared under the same title in *Ekistics,* February 1976, pages 109–13.

Chapter 9, "Planning and Metamorphosis in Japan," originally appeared under the same title in *Town Planning Review,* April 1980, pages 171–76.

Chapter 10, "Office Work and the Evolution of Cities," originally appeared under the same title in *Ekistics,* January/February 1979, pages 4–7.

Chapter 11, "Urban Settlements and Telecommunications," originally appeared under the same title in *Ekistics,* September/October 1983, pages 411–16.

Chapter 12, "The Recent Evolution of Oxford," originally appeared under the same title in *Ekistics,* January/February 1979, pages 33–36.

Chapter 13, "The Ethics of Living at High Densities," originally appeared under the same title in *Ekistics,* February 1966, pages 141–45.

Chapter 14, "Urbanization and Employment: Towards a General Theory," originally appeared under the same title in *Town Planning Review,* July 1978, pages 201–8.

Chapter 15, "The Metamorphosis of the Modern Metropolis," originally appeared under the same title in *Ekistics,* January/February 1982, pages 7–10.

Chapter 16, "Transatlantic Orbits: The Interplay in the Evolution of Cities," originally appeared under the same title in M. P. Conzen, editor, *World Patterns of Modern Urban Change,* 1986, pages 457–72.

Since**Megalopolis**

This book is the result of twenty years of study . . . *Megalopolis* is a vast area. It encompasses many great cities, and its population is now close to 38 million, which is more the size of a nation than of a metropolis. It contains one of the largest industrial belts in existence and the greatest financial and political hubs on earth . . .

What is offered here can hardly be called a description. The writer has not aimed at a portrait of the area and its people, though he believes that it could have been a worthy and exciting enterprise. Rather he has endeavored to analyze and understand the extraordinary dynamics that have created, in a place that was a wilderness three centuries ago, the enormous and powerful concentration of people and activities now achieved in Megalopolis. Nowhere else have men ever built anything comparable, and with such a rhythm.

Exceptional as it is, the urbanization of this part of the Atlantic seaboard of North America has been a signal of a steady trend toward the concentration of dense populations in large urbanized regions, a trend gradually becoming characteristic of this century. The distribution of habitat and economic activities is thus changing; new modes of life are appearing and spreading. This process, which marks an essential turning point of history, has been most advanced in this region, Megalopolis. In this book the urbanization of Megalopolis is presented as a significant experiment, the lessons of which must be taken into account not only by the people living in the area but by those of many other lands as well.

Megalopolis,
Preface

Introduction

The Opening
of the
Oyster Shell

Since *Megalopolis* was published in 1961, the world has been changing fast, largely as a result of continuing rapid urbanization. Several of the basic trends of change within the area of Megalopolis were clear before 1960, and they were described or at least hinted at in that book. In the twenty-five years after its publication, these trends, some spatial, some socioeconomic, were observed elsewhere around the world. Having diagnosed these trends early, I wrote many articles that followed up points made in the original study of the urbanized northeastern seaboard of the United States, describing the evolution of urbanization, analyzing its major characteristics, generalizing from observations first made by 1961. When I started my inquiry in 1956, I already had a strong feeling of the role that Megalopolis was playing as an incubator of new urbanization, as a laboratory for new experiments which would be repeated, with some variation, in many other places. That feeling has since proved to be right.

The articles reproduced in the present volume enlarge, update, and generalize the ideas first expressed in *Megalopolis;* they are introduced by quotations from that book which is already out of print. This presentation, for which I am grateful to Robert A. Harper, shows the continuity of thought over almost thirty years, and proceeds from a particular case in point to more general observations. What began as the study of a spatial, regional complex, increasingly turned to concerns and even predictions emphasizing social and economic developments. Now, a good quarter of a century later, I realize that I was dealing with a mutation in the very nature of the city, and in the behavior of urban society.

The Modern Mutation of Urban Structures

Any city of some size is an extremely complex, multifaceted, multipurpose entity. This complexity has often been examined mainly in considering the components of its standing concrete structures: the buildings, the land use, the engineering infrastructure—all that is often called nowadays the "built environment." In this way the city or metropolitan region is reduced to its most easily perceived and measured tangible form. However, everybody realizes that what makes a city live is the people within it. The city exists by and for the people. A town emptied of population is a ruin, a remnant of past activity, at best a museum like Delos in Greece, Pompeii in Italy, or Monte Alban in Mexico. So, if the description and analysis of a city may start with the environment, natural and built, this is only an introduction to its people, with their activities and ways of life.

This truth is usually accepted, and any assessment of the size and importance of a city begins not with area, or number and height of buildings, but with the number of the population. That is the first characteristic given; the population is 50,000, or one million, or more inhabitants. The measure of size, in fact, involves also the makeup of the population and of the activities that congregate in the place: both must obviously be more varied for a million people than for 50,000 or 100,000. That degree of inner diversity increases considerably the complexity of the system in terms of the built environment to be provided and maintained, as well as in terms of the social, economic, and cultural problems that arise in the daily function of urban society.

Urbanization has been proceeding at an accelerated pace in the twentieth century and will continue to do so, especially in the developing countries where the migration from rural to urban areas has only begun and where the birthrate is much higher. The well-developed countries, however, still often experience some internal migration, largely from small towns towards the larger cities in which the scope of opportunity appears greater. Moreover the large, famous cities of Europe and North America attract migrants from more distant parts of the world, mainly underdeveloped. Flows of emigration out of East and South

Asia, Latin America, Africa have largely replaced the influx of Europeans. The newcomers aim at the better life they hope for in the great cities of the developed nations. These currents keep swelling the population in many a metropolis: Indians, Pakistanis, West Africans, and West Indians in Britain; Algerians, Moroccans, Portuguese, and Vietnamese in France; Yugoslavs and Turks in West Germany; people from all parts of the world in the United States and Canada. Never has there been such a mixing of races and cultures. The homogeneity of a city's community appears forever broken.

For the cities these migrations mean growth everywhere, and many more problems of a socioeconomic nature. At the same time, the inner organization of a city or even of a metropolitan area is being modified by the advances of technology that force radical changes in the division of labor at national and international scales, and in the modes of living, working, and relaxing of large strata of the population. The greatest changes occurred first in the more advanced countries, where the technology was evolved, first applied, and most widely used. The shift in the labor force from mass employment in the production of goods and basic services towards the advanced, specialized services, and the emergence of an "information society" are now well known and recognized, and have begun to be accepted. The developing countries have been slowly evolving in this direction, but as they have only started to take advantage of motorization, automation, electronics, and so forth, most of them are now gradually going through the earlier stages of industrial revolution. Mechanization requires huge equipment, for which massive and continued investment is necessary.

But the advanced economies are forging ahead, reshaping their own structures. I announced and analyzed these trends in my old book on Megalopolis, especially in chapter 11 ("The White Collar Revolution"). By emphasizing the rise in quantity and quality of white-collar employment, and the shrinkage of blue-collar numbers, I also stressed a fundamental social and cultural mutation of urban society. The specialized, highly skilled white-collar workers have other ways of work, behavior, and relaxation, and other interests and concerns than the unskilled or little skilled workers of old. The shift from brawn to brain involved many changes in the way of life; most people overlooked the significance of the new motto propagated since the 1950s for its employees by the great electronics corporation IBM: "Think!"

The present volume gathers many of the articles, written on various occasions, that I wrote after 1961, debating different aspects of this momentous evolution, both in terms of size and in terms of structure, of urban society. The resulting picture varies according to the angle of approach. It also varies from one part of the world to another: ways of building and managing cities result from inherited cultures; people may have the same technology at their disposal but the use of technological means is a product of regional culture. It is obviously an error to assume that all cities tend to be the same around the world even if they use the same materials in their buildings and roadways.

There are so many facets, problems, and variations in the presently ongoing urbanization of the majority of humankind that one must choose a few particular aspects in analyzing this massive phenomenon. To introduce the ideas developed in this book, it seems proper to begin by outlining the consequences of urban growth before proceeding to the new dynamics of the society living in and around the cities.

Growth, Size, and Form

The rapid growth of most cities around the world has been much written about and analyzed by specialists. However the pace of it has entailed changes in form and structure that have often been misunderstood, and the picture obtained from scholarly analysis has become blurred. The complexity of the process appears due to the concurring action of three factors in the past century: first, the rise in the number of people attracted to cities, as mentioned above; second, the concomitant expansion of the financial means of a large proportion of that population; third, the rapid advances in the mechanization of production and transportation. The recent growth has been so fast that it appears increasingly difficult to measure adequately.

Let us consider first the category of the very large cities. By 1800 only some six metropolises (that is, large cities with adjoining suburbs) had reached the size of half a million inhabitants: Tokyo, London, Constantinople-Istanbul, Paris, Naples, and probably Peking. Today we have about two hundred metropolises of a million or more. Despite rules prohibiting expansion in many large cities in the Soviet Union, the number of cities there with more than a million population jumped from three in 1959 to twenty-two in 1986. In fact, large cities are already difficult to count. The suburbs of Washington, D.C., mingle in Maryland around Columbia with those of Baltimore; through the Princeton corridor in New Jersey, the extensions of New York City merge with those of Philadelphia; the continuity of urbanization from Tokyo southward envelops Kawasaki and Yokohama. How should we count in these cases: seven metropolises of more than a million each or three multimillion conurbations? The observer's perplexity increases when speaking of cities *stricto sensu* and looking at the tight clusters of municipal entities, each of which claims more than 50,000 inhabitants by census count.

Increasingly it becomes more realistic to speak of *metropolitan regions* with one or more "central cities."

The difficulties are compounded as censuses announce that the population of the central city—that is, of the central nucleus from which growth started and which usually still is the largest municipal unit, and which gives its name to the metropolis—has been decreasing; it may well fall below the population gathered in the suburban ring. As we grow statistically minded, we cannot help considering the rates of growth or decline of the various administrative units we are examining—municipalities, counties, metropolitan regions, or districts. Now, the rates of growth are usually higher in the smaller towns in suburban areas than in the central, larger, and older cities. If we project them, we see those central places emptying, perhaps melting away. In the 1970s in the United States, population grew more rapidly in "nonmetropolitan areas" than in the metropolitan systems, reversing the trend of the previous thirty years. Some specialists of urban studies began to talk of "counterurbanization" as if the whole urban world of several thousands of years past was over and was going to be replaced by a new fully dispersed pattern of habitat.

By 1985, however, a movement back to metropolitan areas and centers was reported by the U.S. Bureau of the Census. The excitement about the city fading away and a future of counterurbanization had developed mainly in the United States and in the United Kingdom. There was little talk to the same effect on the continent of Europe, in Japan, or in Latin America, although in several of these countries official decentralization policies were in place. Perhaps some schools of scholars and officials put more trust into temporary statistics and the resulting projections than others. One should also account with historical background and current economic conditions: from all we know it is clear, for instance, that cities in the Third World and in the socialist countries keep growing, and the central districts there are not being emptied of population, as happens in the richer countries such as the United States, Canada, Great Britain, and so on. Economic means and standards of living have much to do with the location of residences. The American tradition early on was clearly to separate the areas where workplaces were located, the *downtowns,* from the desirable residential districts which were *uptown,* towards the periphery. And uptown moved progressively outward, farther away from the business centers, as the city grew.

Population growth, obviously, leads a city to consume more ground space to provide housing, places of work, and various services for the increasing number of inhabitants. To some extent space can be saved by increasing density—at work, at home, and in transit. However there are strict limits to densities unless slum conditions are allowed to develop. Rapid and massive population growth causes more space to be urbanized and the city system to expand outward. Economic expansion and greater opulence, even if for a part of the people, lead to greater consumption per capita, extending the city's size in area; suburbs will sprawl beyond older city limits. The city may come to annex the urbanized ring adjacent to it, as occurred over the centuries in all substantially developed cities, which grew by adding such suburban rings to their territory. Many European cities underwent this growth in size, gradually modifying their shape, as is now demonstrated on their plans. Paris is a classic case in point with its rings of boulevards which replaced the successive belts of circular ramparts, until the city reached its present size and form. To extend its territory farther out, the city of Paris would have to annex a wide belt of strongly constituted, densely settled towns and cities adjoining it, but which house a population whose social, economic, and political profile is very different from that of the central city. Hence the strong political resistance to such annexation from both sides, neither wanting to be absorbed into the other.

The case of Paris demonstrates a limit to the traditional process of annexation of suburban rings. Metropolitan systems may be recognized and institutionalized in order to coordinate the administration of a cluster of adjoining cities which must work together while having perhaps diverse interests. A certain division of labor is gradually ironed out among the cities forming one metropolitan system. Many residents of each of those cities work in another neighboring municipality. Expansion of the financial means and of the transportation networks, by road or rail, concur in facilitating the migration of residences farther out to a greener periphery, where real estate is cheaper and is expected to rise in value. Good investment prospects, ease of transport, better environment—all invite this outward movement. Consumer services such as schools and retail trades follow residences to keep close to the consumer. But places of work do not migrate so easily and so fast, though some do; especially manufacturing production and warehousing establishments in need of cheap ground space and easy access now move often but usually beyond the residential belts.

An enormous and dense commuting movement develops within metropolitan clusters. In larger cities this movement often becomes so dense and congested that it consumes much daily time and spoils the quality of life. Urbanites wish they could live as close as possible to their places of work. Some move back towards central cities, where property costs may rise; in other cases corporations or government agencies move part of their offices and personnel to suburban or interurban locations. New cities appear, often creating strings of "emerging cities" in suburban areas. In some cases these "emerging cities," really satellites of major central cities, build up their own downtowns, thus in Washington's suburbia Tyson's Corner and Arlington, in northern Virginia, and Bethesda, in Maryland. This is also true in several places in Long Island, Connecticut, and northern New Jersey, on both sides of New York City. Sometimes this peripheral growth is carefully planned: for instance, the "new towns" around London and more recently around Paris, or the new academic city of Tsukuba on the periphery of the Tokyo metropolitan region. But in the great majority of cases the expansion has not been planned at all and has developed a chaotic sprawl. Frequent and rapid rail connections may foster commuting to the heart of the central metropolis from not-too-distant cities that are large and well-established but smaller than the metropolis: thus from Yokohama to Tokyo, from Rouen to Paris, or from Oxford to London. The result of these trends is to complicate in an unforeseen manner the map of metropolitan regions and to create in some areas seemingly unlimited expansion in space. Old urban shapes may be lost in the process. New concepts are called for to understand what is going on, and the concept of megalopolis has been helpful when applied to the larger of these complex and expanding systems. Hence the adoption of it by the Japanese for Tokaido, which, still extending westward and even northeastward, is today the largest and densest of recognized megalopolitan systems, counting some seventy million inhabitants.

Meanwhile, what is happening in the old, large, central cities? The idea, long propagated, of their dissolution or at least their being reduced to one of the many components of a vast, little differentiated, semiurban tissue, has proved to be wrong and has been abandoned. The major cities, even if undergoing profound change, indeed a real mutation, have remained very lively and very central. The out-migration of residents to suburbia, or beyond, has reduced the population count because censuses count people at their homes, that is, where they sleep. But during office hours on workdays the centers are often as crowded as they ever were, perhaps even over a wider area, because the old business districts have been expanding laterally and vertically; in some very crowded cities, such as in Japan, they have been expanding underground.

In several chapters of this book this mutation is analyzed from several approaches, and in several instances. I like to cite the case of the city of London, this ancient downtown of the English capital, where the census population dropped from 250,000 in mid-nineteenth century to some 5,000 to 7,000 in 1960–80, but the number of people present at midday on an ordinary working day is estimated at about 300,000, if not more. Some cities, particularly in Japan where commuting takes on huge proportions, have had counts made of both daytime and nighttime populations. The ratio of one to the other may be quite high, close to ten or higher in the central districts of major cities. In the square mile of the city of London it approximates thirty to forty. However the same night/day ratio calculated for the adjoining city of Westminster and its surroundings should be much lower. Although it is largely an area of offices and institutions mostly closed at night, there are many more people who work there at night and even sleep there, not so many in actual residences, but in large and numerous hotels.

The role of hotels and other lodgings for temporary visitors in many major cities brings us to another aspect of the sorts of people who gather there. The central cities have always been crossroads, meeting places; that was the main function of their centrality. That function has grown enormously, partly because of the stupendous expansion of tourist travel in our time, and partly because the major old centers of business have kept that function, and have even concentrated the crucial activities of information gathering and of dispensing modern wisdom. Despite all the endeavors at decentralization, all the paraphernalia of telecommunications, all the attempts at delegating certain functions to smaller or newer centers, the larger well-established crossroad cities keep their power to attract large and dense flows of people from far beyond commuting range for special business. These visitors are transients but not tourists. They come to transact some business that is important to them and which they feel could not be done as well, if at all, without spending some time in that great central city.

The business transients may come for short visits—usually they still spend at least one night in the crossroads city. Many among them return there periodically, at more or less frequent intervals. This movement may be likened to irregular long-distance, often international, and even intercontinental commuting. Many institutions from distant lands—governmental, financial, or industrial, some even of a cultural nature—are known to maintain permanent lodgings for members of their management, or associates, in London, Paris, New York, Tokyo, Washington, Brussels, Rome, or even Geneva and Zurich. These are great transactional cities, great lobbying centers; most of them are also political capitals. Each of these major centers attracts on an average day thousands of such visitors on business. Many lesser centers have nevertheless equivalent functions, even if on a smaller scale and for not so worldwide a drainage area. These observations call for examining the new dynamics which are developing in lively cities.

The Hinge Function and Networks

The essential reason for the mutation in the nature of city centrality is an expansion that is unrelated to the size, shape, or number of residents of the city and that is therefore a very novel trend. It may be called an *expansion of the horizons* of urban activities. First, the expansion affects geographical horizons: in days of yore a city's center connected the city itself with the surrounding region which depended on it for various services and for communications with the outside world, to the extent that this region and city needed the outside and maintained relations with other places. The range of these relations seldom extended very far, unless the city was a political capital of substance, or a very active seaport. Even in the latter case the networks of external relations were usually rather limited. Only a few selected cities in specially endowed locations were and long remained great crossroads with far-flung intricate networks.

Geographical horizons extended gradually with international trade, exploration, and improvement of the means and security of transportation, especially by sea. The expansion of horizons was made possible by geographical knowledge and by transport technology, but it was really fostered or restricted by the community's attitude towards the outside. How much did the city or the community want to deal with outsiders, foreigners, exotic people? The reaction to the opportunity offered by science and technology varied greatly with nations and cultures, and even with local communities. Thus western and southern Europeans showed generally a much greater willingness to travel afar, establish relationships with strangers, and settle in new, exotic environments than the peoples of China, India, or Japan, who, even though they knew how to navigate and strike across the sea, and were familiar with long-distance caravan trade, preferred to stay closer to home. The Romans established settlements in India in ancient times, but the Indians began coming to Europe only in the last 200 years. Traders from Venice, Genoa, or Lombardy were established in Chinese cities or in Southeast Asia in the Middle Ages; Marco Polo and his family were no exception, but Chinese merchants were not known to come to European cities before the eighteenth century, and even then were often brought in by European partners. The roads of the silk or spice trade were known to Asians for a long time. They did not seem interested in going far out to establish new connections. They left to middlemen the task of creating and maintaining these networks.

Within a nation or a culture some communities proved to be more adventurous, more eager to enlarge their horizons than others. Thus in France, Bretons and Normands were more adventurous than others, and people from Paris and Lyon much more than those from the cities of the Loire Valley or Languedoc. It would be easy to multiply the examples of such differences in outlook, in attitudes. We may call them cultural, for they must be rooted in local cultures. However even cultural attitudes evolve and may change radically under the impact of certain events. Today, Indians, Chinese, Japanese, and Koreans migrate much more easily, travel in large numbers all around the world, and mix willingly with other nations, though differences remain; the Japanese, for instance, emigrate much less frequently and more reluctantly than the Chinese or Indians.

Here again geographical and historical differences may be observed. Attitudes towards travel and migration have varied in each nation during successive periods of history. The French and the British began to travel afar, explore, and settle in distant lands from the sixteenth century on; in the French case one may even go back to the Crusades from the twelfth century on. But the Greeks and Italians had begun long before. Old cultural links establish lasting lines of communication, cultural orbits that survive many crises. Thus South Americans gravitate more towards Spain, Portugal, and France than towards countries of northwestern Europe. Australia, New Zealand, Canada, and India remain to a large extent in the British orbit, despite a special relationship developing with the United States. The English-speaking world forms a huge cultural orbit of its own.

Modern cities evolve their networks of connections along diverse lines, but among these, old cultural and political relations remain paramount. However they also compete for markets and customers of the services they offer, or for establishments and personnel offering specialized services. The quality and diversity of the specialists in various fields cannot be the same everywhere. In past history the importance of a city depended on the size, wealth, and cultural influence of its "orbit," that is, the area for which that city was the main center. If the city was a political capital, the orbit was obviously the national territory plus the dependent lands, if any. If it was a seaport, the orbit of the city was its hinterland plus the network of maritime connections it had established. If a specialized industrial center, its orbit was composed of its markets plus a certain surrounding area gravitating to it for the usual urban services.

The larger and more successful cities were usually of all three kinds at the same time, with preferably a variety of industrial specializations. The greater the diversity of specialized services that the place could offer, the higher would be the probability of its vitality and success as a crossroads and socioeconomic center. That was how a powerful and successful city would attract more people to it to work, transact business, and use its ancillary services—the latter extending from health care to entertainment of all sorts. Thus the "hosting environment" is an important characteristic of a transactional city, and that character developed early in large political and commercial centers. Not all the elements of transactional activities and environment have been virtuous. Hence the reproaches and condemnations heard throughout the ages against large, blossoming cities, to begin with the outcries in the Bible against places such as Babylon and Nineveh.

The organization of services, especially those that require and provide specialized skills and information, is always of decisive importance for the role, influence, and prosperity of a city, however large or small the orbit it serves. The ability to attract such highly competent personnel is of course linked to local culture, wealth, and hosting environment. Good climate, exciting regional entertainment, well-organized means of access, political stability—in short, a high quality of life, is indispensable to the development of new centers of transactions, as is illustrated by the case of the French Riviera, which attracts research, many laboratories, institutes, and international conferences. But the rapid emergence of such new centers is rather uncommon. The process is usually gradual. In contrast, great old cities, leading crossroads for a diversity of activities—transactional, cultural, industrial—have a better chance of preserving their centrality for centuries, even though the nature of the centrality may evolve: thus Rome, Constantinople-Istanbul, Alexandria, Venice, Milan, Lisbon, Paris, London, Moscow, Amsterdam, Cologne (of which Bonn was long just a satellite), Kyoto, Osaka, Canton, and in the New World, Boston, Montreal, Mexico City, Lima, Buenos Aires, and Rio de Janeiro.

The question arises: What determines the orbit gravitating around the center? To what are the scope and strength of the centrality due? Much that is written in the preceding pages and in other chapters of this book attempts to answer these questions and to analyze the evolution of a city's centrality. At first look it appears that this century has produced a major shift in the role of urban centers. It has modified the role of a city as a hinge between the region surrounding it and the outside area with which the population of the city and its region maintained regular relations. In the past a city first of all served its region and acted as a hinge linking the different parts of that region. That function defined the orbit of the city and its centrality. On a secondary plan, the city also acted as a hinge linking the various components of its orbit to places outside it with which it had business to be transacted. The internal networks of the orbit were more important by far than the external networks. In recent times this relationship has largely been reversed. Almost every region of some size on the globe has become so dependent for its prosperity, security, and progress on other, often distant regions and places, that the long-range, distant networks of relationships must be reckoned as essential. More than a regional center, a central city is the hub of relations linking together the partners in a diverse, vast weave of cities, regions, and countries.

Thus the evolution of urban centrality leads to the breaking up of much of the tight regional compartmentalization of humankind. This evolution developed gradually through many stages recorded in history. As we have already indicated, it was brought about first through exploration, then through trade, often also through conquest that established empires, and finally it was facilitated by the progress of technology and knowledge. Through the ages there has been much interplay between all the factors and methods of building up and extending networks. The aim of a political empire was usually to achieve certain economic and cultural integration of the different parts. Military expansion was often prompted by the desire to secure trading routes and control markets. Modern urban networks may carry the imprint of past empires: cities in areas that at some time belonged to the British or French or Dutch colonial systems preserve privileged relations of various kinds with London or Paris or Amsterdam. A few years ago, for instance, a telephone call from the Ivory Coast, formerly a French colony, to neighboring Ghana, formerly a British colony, had to be routed by way of Paris and London. This example illustrates the interplay of politics and technology in shaping existing networks. Trade, language, and investments usually reinforce old infrastructures.

It could also be argued that external networks have been of greater importance than regional ones for certain categories of cities, mainly great international trading centers, such as Venice, Genoa, Milan, Liverpool or Antwerp, Singapore, and Boston, and for the capital cities of great empires, such as Rome, Constantinople, London, Paris and Lisbon, to mention a few. These capitals, whose roles are sketched in another chapter of this volume, usually retain the direction of vast extended networks well after they may have lost most of their distant dependencies, owing to the lasting vitality of economic and cultural relationships. In my original work on Megalopolis, I developed, almost as the nucleus of a general theory, the concept of the hinge as a major function of the main cities of that remarkable region, a hinge around which the American economy revolved. That economy grew so fast, however, and on such a scale as to make the national system of the United States paramount in the development and prosperity of the megalopolitan cities. Only in the cases of Boston and New York would their international linkages, extending early around the world, be considered of essential importance, and indeed decisive, for their growth and national role.

Some cities in extending faraway connections have been more daring and adventurous than others located in the same part of the world. It has been observed that great cities were often seaports, especially when located at or near the mouth of navigable rivers. Planners early in history recognized the advantages of such a position, as is evidenced by the choices made by Alexander the Great, a notable city builder, who sited one Alexandria on the delta of the Nile and another at the mouth of the Indus. The chapter that follows on orbits traces the origins of long-range urban networks around the Mediterranean.

Probably other networks linking a number of cities developed early in China and India. We have, however, little detailed historical information on the urban and economic past of these great civilizations. Recording the past and the present has been, it seems, a speciality of Europeans, as well as the exploration of distant lands. Hence the central role of people of European origin in starting the trends that, as we have seen, have led to our present information society. Other old cultures, especially Japan, have realized recently the importance and creativity of information gathering and analyzing, and are vying with Europe and North America in these fields.

The importance of seaside location has been decreasing gradually with the constant improvement in the means of transportation by land and by air, and the networks of telecommunications. Airplanes and telephone calls now cross maritime and continental space with equal facility, though restricted by politics and organizational skills much more than by the physical features of the planet. However, owing to a long-established tradition of hinge activities at the contact of land and sea, and to old networks of overseas linkages, gathering and exchanging information, the great seaports have generally preserved their dominating role as crossroads and transactional centers.

The majority of the large cities we have mentioned are or have been seaports. The coat of arms of the city of Paris, which is no longer accessible to modern seagoing vessels, still shows a ship, tossed on the waves, which floats and does not sink. Moscow, located deep inland, is linked by a monumental system of canals and rivers to several seas. Chicago and Detroit, like Toronto, owe a great deal to their position on the Great Lakes, a water system comparable to an inland sea and now connected for navigation to the Atlantic Ocean by the St. Lawrence Seaway. Mattei Dogan, in an introductory chapter to a two-volume survey entitled *The Metropolis Era,* discusses "Giant Cities as Maritime Gateways" and concludes: "To establish that among the 300 giant cities of the world more than two-thirds are on the water is a significant fact which helps us to understand better how our world is built" (M. Dogan and J. D. Kasarda, 1988, p. 54).

Dogan revives the theory earlier offered by the American economist C. H. Cooley in 1894, and elaborated by the French geographer Paul Vidal de la Blache (1910), that cities locate at points where a break in transportation occurs. This principle certainly applied generally in the past. It should be observed, however, that such breaks between water and land transport exist along very extended coastlines and large rivers, but that at only a few points on these long lines of access to navigable water did cities emerge and grow. The choice of the point where the break in transportation was organized depended on a series of factors concurring—topographical, political, social. Physical geography plus considerations of security can hardly explain large cities such as Singapore and Hong Kong rising on small islands off a continent. Rather, the explanation lies in different cultural and economic networks coming together in a place favorable to the establishment of a crossroads and emporium: thus the British and Chinese networks in Hong Kong, the British, Chinese, Malayan, and Indonesian in Singapore. In antiquity a great city flourished for 600 years on the small and craggy island of Delos in the Aegean Sea. When circumstances excluded it from the predominant networks, it fell into ruins. Now an archeological museum, Delos reminds us that cities are human artifacts and exist by participating in systems of relationships, not just as eagle nests.

Those systems of relationships must be serviced by the city in ways that are useful to and appreciated by outsiders. The range of the catchment area for outsiders has expanded rapidly in the twentieth century, as is shown by our outline of the modern processes of growth, migration, and network building. The expansion of the catchment area has also meant the coming together of more peoples, cultures, and cities. Rather than being simply the center of a region, the city has become a participant within a partnership of many cities. Probably it always needed to function that way. But the city is only now becoming fully conscious of the new dynamics of a world increasingly woven tightly together.

The Opening of the Oyster Shell

In the beginning of his *Politics*, Aristotle said that cities were started by families settling together in one place for the sake of security, then they remained there for the sake of a good life. The search for security and a better life still goes on. Even trading cities opened only gradually and recently. In 1950 the executive secretary of the Chamber of Commerce at Le Havre, a large French seaport, who was a learned and thoughtful man, recalled that his grandfather had had to be within the city walls by sunset, otherwise, as the gates of Le Havre were closed for the night, he would have had to stay outside.

The closing of city gates at night is an old custom, the security reflex of a tightly organized community. It seemed natural that a city would strive to be such a community. Strangers, the *metecs,* the foreign merchants had specially reserved quarters, often outside the walls, forming suburbs or ghettos. Gradually in recent centuries the urban communities of Western cities, particularly those which were capitals of empires or trading centers, began to open up. Perhaps they felt strong and secure enough; perhaps they had convinced themselves of the virtues of a gradual assimilation of the newcomers into their community. The process helped to break up ethnocentricity and to develop more universal features in the cultures of the West European and North American nations. In a famous satire of the 1730s entitled *Persian Letters,* the French writer and jurist Montesquieu described the way that Paris society received a visiting nobleman from Persia: "How could one be Persian?" exclaimed the French gentry; and the refined Iranian was just as astonished by the French, the Spaniards, the Portuguese. In the ensuing 250 years urban communities have continued to open up, though segregation, misunderstanding, and friction persist. The "melting pot" process, pioneered by America, has not yet produced a fully homogenized alloy. The Canadians prefer to speak now of a "mosaic" when describing their nation.

The new city hall of the large Canadian metropolis of Toronto, which rises above a wide open plaza, is an evocative symbol. It was designed by a young Finnish architect. With its two high, curved office towers encasing a round cupola over the council chamber at their base, the city hall, when examined from a distance, evokes a huge oyster opening its shell rising towards the sky. To an analyst of urban affairs it offers a powerful image. It may be hinting, first, at the building's function of housing the governments of both the central city and the metropolitan area of Toronto, and represent the opening up of an old city. Second, it may be hinting at the opening up of the local traditional society to the varied components of the population of Metro-Toronto, comprising newcomers from many countries and cultures—an involved mosaic. But the symbol of the opening oyster shell rising into the sky evokes even more: the interests and connections of the city which extend far beyond the traditional Canadian and British orbits. Toronto has become and wants to be a "world city," challenging in that respect its old rival Montreal, which, being bicultural and a great oceanic port, has had a more cosmopolitan tradition.

The term "world city," little used in the past, has recently come into vogue. It is indicative of the process widening a city's horizons. The term is particularly popular in West Germany, where several cities claim to be a *Weltstadt*. Munich has been advertising itself as a "world city with a soul!" The word *Weltstadt* seems to have been coined (according to the *Grimm Deutsches Worterbuch*) by Goethe himself, who in 1787 applied it first to Rome and later also to Paris. Afterwards the term was often used in German literature to designate cities with broad geographical interests and connections, not specifically for the extent of the city's cultural influence, which is what Goethe seemed to have had in mind. In 1915 the Scottish planner Patrick Geddes used "world city" to designate vaguely very large urban systems with widespread networks, such as the Boston–New York–Philadelphia system.

The term began to be used more frequently in English in the 1970s, being first applied to the largest urban centers with truly worldwide relationships and influence. Increasingly, however, the use has spread, and cities proliferate which want to be "world cities" in some respect. To be able to extend the business networks of a community to most of the world is of course a logical desire for any transactional center or growing corporation. Many large corporations merit being classified as multinational. The increasingly involved division of labor among individuals as well as organizations and smaller firms, as they produce and distribute products in a competitive and demanding environment, also causes a greater dependence of each specialist on many others around the world.

Conclusion

Every city tries to be a microcosm of the astonishing variety of humankind. No longer is it fashionable for a city as a whole to aim to be a homogeneous, tightly knit community, though some small sections of it may preserve such structures. New York City is probably the most spectacular example of this trend in recent times. A distinguished Greek planner, Panayis Psomopoulos, wrote me in July 1988, after a visit to New York which had brought him out of Manhattan to look at Brooklyn: "New York is the city of the world, because it combines on the same spot all the patterns and life styles of all cities, large and small, wealthy and poor, no matter in what continent."

Many other cities, particularly in the wealthy countries, experience similar trends even if on a more modest scale. Success, wealth, and power attract crowds of those who do not have such benefits but hope to achieve them once implanted in the place that breeds them. The result often appears to be chaotic. To a modern scientifically trained mind the complexity and fluidity of the current urban phenomena are frustrating. How could order be brought out of such chaos? In many places, particularly on university campuses, the young generations call for basic reforms in all fields, from syllabuses to ways of behavior and trends of thought. They seldom realize that most of the present trends have long existed somewhere deep in urban society.

The difficulty today resides in the speed of change, in the unexpected shifts of trends, in the fragility of forecasts, in the tide of rising expectations, in the opening of closed societies. Things have been made worse by the neglect to which most cities in the world have been subjected. While plans and surveys have proliferated, consequent action has in general been slow and scattered, as those in charge have been discouraged by the difficulty of the task. Once a good plan to improve the built environment of a metropolis is readied and agreed, it takes ten to twenty years to construct it, and in this time needs, means, and problems change considerably. Moreover physical change lags behind social change; the main barriers to attempts to adapt to the latter are in the minds of people.

Still, in chaotic and disconcerting ways, change develops in and around people and within all strata of society. New cultures, new structures are gradually emerging in the lively and exciting cities of today. The new forms differ from place to place; they cannot be the same in New York and Beijing or Moscow, in London and Tokyo, not even in Paris and Brussels. They are not yet stabilized and may not be for some time to come. Much of what is happening shocks our established taste and threatens our expectations and old scales of values, even more than modern youth may perceive. The city is in permanent revolution. It is not easy and it may be unpleasant to many to live in the midst of it. But if so many cities continue to attract and retain larger numbers of people, at least in daytime, it can only mean that they hope and strive for a better future, and know somehow that the past is past and that a new and better world is coming and may be achieved through participation in this immense, chaotic urban transition.

Jean Gottmann

Bibliography

Following is a brief list of some suggestions for background and further reading:

Conzen, Michael, ed. "World Patterns of Modern Urban Change." Department of Geography, University of Chicago, Chicago. Research Paper No. 217-218, 1986.
Dogan, Mattei, and John D. Kasarda, eds. The Metropolis Era. 2 vols. Beverly Hills, CA, and London: Sage Publications, 1988.

Gottmann, Jean. *Megalopolis. The Urbanized Northeastern Seaboard of the United States.* New York: Twentieth Century Fund, 1961.
————. *Megalopolis Revisited: 25 Years Later.* College Park, MD: University of Maryland Institute of Urban Studies, 1987.
Gottmann, Jean, and Robert A. Harper. *Metropolis on the Move: Geographers Look at Urban Sprawl.* New York: J. Wiley & Sons, 1967.

Part One   **Urban Origins**

This particular type of region is new, but it is the result of age-old processes, such as the growth of cities, the division of labor within a civilized society, the development of world resources. The name applied to it should, therefore, be new as a place name but old as a symbol of the long tradition of human aspirations and endeavor underlying the situations and problems now found here. Hence the choice of the term *Megalopolis*, used in this study.

Some two thousand years before the first European settlers landed on the shores of the James River, Massachusetts Bay, and Manhattan Island, a group of ancient people, planning a new city-state in the Peloponnesus in Greece, called it *Megalopolis*, for they dreamed of a great future for it and hoped it would become the largest of the Greek cities. Their hopes did not materialize. Megalopolis still appears on modern maps of the Peloponnesus but it is just a small town nestling in a small river basin. Through the centuries the word *Megalopolis* has been used in many senses by various people, and it has even found its way into Webster's dictionary, which defines it as "a very large city." Its use, however, has not become so common that it could not be applied in a new sense, as a geographical place name for the unique cluster of metropolitan areas of the Northeastern seaboard of the United States. There, if anywhere in our times, the dream of those ancient Greeks has come true.

Megalopolis,
"The Main Street of the Nation"

One

Orbits:
The Ancient
Mediterranean
Tradition of
Urban Networks

Some fifty years ago, I entered on a geographical career, intending to specialize in the human geography of the Mediterranean. I was trained in France where, at the time, the first two university degrees in geography and in history were joined. So that historical geography or geographical history always seemed to me to be natural approaches. World War II sent me to America and started me on a transatlantic transhumance. In that orbit, I have specialized in large cities and urban regions. Analyzing these I have traced the roots of most modern, large-scale systems of urban settlement to ancient patterns that sprang up first around the Mediterranean. From there they spread out to wrap up the planet.

To understand the evolution of the contemporary ways of the world, networks of cities are fundamental. Too often, however, a city is considered only in the framework of the surrounding region. The question has arisen, worrying geographers, historians, sociologists, and politicians, whether a city lives, works, and lasts or falls mainly as the center of a

Presented as the Twelfth J. L. Myres Memorial Lecture, Oxford University, Oxford, England, 2 May 1983.

region, determined by local circumstances, or chiefly as a partner in a constellation of far-flung cities. This is not, in fact, a new problem born in our time. It is an ancient problem which has been with mankind since the dawn of history. Gordon Childe would probably have said since the Neolithic.[1] The cradle of the systems that may be called urban networks or constellations of cities working together is, of course, the ancient Mediterranean.

It was among Mediterranean people that the debate developed of what was preferable: the large polynuclear framework or the secluded, insular compartment. Which is the essential orbit? The tortured, fractured topography of the Mediterranean basin, where mountains, sea, and deserts have divided the good land into small separate cells, may well be at the source of the dilemma local populations have had to face. And the debate has raged for ages, especially among the Greeks, including Homer, Plato, and Aristotle. But I should not engage in name-dropping now; let me come to specifics.

Forty years ago, in May 1943, Sir John Myres delivered in Cambridge the Fraser Lecture he entitled: *Mediterranean Culture: An Essay in Geographical History.*[2] To set the scene, he started with the *Orbis terrarum* around the Midland Sea; disposing his actors, he quickly came to cities and singled out two major categories of towns: first, the "bazaar cities" from Athens and Corinth to Carthage and Venice, and second, the "sanctuary cities" (the *hieropolis*) from Jerusalem to Compostella.

Later in that lecture he acknowledged that the functions of bazaar and sanctuary may very well coexist and complement one another in the same city: the market and the temple. The orbit of a city may be relatively short, of regional scope. Still, in all cases worth mentioning, those that mattered in history, the orbit extended farther, lengthened, and encompassed other cities and regions with which regular linkages had been established. Indeed, a city is more often a hinge joining the two orbits: the regional and the wider.

Let us first look at the examples of two remarkable islands in the Aegean Sea: Santorini and Delos.

In 1967 the excavations directed by the late Spyridon Marinatos on Thera (or Santorini) finally located Akro-Thera, an ancient Pompeii-like city of the Aegean, buried under the ashes of the powerful volcanic eruption which, circa 1500 B.C., exploded the island and caused severe disruption through a large area of the Minoan world. I was privileged to visit the excavations with a group conducted by Marinatos in 1972. Much of the marvelous pottery and wall paintings found in the ancient town is now in the Thera collection at the National Museum in Athens. The highly civilized people who lived more than 3,500 years ago on that small island had an active maritime life and developed a network of rather distant connections. Two rhytons were found there, made of ostrich eggs decorated with faience suggesting trade relations with Africa. Ostrich eggs are known to have been valued very early by Mediterranean populations. The wall paintings testify to contacts with environments of tropical appearance at a time when the Mediterranean climate could not have been of that sort. Especially significant for my purpose here is the frieze, found decorating at least three sides of a room, which pictures three seaside towns, with ships plying at sea between the towns, entering the harbors, obviously linking different towns together. At one place there appears to be a battle at sea. In another town, cordial welcome seems to be extended to the incoming ships.

Marinatos, in his report on the excavations for the summer session of 1972,[3] tried to identify the three towns on the frieze. One of these is certainly Thera, but where may the other two have been located? Careful analysis of minute detail led him to designate the painting as the "Lybian frieze" depicting probably relations with towns in Cyrenaica, the closest North African shore, and known to have participated in the Minoan world. Some exciting debates may still be forthcoming on the identification of the three towns. Marinatos's successor, Professor Christos Doumas, seems to doubt the Lybian diagnosis and mentions other possible connections; he rather inclines towards direct or indirect linkages with Egypt. This could be supported by the type of monkeys painted on the wall of another house and by ostrich eggs in rhytons.[4]

At present, we may describe this ancient painting as the oldest map known that shows more than the plan of a building or a small area such as a farm estate. Here, three towns are shown linked by sea-lanes, with indications of the topography of the harbors and hinterland scenes depicting the animal life there. The topography is different behind each of the three towns and so are the animals shown. Behind one of the towns, blue ribbons certainly represent a river or water channel. One such river seems to separate the island on which the town is built from the mainland; but the same river extends inland, and marvelous wildlife scenes with lions, deer, and birds amidst exotic palm trees are painted along the stream. The thought arises that this town might be located in the delta of the Nile.[5] Examining the details, one cannot help being reminded of some of the early maps of the Atlantic shores of America in the sixteenth and seventeenth centuries A.D. Indeed, this frieze must have cartographic meaning. It is a historical and economic map of the time before abstract symbols and grids were adopted. I have secured the agreement of Dr. Helen Wallis, of the British Library, a distinguished authority on the classification and identification of old maps, to designate this frieze of the three towns from Akrotiri as the most ancient map known at present of a large-scale area.

The maritime activities and networks of Thera in the sixteenth century B.C. may serve as an introduction to a brief look at the much more impressive and better known activities and networks of Delos in the first millennium B.C. Delos is a typical hieropolis. It is located on a small island, obviously devoid of resources, save perhaps a fairly central location in the Aegean. The Homeric Hymn to Delian Apollo tells us remarkably well how the local population compensated for the hard and rocky soil, the lack of local resources, by building on the sanctity of Apollo's birthplace.

I quote from the translation in the Loeb Classical Library (To Delian Apollo, 140–175):

Many are your temples and wooded groves, and all peaks and towering bluffs of lofty mountains and rivers flowing to the sea are dear to you, Phoebus, yet in Delos do you most delight your heart, for there the long robed Ionians gather in your honour with their children and shy wives: mindful, they delight you with boxing and dancing and song, so often as they hold their gathering. A man would say that they are deathless and unageing if he should then come upon the Ionians so met together. For he would see the graces of them all, and would be pleased in heart gazing at the men and well-girded women with their swift ships and their wealth.

Then follows the praise of the girls of Delos, Apollo's handmaidens, who "can imitate the tongues of all men and their clattering speech." The Hymn describes the festivals at the great crossroads of Delos and the bard concludes: "As for me, I will carry your renown as far as I roam over the earth to the well-placed cities of man, and they will believe also; for, indeed, this thing is true."[6]

There is little doubt that few small craggy islands have been known to achieve such a thriving combination of sanctuary and market functions as did Delos. It was a great emporium, a multinational center in the middle of the Aegean, extending its trade to the whole eastern Mediterranean for many centuries. Its orbit was finally incorporated into the Roman one which restructured the life of the Mediterranean. But when it rose against Rome, Delos was crushed commercially and politically. Moreover, the rise of Christianity destroyed the centrality of Apollo's birthplace. The gradual coalescence into one system of the Orbis terrarum was also bound to decrease the advantages of the insular position distant from larger lands. The sea-lanes needed tighter joints with land routes, and there are many examples of how that happened.

The most famous episode of that process takes us back to the tenth century B.C. and outside the Greek world. We find it in the Bible (1 Kings 9: 26–10:15) in the account of the reign of King Solomon. There is little doubt that Solomon built up a large political and commercial orbit centered on Jerusalem. That orbit went far beyond the borders of what may have been the Solomonian empire. Alliances with Tyre and with Egypt gave Jerusalem a commanding intermediate position on the northeast-southwest routes between the sea and the desert. Then the creation of the port of Etzion-Gueber, on what is now called the Gulf of Akaba, to send fleets on the Red Sea in cooperation with Tyre, a great maritime Phoenician trade center, endowed Jerusalem with a commanding role on a transisthmic northwest-southeast route.[7] The city of Solomon's great temple also became a great caravan city, connecting land and sea networks.

The biblical text curiously weaves together in a few paragraphs two famous episodes: the sending of fleets from Etzion-Gueber to the land of Ophir, and the visit to Jerusalem of the Queen of Sheba. As a conclusion to both, much wealth came to Solomon. The isthmic route opened up great trade perspectives. Where was Ophir? Wherefrom came the Queen of Sheba, who brought so many spices and precious stones (1 Kings 10:10)? Could she have been the representative of a powerful caravan syndicate controlling routes along the Red Sea with which the sea trade to Ophir would compete? Or was her realm around and beyond Ophir? Once more we are left guessing in front of the map. Ophir must have been around or beyond the Bab el Mandeb.

Solomon's legend extended far to the Southeast. In his book on the Aflāj of Oman (1977), Dr. John C. Wilkinson provides an amusing illustration of this. Traditional modes of irrigation in the interior of Oman are based on the water supplied by extensive networks of ancient, artificial, subterranean channels called qanāt aflāj. They belong to a system of water supply found in various parts of the great Afro-Asian desert belt from the Western Sahara to Central Asia. Dr. Wilkinson reports on the strength of Arab chronicles and local beliefs that the qanāt were built by Sulayman B. Dawud (Solomon, son of David), who one day was carried by the winds across Oman on his daily trip from Persepolis to Jerusalem. He saw the castle at Salut and "ordered the spirits to investigate . . . Then Sulayman entered Oman and, at that time, there were only nomads living there. He stayed ten days, on each of which he ordered his spirits to dig a thousand nahr (qanāt): hence the ten thousand aflāj of Oman."[8]

Indeed, King Solomon must have astonished his contemporaries with the speed and efficiency with which he got things done. Jerusalem must have known phenomenal growth in his reign. The city of David was a respectable regional center by the standards of the time, but Solomon's capital became a great metropolis with a magnificent temple and royal palace; a vastly expanded political and commercial orbit had been obtained, great wealth accumulated, and new satellite cities acquired in several directions.

The fame of the king's power and wisdom has endured 3,000 years, but the political system he created did not survive him for long. The great works, far-away expeditions, and expansionist policies were a heavy burden to bear for his people; the "yoke was grievous," says the Bible. The great wealth that flowed into Jerusalem was not shared equally; under Solomon's son and successor, Rehoboam, the people of Israel protested. Ten tribes rebelled, and the kingdom split into two (1 Kings 12). The question may thus be asked whether Solomon's policies were wise in the long run or whether the enlargement of the orbit was bound to lead to political trouble.

Five centuries later, Athens, the great Greek metropolis, which, from the small and poor peninsula of Attica, had extended its power, influence, and trade in all directions, was experiencing trouble from within, despite and perhaps because of its great achievements and opulence. The debates must have been widespread as to what might be the best geographical framework to obtain a happier political life. The geographer cannot disregard Plato's doctrine for the ideal polis as set forth in The Laws (I quote from the translation by A. E. Taylor, dedicated to New College, Oxford, published by Dent, London, 1960): "The territory should be large enough for the adequate maintenance of a certain number of men of modest ambitions and no larger; the population should be sufficient to defend themselves against wrongs from societies on their borders, and to assist their neighbours when wronged to some purpose" (Book V, 737). Earlier, discussing in Book IV with Clinias, the Cretan who seeks advice, how the city should be located, the Athenian advises that the population should be kept away from the sea:

It is agreeable enough to have the sea at one's door in daily life; but, for all that, it is, in very truth, a briny and bitter "neighbour". It fills the city with wholesale traffic and retail huckstering, breeds shifty and distrustful habits of soul, and so makes a society distrustful and unfriendly within itself as well as towards mankind at large. In view of this situation, there is further comfort, however, in the universal productiveness of our site. Clearly, since it is so rugged, it cannot at once produce everything and yield much of anything. Were that the case, there would be the opportunity of export on a large scale, and, once more, our city would abound with currency in gold and silver. Now, . . . nothing is a more serious impediment to the development of noble and righteous character in a society. (Book IV, 705)

Small scale, austerity, isolation, restricted maritime and trading activities, such is Plato's recipe for a righteous and stable society. This doctrine of political geography has often been offered as great wisdom to this day. It was, however, seldom put into practice by the Greeks, or by Mediterraneans in general, when they could avoid it. Plato's best disciple, Aristotle, already began diluting the Master's puritanical isolationism in his *Politics.* Certainly he condemned greed, but he allowed for some naval power and sea trade. To his princely pupil, Alexander of Macedon, he seems to have suggested that the virtues of the Greeks, once united, would easily allow them to dominate Asia as well as Europe.

So Alexander went on to his sweeping conquests east and south, extending his empire to the Nile and the Indus, setting his capital in Babylon, creating new seaport cities near the mouths of great rivers, spreading Greek culture, coinage, and credit methods. What ensued has been better told in seven classic volumes by M. Rostovtzeff[9] than I could do here. But I owe a special debt to Professor Nicholas Hammond, of Cambridge, for drawing my attention, thirty years ago, to the role of the network of large cities, great centers of long-range and cultural activities, in Alexander's Great Design for his vast multinational empire, which was to be a sphere and era of harmony and prosperity.[10]

The Platonic model of the small, equal, self-sufficient and self-absorbed, juxtaposed territorial units may be easily opposed to the Alexandrine model of a vast, expanding, pluralistic political and cultural system, bound together and lubricated by the active exchanges and linkages of a network of large trading cities. The former model offers a set static ideal, the latter a dynamic, kinetic one. Both designed theoretical orbits aiming at achieving harmony and happiness for the people. Both have served as central icons in political philosophies probably long before and certainly long after the Hellenistic Era. The Platonic and the Alexandrine models are very useful, I believe, to analyze the past and present conflicts in political philosophy and in political geography.

Alexander did not live long and his empire was promptly divided up after his death. Still, the impact on Mediterranean culture and organization proved lasting. Within three centuries Rome had taken over, extended the *Pax Romana* around its *Mare nostrum,* and made the *Orbis Terrarum* its own. To the urban network greatly expanded, better interwoven on land as well as at sea, was superimposed a military and juridical structure without precedent at least in the West, though a similar organization may have already existed in China.

And Rome kept extending its orbit by conquest, trade, settlement, and road and city building, northwards in Europe, southwards in Africa, and eastwards in Asia. I do not need to quote here Sir Mortimer Wheeler on Roman settlements in India, or Maspero the Younger on Roman trade with China.[11] Roman dynamism naturally provoked some turbulence within and around its orbit. From Jerusalem, destroyed and rebuilt, a new religion was gaining from city to city throughout the empire. With the emperor Constantine a great change came early in the fourth century. Not only did the empire become officially Christian, but its capital was moved to a new location, a new city, a New Rome. Officially, Constantine chose the location of Constantinople inspired by a divine vision, as A. Alföldi has described.[12] But the geographer feels more relevant the analysis provided by Sir John Myres in his lecture to the British Association, Section E, in 1923 on the Marmara Region:

If the New Rome was to defend the empire as a whole, it must be as near as possible, not only to the Danube frontier and to the north-western trunk-road by which Aquileia and Milan were to give and receive reinforcements, but to the Euphrates frontier as well. If it was to be a great centre of population, it must be fed; so it must stand on the seaboard, within reach of the corn of Egypt as well as to stop sea-raiders out of the north; so it must be a naval arsenal, with direct access to the Pontus and also, as direct as might be, to the Levant. In case of accidents to resources from overseas, it must have local supplies, and a local reserve of men; so it must command the Thracian cornlands and highlands, as Lysimachia and Adrianople had done, but without the risk of isolation which hampered both of these . . . It must be essentially Greek for it was to dominate the sentiments as well as the interests of the Greeks.[13]

How complex was the weave of factors and forces to be coordinated! How skilful the Romans must have been in building up and extending the immense network of cities, including all the provincial and regional capitals, on which rested the inner structure of the empire. With the New Rome, "once again, perhaps, a great statesman builded better than he knew." Constantinople remained a great political capital, Roman, Byzantine, then Ottoman, for 1,600 years from 330 to 1922 A.D., a record in longevity for a great capital.

Meanwhile, the first Rome, although taken, ransacked, and shrunk, knew how to remain a great world centre, religious and political, less concerned with material problems than with inner life. And Constantinople started a chain of new Romes. Many capital cities have since claimed the title of a new Rome. Vienna and Moscow, among others, wanted each to be the Third Rome. Indeed, the unity, prosperity, and relative peace that Rome was able to establish for a time over the whole Mediterranean orbit bequeathed a powerful legend and model for many cultures. No other city to date may claim an equivalent reputation, even though much of the Roman inheritance originated in other cities of the empire. The orbit was so well knit and structured, despite its vastness, that the image left to succeeding generations was almost monolithic. This could have only been achieved by intense inter-city trade and the standardization of institutions in the main cities.

In fact, the history of the Roman Empire was hardly a quiet one, especially on the periphery. The legions were left little time to loaf. The pressures already intensified in the third century A.D. Real decline developed in the fourth, despite the splendor of Constantinople for almost a millennium afterwards. The barbarian invasions and migrations rapidly fragmented the cultural and economic unity of the Mediterranean so gradually built up from Alexander to Hadrian. The disruption, recession, and the great insecurity that ensued and lasted must have been deeply resented. It seems indeed likely that the ease and speed with which the Moslem Arab conquest spread in the seventh century from the caravan cities of Arabia, heirs to the Nabateans, first in a circum-Mediterranean movement, and then eastwards along the routes of silk and spices, could best be understood as welcomed by the populations that yearned for stability, order, and the restoration of ancient urban networks.

The Italian and Greek populations resisted the Moslem onslaught better than most other Mediterranean cultures. The Mediterranean world soon seemed clearly divided into two apparently irreconcilable halves: the Christian and the Moslem. Soon, however, some networks revived and transactions trickled through that curtain between two faiths. In 800, Charlemagne, Emperor of Occident, exchanged gifts with Haroun al Rashid, Caliph of Baghdad, but not with Hakam, the Caliph of Cordoba; for even the political unity of Islam had already been broken. Mediterranean fragmentation continued, shifting and evolving, although economic networks survived and, in various ways, along diverse roads old and new, carried on with trade, cultural, and information exchanges. The Mediterranean realm was rightly called by one geographer the land of discontinuity, and by another the land of joints.[14]

The Middle Ages in the Mediterranean was another era dominated by urban networks and urban rivalries.[15] These developed in the Christian parts as well as in the Moslem lands, though we know much less about the latter. The most extraordinary life and the greatest activity was then in Italy, a land of city states rivaling and fighting one another, while maintaining networks and trade in certain orbits which they harshly disputed to one another. There were long and bloody duels between Milan and Florence, Venice and Genoa, to mention only the most famous. No story of a people is more extraordinary nor more extolled than that of Venice in the 1,000 years from the seventh to the seventeenth century: a city that was never very large, born and based on islets in a lagoon, that dominated the trade of the Orient, deflected a crusade to take Constantinople in 1204 and divide what was left of the Roman Empire, while preserving its relations with infidel Egypt.

The urban networks of the Italian cities were multiple, economic, financial, cultural. But it had been early accepted among them that Rome kept the monopoly of the *hieropolis* function and that the Bishop of Rome was the supreme spiritual pontiff of the whole orbit of Christianity. While fighting bitterly among themselves on many matters, the Italian city-states agreed on that Roman supremacy, which helped to maintain a certain unity of the global orbit. We are still reminded of it in the pontifical blessing *"urbi et orbi."* The cultural and economic centers moved, meanwhile, between a half-dozen major cities. The greatest achievement of the medieval network of Italian cities came in the fifteenth century when they began losing their predominance in the Mediterranean orbit as more centralized sovereign states were taking over in all directions: the Ottoman Empire, Portugal, Spain, France, and England.

The vast crossroads of trade routes, of the gathering and redistribution of wealth, information, skills, and ideas produced then and diffused the Italian Renaissance.[16] It came, of course, gradually, but the marvelous artistic and intellectual explosion changed the course of history. No doubt the late sixteenth century A.D. opened up the decline of the role of the Mediterranean and the seventeenth century shifted the centers of the main orbits elsewhere: the new orbits were to be centered first in Lisbon which dominated the trade with the East Indies, and Seville, which controlled most of the trade with American shores.[17] Then the directing centers shifted definitely away from the Mediterranean to the northwest, or northeast.

However, the Mediterranean cities, especially Greek and Italian, having created and incubated what certainly became the most skilful and useful system of trade and credit, based on geographical, mathematical, and psychological knowledge, put their nets at the disposal of the stronger powers from the fifteenth century on. By then, they had lost the control of the routes to Asia, and the Portuguese had rounded the Cape en route to the Indies. From Genoa, Columbus went to Cordoba to obtain the approval of Isobela la Cattolica for sailing westward on the Ocean. John Cabot was a citizen of Venice. Amerigo Vespuce and Verrazzano felt they were extending the Italian orbit while navigating in the service of other sovereigns. However, the Italian early monopoly on the spices trade and on discovery was soon lost. The financial skills of Milan, Venice, and Florence had been learnt by many others. Still, the Bank of America was founded in San Francisco by a Mr. Giannini, two Mediterranean-sounding names, and there originated also the Visa credit card. Those Mediterranean cities have provided us with more than tenets of political philosophy.

None of it would have happened had the Platonic model of isolation prevailed.

In fact, today, as most empires have come to an end or to a mutation, and the role of the nation-state has weakened, new orbits shape up once more, largely structured by networks of transactions, by communities of beliefs, and by interests between institutions and groups better identified by the cities or regions where they are based. The modern gradual evolution towards an interlocked world system is increasingly dependent on interwoven urban orbits. The roots of modern problems and of basic philosophies are perhaps more obviously Mediterranean today than they were in recent centuries.

Still, the geographer must ask one question: Why the Mediterranean and its ancient cities? Why did the tradition of large, far-flung networks of cities originate in that region? It is generally true of cities that each of them works as a hinge between the region of which it is the center and the outside world, between the local and the external orbits. Mediterranean cities have developed first the latter with impressive scales and consequences. And they taught the rest of the world how to achieve this. There have been other great cultures, just as ancient, with splendid art and techniques, with denser and highly skilled populations, notably in China and in India. However, it is the Mediterranean-born culture that has swept around the planet and reorganized it in one orbit, diversified, partitioned, complicated as Mediterranean orbits always were, but now conscious of its unity.

Could this have been caused by the challenge of a difficult physical environment, with an uncertain rainfall, a mountainous topography, high seismicity, few good soils, a difficult sea? Similarly challenging circumstances may be found elsewhere: in Indonesia or in Japan, for instance.

I am frequently reminded of a round table in Tokyo in 1972 at which a few Westerners, none of them truly Mediterranean, faced an assembly of Japanese scholars discussing the future of their country. One of the Japanese made a point very strongly: "We are different from you," he said, "do not expect us to adopt entirely your ways and your views. Remember, you came to fetch us. We did not go to fetch you in Europe or in America. We knew how to navigate and to strike across the sea; but we were not interested."[18] The Chinese sometimes make similar remarks. Indeed, there had been Mediterranean merchants and settlements in India and Southeast Asia in Roman times, possibly earlier. There were no Indian or Chinese establishments in days of yore in Mediterranean cities.

Some people like to travel more than others. The main lesson that Ulysses brought back from his wanderings was the knowledge of the diversity of the places he had visited and of their inhabitants. This is what he told Penelope about, when they were reunited. This is what the frescoes of prehistoric buildings at Akrotiri seem to describe. Does this ancient Mediterranean tradition express basic curiosity or even more, the impulse to learn how to deal with others, how to overcome distance, and perhaps even how to overcome human diversity? The will of individuals to liberate themselves from their original environment even if it is the Garden of Eden? I am afraid I have got out of my prescribed orbit.

Notes

1. See V. Gordon Childe, *Man Makes Himself* (London, 1936).

2. John L. Myres, *Mediterranean Culture: An Essay in Geographical History* (The Fraser Lecture, 1943) (Cambridge, 1943), 52.

3. Spyridon Marinatos, *Excavations at Thera VI* (1972 Season), Athens Archeological Society, Publ. 64 (Athens, 1974), 60, 112 plates.

4. Christos G. Doumas, *Santorini: The Prehistoric City of Akrotiri*, Editions Hannibal (Athens, 1981?), well illustrated, and by the same author, *Santorini: A Guide to the Island and its Archeological Treasures*, Ekdotike Athenon S.A. (Athens, 1982), 128, 91 illustrations in color. Professor Doumas writes in the latter: "Shipping was without doubt one of the principal preoccupations of the island population. More particularly, in the Cyclades, seafaring had begun in at least the 7th millennium B.C. We do not have proof of the export of Theran products to other places. This, however, does not preclude the possibility that Theran boats were engaged in transit trade between other lands of the Mediterranean (e.g. between Crete and Egypt or Anatolia) . . . It can be maintained that, in prehistoric Akrotiri, even as early as the 16th century B.C., a kind of urban *bourgeoise society* had developed, a consequence, as in more recent times, of commerce and shipping." (p. 58 of *A Guide to the Island and* . . .) The ostrich eggs and the Ethiopian species of monkeys appearing on a wall painting in another house seem to have been diffused by trade from Egypt in the eastern Mediterranean.

5. This remark is entirely my own. I have not had an opportunity to discuss this point with the competent Greek archeologists. I am greatly indebted to Professor Doumas, Mr. Panayotis Psomopoulos, and the National Museum in Athens, for a beautiful color photograph of the frieze on one of the walls of Room 5 of the West House in Akrotiri, which I was able to display at the Myres Memorial Lecture in New College, Oxford. On Delos I wish to refer to the classic volume by Pierre Roussel, one of my teachers at the Sorbonne, *Delos* (Paris, 1925), and his essay "La population de Delos a la fin du IIe siècle av. J. C.," in *Bulletin de Correspondance Hellenique*, LV (1931), 438–49. Also to the interesting study by Alexandre Papageorgiou-Venetas, *Delos, Recherches urbaines sur une ville antique*, Deutscher Kunsterverlag (Munich, 1981) (good bibliography).

6. Quotations from "To Delian Apollo" in *Hesiod, the Homeric Hymns and Homerica*, with an English translation by H. G. Evelyn-White, William Heinemann (London, 1967), 336–37.

7. The importance of isthmuses and transisthmic routes was stressed in many works by historians and archeologists. Sir John Myres also mentioned

transisthmic routes. The classical theory about these may be found in Victor Bérard, *Les Phéniciens et l'Odyssée* (Paris, 1926), 2 vols. See also J. Gottmann, "L'homme, la route et l'eau en Asie Sud-Occidentale," in *Annales de Géographie* 47 (15 November 1938), 575–601.

8. John C. Wilkinson, *Water and Tribal Settlement in South-East Arabia: A Study of the Aflāj of Oman* (Oxford Research Studies in Geography) (Oxford, 1977), especially Chapter 6.

9. M. Rostovtzeff, *The Social and Economic History of the Hellenistic World* (Oxford, 1941), 3 vols.; also his *The Social and Economic History of the Roman Empire* (Oxford, 1926), 2 vols.; his *Caravan Cities* (Oxford, 1932); and his *Ptolemaic Egypt* (Cambridge, 1928).

10. N. G. L. Hammond has been the leading specialist on Macedonian ancient history. In 1952 we both coincided at the Institute for Advanced Study in Princeton, N.J., for a period of research. As I was already working on modern urban networks and interested in their ancient background in the Mediterranean, Professor Hammond stimulated my research in this direction by outlining the thinking and planning of Alexander on cities, their location and interaction. See also his monumental work, *A History of Macedonia*, and, more especially, his *Alexander the Great, King, Commander and Statesman* (London, 1981). Also W. W. Tarn, *Alexander the Great* (Cambridge, 1948), 2 vols.

See also G. T. Griffith, ed., *Alexander the Great: The Main Problems* (Cambridge, 1966); also E. Badian, ed., *Alexandre le Grand* (Entretiens XXII of Fondation Hardt) (Geneva, 1975); also R. Lane Fox, *Alexander the Great* (London, 1973). For the Exhibition entitled *The Search for Alexander* at the National Gallery of Art, Washington, D.C., in 1980–81, an interesting catalogue was published with an essay by Nicholas Yalouris on "Alexander and His Heritage."

I have used repeatedly in various papers the dichotomy of the Platonic and Alexandrian models of the city; to begin with, in *The Evolution of Urban Centrality: Orientation for Research,* Research Paper No. 8, School of Geography, University of Oxford (1974).

11. Sir R. E. Mortimer Wheeler, *Rome Beyond the Imperial Borders* (London, 1954); and *Impact and Imprint: Greeks and Romans Beyond the Himalayas*, The Earl Grey Memorial Lecture (Newcastle-on-Tyne, 1959); and Henri Maspero and Et. Balazs, *Histoire et Institutions de la Chine Ancienne*, revised by P. Demieville, (Paris (Musée Guimet), 1967); see also the several volumes by Needham, et al., *Science and Civilisation in China,* Cambridge University Press.

12. A. Alföldi, *The Conversion of Constantine and Pagan Rome* (Oxford, 1948). I have also read with interest the essay by Jaroslav Pelikan of Yale University, "The Two Cities: The Decline and Fall of Rome as a Historical Paradigm," in *Daedalus* (Boston, Summer 1982), 85–91.

13. John L. Myres, "The Marmara Region" in his book *Geographical History in Greek Lands* (Oxford, 1953), quot. 251–52.

14. Jules Sion called it the "land of the discontinuous" in his essays "Sur la Civilisation agraire méditerranéenne," in *Bulletin de la Société Languedocienne de Geographie* (Montpellier, 1940), 20–45, and André Siegfried used the expression "pays de l'articulation" or "land of joints" in his volume *Vue Générale de la Mediterranée* (Paris, 1943) (trans. by D. Hemming, *The Mediterranean* (London, 1948).

15. Vast libraries have been published on the economic and political history of the decline of the Roman Empire and on the medieval and Renaissance periods in the Mediterranean. I shall not attempt here a bibliography. It seems enough to refer to the two editions of the *Cambridge Economic History of Europe* (Cambridge, 1967–77), especially vols. two, three (1971); four (1967); and five (1977). Each volume contains a rich bibliography.

16. I have also consulted: R. S. Lopez and I. W. Raymond, *Medieval Trade in the Mediterranean World* (New York, 1955); R. S. Lopez, *The Three Ages of the Italian Renaissance* (Charlottesville, 1970). On Venice especially Frederic C. Lane, *Venice and History* (Baltimore, 1966), and *Venice: A Maritime Republic* (Baltimore, 1973), as well as Lord Norwich's *A History of Venice* (London, 1982).

17. The books referred to above by Lopez and Norwich and volume five of the *Cambridge Economic History of Europe* elaborate these points.

18. I am referring to the discussions in *The 4th International Symposium on Regional Development* of the Japan Center for Area Development Research, Tokyo, January 1972, especially the remarks by Professor Osamu Nishikawa.

.

Part Two   **Urban Centrality**

The natural setting of Megalopolis provided a favorable location for the development of a great hub of relationships.

Historically, of course, this was the main gate through which came the great flow of immigrants that settled the continent and formed the American nation. Many people, especially in Europe, readily infer from this history that the abundance of cheap labor and skilled manpower supplied by the immigrants led to easy industrialization, and that on the resulting concentration of manufactures and on the large consuming market was then founded the greatest commercial and financial concentration of our time.

Although one could hardly overestimate the immense potentialities brought to this seaboard by the influx of immigrants, it must be recognized that the range of opportunity was broadened, for them and for those who had been there longer, by early and shrewd endeavors at large-scale commercial organization. These were first undertaken by the European sponsors of the first settlements, such as the Virginia Company, the Company of Massachusetts Bay, and the Dutch West Indies Company. The settlers quickly learned, however, how to organize for their own purposes instead of becoming merely outposts of European trade. Their endeavors to carry on an autonomous commerce started the American economy on the course that led first to independence and later to financial supremacy.

As the American economy grew, each of the main seaside cities developed a network of trade relationships on the continent and on the high seas. Standing at the contact of these two realms, the seaports assumed the role of *hinges* linking the development of these two foundations of the national economy. From period to period, the main weight of this seaboard's interest has oscillated from sea trade and overseas ventures to continental development and back again. Whether the general circumstances threw the door of the American economy open toward the outside or closed it to turn the main endeavors inland depended on decisions made in that *hinge,* the string of eastern cities. They alone in the country had enough capital, skill, and authority to elaborate such policies and profit by their application . . .

As manufactures were then [in the nineteenth century] favored, they naturally developed in or around the large Northeastern cities, where there was enough capital to finance them. The steady flow of abundant and cheap immigrant labor and the proximity to the consuming markets of the most densely settled and developed section of the country combined to foster the growth of the factories . . .

This inland progress [of developing the continental United States] was to a large extent financed by Northeastern seaboard interests, especially by New York and Boston bankers; and the seaboard money markets were, of course, gathering more strength and profits as a result of the country's growth. The concentration of national credit and money management in the four large cities of Megalopolis was already obvious, and the hinge function was especially well illustrated by the flow of capital . . .

[In the twentieth century] Megalopolis was able to rise so quickly to such eminence in the international economic system both because of its network of overseas relationships and because it kept the reins of direction of the national economy. This managerial role was not independent from the financial one, and both had been built up, maintained, and reinforced through three centuries of stubborn and daring endeavor. Newcomers and well-established native people cooperated through the whole period to broaden the scope of opportunity in all directions, to "trye all ports," and to organize a system of entangled connections by sea, by land, and by air, reaching to every small town on the continent and to the ends of the earth abroad. These Megalopolitan endeavors were aided by competition between the old, early established seaboard cities, by the continent's development, and also by the course of history overseas. This same opportunity was open, however, except the heritage of the past, to many other great cities or developing regions on other seaboards in America and elsewhere. The physical advantages locally available to Megalopolis in terms of climate, topography, and proximity to Europe were important in the early stages of American history, but they have not been of serious purport in the last hundred years, for the technology of transportation and manufacturing have reduced to very little indeed the practical influence of local physical circumstances . . .

The story of the continent's economic hinge has revealed the successive stages of Megalopolis' efforts to become larger and wealthier, and this growth has involved the development of large *downtown* areas in the cities. They grew up from wharves, in the port cities, as well as from the market-place hubs of traffic and commercial transactions, from the centers of government and education, and from the sites of worship or recreation. Since time immemorial the city has supplied to the surrounding countryside properly serviced sites for the exchange of goods and

ideas, for the administration of justice and
politics, for the celebration of religious rites
and other collective traditions, for education
and relaxation. The crowding of people and
the gathering of wealth in the cities of Megalopolis caused all these functions to be carried out on an impressive and rapidly
widening scale.

Megalopolis,
"The Continuous Economic Hinge"

Two

Urban Centrality
and the Interweaving
of Quaternary
Activities

The city, the *urbs,* has been for a long time the central place *par excellence* in the organization of inhabited space. In the past the city may have been small, but its central functions in terms of administrative, commercial, and social activities made it the focus of the surrounding countryside, which was organized largely by the transactions and the decisions made in the urban center and along a network of means of access to that center.

Traditionally the best known urban activity was the market, where goods were exchanged at the crossroads of the city. However, there have been parts of the world and periods of history in which the market function was not so centralized and rooted in space as it has usually been in Europe and Asia. Thus the settlement by plantations of the southeast United States, particularly Virginia and the Carolinas in the seventeenth and eighteenth centuries, resisted the setting up of regional central markets. Some urbanization took place in those areas nevertheless, but, except for a few large seaports, the cities of the southern United States arose around the courthouse square. The judicial and

Reprinted from *Ekistics,* May 1970, 322–31.

administrative function replaced here to some extent the marketplace as a generator of urban centrality. In the cities of the Old World, the castle (which in the past often assumed the judicial function) and the market were close neighbors, the former policing and protecting the latter, in the old cores. In the New World, the courthouse and the business district were also eventually found side by side.

The Industrial Revolution concentrated in cities the rapidly developing function of manufacturing production; industrial plants and warehouses seemed to take over the urban centers; the market for the labor employed by the manufactures came to dominate the inner life of the cities, and during the nineteenth and early twentieth centuries urbanization became synonymous with manufacturing plants, concentration, and growth. Since 1950, with mechanization, automation, great mobility of people and goods, it has become possible for the plants to disperse around the cities, to move to small towns, or even to crossroads in seemingly rural territory, with more advantages than drawbacks for the process of production. Manpower can commute to the plant from a wide radius around it, the workers' residences being scattered in rural territory. A large plant may attract a shopping center to its vicinity, developing a multifaceted function of purely local centrality. This would still be more on the scale of the village of the past than on the scale of a city. The cities meanwhile in this era of postindustrial development keep on growing at a faster rate than ever, and the largest urban concentrations have in the recent quarter of a century attracted more people than ever.

Concentration or Diffusion for the City?

The dispersal of urban functions across the land has led some authors to question the centrality function of the modern city. Prefacing a new edition of Max Weber's classical essay *The City*,[1] Professor Don Martindale, of the University of Minnesota, implied that the solidly organized community and central place Weber was talking about was disappearing. What used to make the tight organization of the urban community was becoming diffused across the country, and the nation was replacing the city as the framework of economic or social evolution and of the organization of space. This way of thinking seems to have been largely propagated by a school of sociologists from the American Middle West. Settlement has been very fluid in the central and western parts of the United States for more than a century. Still, in these very regions, the student of landscapes can hardly deny that large cities have been growing larger, that some small cities have been lagging and decaying while others developed fast, and that in many centers new skylines sprang up and proliferated, fostered by the anxious and eager endeavors of local communities vying with one another.

So much investment and energy poured into the old cores of cities and into a few spots selected to serve as new cores in larger metropolitan systems indicates some need for grouping together the activities which correspond to the centrality function, traditionally located in central districts. But both the theoreticians of urban analysis, who seemed overwhelmed by the suburban sprawl and interpreted modern urbanization solely as a process of diffusion of the city, and the politicians of most countries where urbanization developed fast, worried about the increasing concentration of population and employment in and around a small number of the large urban centers in their respective countries. In the United Kingdom, it was the flow towards greater London and the surrounding counties in the Southeast; in France, it was the growth of the Paris region; in the Netherlands, the growth of the "Randstadt Holland," and more particularly of Amsterdam; in Switzerland, Zurich and, to a lesser extent, the Lemanic belt from Geneva to Montreux; in Canada, the region extending from Montreal to Windsor, Ontario (which still drains population and employment to a degree that alarms other parts of Quebec and Ontario) is looked upon with suspicion by the rest of the country. In the United States, the trends were more diversified as the national territory and economy were so much vaster and undergoing faster change; on the whole concentration continued to develop in a small number of areas which were acquiring in the process more central functions, while larger areas within the country were being thinned out.

All around the world, about 400 million people were added to the population of metropolitan areas of 100,000 and more during the last twenty years. Probably 200 to 300 million more will be added to these agglomerations during the 1970s. Obviously, many more buildings, taking up more land around old cores or between older cities, have to be added to the standing mass. The master plan for the Region of Paris,[2] published in 1965, indicated the need of building during the following ten years as many new housing units as were counted by the 1962 census in the city of Paris proper. Some people saw in this an indication that something equal to the old city of Paris had to be built anew and outside it. Certainly most of the new residential units have to be built outside the municipal limits of Paris, adding to the suburban sprawl. But the city of Paris is much more than a grouping of residences and of services of the kind that cater to the daily needs of residents. The differences between the residential function and the sum total of the Parisian community was made up, in part, of the conglomeration of industrial plants inherited from the period of manufacturing concentration and, in part, of those special functions and services which gave the city its national and international centrality. This encompasses government, finance and business management, higher education and research, mass media, and entertainment of all kinds. Specialized trades and large-scale merchandise marts are also an important element of the system. Some components of this system could be decentralized and sent away. The Citroën Automotive Works are to be moved to the outer periphery, north of the city. The central produce market of Les Halles has been moved to the southern suburb of Rungis near Orly Airfield. Many smaller industrial establishments and some large government offices have been "decentralized" to more distant locations. For some thirty years legislation has fostered decentralization of industry and restricted the growth of other kinds of land use in the Paris region, including offices. Nevertheless, total employment in the region kept on growing at a faster rate than the national average until very recently. The same trends of concentration were observed and similar legislation enforced in greater London with rather similar results. In the late 1960s it seemed that the flow of people and employment concentrating in the London and Paris conurbations was slackening and that other urban regions in the two countries were growing as fast or faster. Whether this slowdown in concentration was the result of legislative and economic incentives, or a reaction against the overcongested environment of the great metropolises, or whether deeper economic and social forces had determined this shift in trends, has not yet been elucidated.

What remains clear is that while the intense concentration of centrality functions in great international hubs, such as London and Paris, is somewhat decreasing in relative terms, more concentration develops around a few other cities in England and France, where lagging centrality is picking up. We are still far from being able to acknowledge objectively a decrease in the centrality function of large cities, at least of some of them. In fact, trends similar to those in American cities may be observed in the leading cities of Western Europe: in the central cores land speculation remains very lively; land values have been rising; more construction is taking the place of office buildings, civic centers, arenas, theaters, museums, and hotels. The redevelopment leads, however, to an urban core of a more specialized kind. The core is losing some of the manufactures, crafts, residences, and, in some cases, shops, that it used to have. But it is developing in other ways typical of the centrality of a great crossroads system. The economic activities which keep on agglutinating in the urban centers or in their vicinity belong to a somewhat different gamut than before. What those activities are, and how interwoven they are, is now being studied in the major cities of Europe, and the answers obtained should help us understand the new meaning of urban centrality.

The Interwoven Quaternary Activities

Fundamental linkages exist between a good many of the economic activities now expanding in the centers of those cities which are still vigorously growing. In previous writings, I suggested that the common characteristic of these economic activities was that they were mainly concerned with and operated through abstract transactions, which by more or less remote control directed the processes of production and distribution. These transactional activities were traditionally carried on in urban locations and were the product of administration (including the administration of justice), politics, business management, the gathering and interpretation of information—and therefore of the mass media, but also of scientific research, higher education, the performing arts, and the specialized commercial trades aiming at special categories of customers.

All these activities are at some stage interdependent. This we know by logical deduction as well as by empirical observation of the way in which each of these activities operates. We have not tried, however, to analyze systematically the linkages between all those economic activities. In the past, the total number of personnel involved in transactional work was very small. The managerial and professional occupations represented a negligible fraction of the labor force, even in the most advanced countries. The total amount of information available to this specialized and scarce personnel was rather limited and processed at a few major nodes of traffic. The concentration of wealth, power, and knowledge would therefore group the few competent people at selected spots well served in terms of information flow. Large seaports and major seats of political power used to be preferred locations for such concentrations.

The characteristics of transactional work have changed, especially in quantitative terms, during the twentieth century. Rapid progress in the technology of transport and communications on the one hand, and in the geographical expansion of the economically developed world on the other hand, have been the main factors inflating the quantity of decisions to be made, the variety of factors at play in the decision making, the volume and intensity of the flow of information in all fields; to handle this work, the personnel needed to manipulate the data, make the decisions, and perform transactions expanded in parallel. The managerial and profession occupations represent now a substantial proportion of the labor force in advanced countries: about 13 percent in England and Wales (1966), 15 percent in France (1968), 10 percent in Switzerland (1960), 12 percent in the Netherlands (1960), 17.5 percent in Sweden (1965), 21 percent in Canada (1968), and 21.8 percent in the United States (1967). These figures are not quite comparable, as the definitions of occupational categories vary from country to country; but the general picture is clear: the "high status" occupations requiring personnel with special training and qualifications form the most rapidly expanding sector of the labor force.

In the early 1950s, the educated public opinion was stunned to learn from a report prepared by UNESCO that of all the scientific and technological personnel that ever lived, about 97 percent were alive; this percentage may have been established on the basis of debatable estimates about past centuries; still, there was little doubt that it was close enough to the truth. By 1966 the total number of the people employed as faculty by the higher education establishments in the United States rose to 657,000, about 1 percent of total nonagricultural civilian employment, and surpassed the number of all employees in the mining establishments in the country, which remains the largest mining producer in the world. Higher education establishments cannot be found in every village. They are often grouped in or near large urban agglomerations, and such gatherings will attract to their proximity other activities, such as research laboratories and institutes, libraries, museums, specialized trades, and so on, all requiring rather specially trained personnel. There is a sort of cycle and snowballing effect in the interweaving of transactional activities.

The function of urban centrality is returning closer to what it used to be before the Industrial Revolution started; it is again dominated by transactions and by executive, legislative, judicial, and commercial functions. However, two new categories of academic work and research have to be added to the constellation of activities generating urban centrality. And at the same time, a new revolution brings about a novel organization of the labor market for a highly qualified and specialized personnel, which in turn needs the assistance of large numbers of specialized clerical staff. This labor problem becomes one of the major factors of concentration for new jobs, adding to the situation inherited from the past, in which the networks of information were centralized in hubs of power and accessibility.

The old classification of occupations and economic activities in three sectors—the primary, producing raw materials; the secondary, processing them into finished goods; the tertiary, consisting of the services—is no longer adequate. We must recognize a *quaternary* sector of economic activities corresponding to the transactional work which now employs a large and growing part of the labor force. Studying the concentration of white collar workers in Megalopolis, I suggested in 1961 this new *quaternary sector* for labor statistics.[3] It is being gradually adopted as a useful distinction to assess modern trends. In the occupational structure, the quaternary sector is usually meant to include only the managerial, professional, and higher level technical personnel. In fact, it ought to be extended to a part of the more numerous category of occupations designated as "clerical." Perhaps, as time goes on, the upper strata of the clerical occupations will be increasingly taken over by personnel with higher technical skills and academic degrees qualifying in the professional category. At present, however, many clerical workers participate in the data gathering and interpreting process which integrates them with the quaternary rather than the tertiary sector of services. The tertiary sector would remain essentially concerned with the transportation and manipulation of goods, with domestic services, and with the less qualified operations of distribution and sales.

The quaternary sector permeates not only the services but also some of the secondary sector. Publishing, for instance, is considered a manufacturing industry and therefore belongs in the secondary sector of economic activity. A large part, however, perhaps the majority, of employment in publishing firms consists of managerial and editorial staff belonging rather in the quaternary sector. This also is the case of the research personnel of large manufacturing concerns. Research, even in a technical laboratory, is part of the process of data gathering and analysis and this is largely a transactional activity.

To understand the modern *community at work* in the central city, we must observe the interdependence of the quaternary activities. They have a trend to group themselves together. The large cities have a well-known internal geography of adjoining districts which are highly specialized: the financial district, the press and mass media district, the law courts district, and the corporation headquarters area are all subdivisions of what is usually designated as a central business district (C.B.D.). In recent years, the unity of this C.B.D. has been broken up in many cities into two or more groupings. But these different groups remain very much interwoven in this daily work. The interweaving of the quaternary activities has determined the rise of the skylines, the expansion of office buildings, and the very intensive traffic between the various components of the quaternary community within the metropolis, on the one hand, and between several central cities, on the other. This is why decentralization of the upper level of the services has been more difficult to achieve than the dispersal of manufactures or of rank and file offices. This is also why the cities with a large quaternary sector are so bustling and struggling against congestion.

Analyzing the Linkages

During my inquiry into the urbanization of Megalopolis on the northeastern seaboard of the United States, in the late 1950s, it had become quite clear that through their interweaving the quaternary activities were responsible for the lively centrality still observed in the cities of Megalopolis. The largest and most striking case was that of Manhattan. As my study proceeded parallel to, but in coordination with, the survey of the New York Metropolitan Region directed by Raymond Vernon, we pooled our interests and means to attempt a study of the office function of New York City and particularly of Manhattan. This study proved to be quite difficult to do, particularly as attempts at showing the linkages between the various activities carried out in the offices and between office work and related facilities in Manhattan met with the obstacles of secrecy imposed by competition or by confidential aspects of transactions. The New York survey gave up the plan to devote a volume to "the front office of the nation." Still, the question was rapidly sketched in the general volume by Edgar M. Hoover and Raymond Vernon, *Anatomy of a Metropolis* (1959)[4] and in the more specialized volume on banking by Robbins and Terlecky, *Money Metropolis* (1960).[5] To better understand the impact of the interweaving of such activities in the whole network of megalopolis, I proceeded with some analysis of this matter and summed up my conclusions in my book, *Megalopolis;*[6] this led me into the occupational structure, the consideration of linkages measured by the flow of telephone calls and airline connections, and the definition of a quaternary sector. Later, as the debate developed in the 1960s concerning the growing concentration in urban regions and the dilution of urban centrality through the sprawl, I returned to this problem and approached it through the architectural symbol of the skyscraper and the thickening skyline, typical of modern expansion in central cities. This was summarized in the article entitled "Why the Skyscraper?"[7] with a suggestion of transactional work as now characterizing urban centrality.

In the 1960s research by specialists in urban affairs on central business districts evolved and expanded fast. The previous concern with the delimitation of the C.B.D. in space (as outlined by Raymond Murphy and Vance) yielded to a focus on the location and migration of the offices, which were being recognized as a major and rapidly expanding urban land use. Some work on the offices was conducted in America, chiefly through locational analysis of some specific functions such as in William Goodwin's article on "The Management Centers in the U.S."[8] Other analysts were concerned with the geography of the business firm, and stressed the factors determining location of the various components of the firm, particularly the headquarters, branch offices, and so on. The concentration of offices in and around a major metropolis and the need to decentralize by dispersing them to other centers within the nation was more studied in Europe than in North America. The American concern in this area seems to have been determined mainly by fluctuations in land values and the provision of transport facilities. In Europe it was a deeper and more political concern of reviving the vitality of provincial centers. To achieve it, it seemed necessary to stop, or at least slow down, the brain drain and economic drain caused by the concentration of quaternary activities in one part of the country, such as around London, Paris, Amsterdam, or Stockholm.

The work of British geographers and planners in analyzing the location and migration of offices has grown to be an outstanding contribution to urban studies. Most of the work, however, has been done on central London and on the decentralization of offices from London. Location has been an overriding concern in most studies, although some of them (such as the inquiry directed by John W. House in the northeast of England) have paid considerable attention to the circumstances in the local environment inducing migratory trends of quaternary personnel.

Data available from the Location of Offices Bureau and from various studies by academic investigators concur to show that decentralization of offices has been a difficult trend to bring about. In the 1950s the concentration went on in greater London and its surroundings; increased legislative and administrative pressure to decentralize, added to the higher costs and worse congestion in London, seem to have given momentum to the outward migration in the 1960s, and this trend is expected to be sustained in the 1970s. Still, both official reports and scholarly studies show that the vast majority of offices moving out of central London have gone to the periphery of the London region, within a sixty-mile or one-hour-by-train radius, rather than to more distant locations in large provincial cities. Greater mobility within a metropolitan system makes it possible to keep contacts between points in Hemel Hempstead and the London West End, or Croydon and the London East End, with little more time spent on the trip than between points in the East End and West End. Nowadays, a professor at the University of Oxford is required by statutes to reside within ten miles of Carfax, the central crossroads of the city, where the Town Hall stands; a century ago this distance was set at one mile only and ten years ago at four and a half miles. The great ease of transport allows for such extension of the notion of proximity; it is only in the central sections of the larger and more congested metropolises that increased congestion has hardly allowed for improvement in overcoming distance unless a special direct link (such as a well-served underground rail line) exists between the two ends of the trip.

Central functions in London have kept on developing, devouring ground space, pushing high towers into the air, along a traditional east-west axis of traffic, parallel to the river, and continuing westward the link between the merchants and government, a duality that laid the foundation of London's greatness. Recent work by John Goddard of the London School of Economics has well analyzed the patterns of office location in central London. The concentration is striking of financial and related offices in the one square mile of the City, next to the blocks around Fleet Street where publishing and professional offices congregate (1968).[9] P. W. Daniels, of University College, London, has sketched the outward movement of offices (1969).[10] Attempting a synthesis of the situation, the Joint Unit for Planning Research, directed by Peter Cowan, set forth the results of a wider inquiry (1969).[11] The authors show in conclusion that despite decentralization, office employment and new office space have both kept on increasing in the Greater London Council (G.L.C.) area; office expansion proceeded at a much faster rate, of course, in the suburban ring surrounding the G.L.C. area.

However, the Cowan team observed "that the office function is closely tied to changes in society, and that its present ascendancy in the centres of our cities is the outcome of a particular phase of urban life, in which communications are highly important but the technology of communications is still developing." Like so many other analysts of office concentration, they declare their readiness to assume that as present trends develop and the technology of communications improves, "we may find that a larger number of office jobs disappear from the centre of the city, leaving only an elite core behind. Eventually, with further technological advance even this elite may leave the city centre. Home decision-making may be the rule, and office work may become a cottage industry."[12]

One cannot help wondering at this stage how much wishful thinking or decentralizing optimism is responsible for such remarks. Every time I have affirmed the results of my findings, particularly in America and in France, but also in other countries, including Japan, as to the obvious concentration of contemporary quaternary activities in a few central cities, the question has been thrown at me: "Isn't dispersal going to occur soon owing to progress in the technology of communications?" It is noteworthy, and the Cowan team recognizes it in their book, that no signs are as yet present that transactional quaternary work can be dispersed in ways restricting or avoiding direct personal contacts. In fact, such contacts are proliferating on a scale and at a frequency hardly imaginable a quarter of a century ago. Scientific and technological work is increasingly pursued as teamwork; decision making multiplies consultations, conferences, and committees.

Indeed, the transactional activity of a larger center is no longer measured only by the payroll or the floor space of the offices gathered in and around the place. One ought to take into the tableau the movement of participants in the transactions who come into the center from the outside. The movement in and out of central London, of people who do not live or have their employment in the G.L.C. area, is enormous and expanding. It is very difficult to measure it quantitatively and, even more, qualitatively, that is, in terms of its role in the total volume of transactions that are actually negotiated or considered in London. The equipment that services these participants in the work of London offices, though outsiders in terms of statistical count, occupies a large part of the central city. It includes the hotels of the West End, restaurants, theaters and other establishments of the performing arts, specialized shops, luxury department stores, hospitals, museums, libraries, and so forth.

The analysis of quaternary activities is indeed poorly served by studies which limit themselves to one category of land use. The work on office location and growth pursued by so many geographers, architects, and planners brings a worthy contribution in terms of improving the precision of our knowledge about land use patterns in the various cities covered. In this respect the work on London is probably the most advanced, although some good analysis has been conducted on central Paris (for the "Schema Directeur" prepared by the District of the Paris Region in 1965, and by the team of the Atlas of Paris under the direction of Jean Bastié and J. Beaujeu-Garnier). There has also been pioneering work done by Jean Labasse on the financial function in the centrality of Lyon, and a good study of land use in the center of the city of Manchester by R. A. Varley (1968).[13] Important work on the location and decentralization of offices has been done in Sweden. Land use patterns plainly demonstrate the trend of transactional activities to agglutinate in central places well serviced for the purposes of the trade and endowed with good facilities for receiving and entertaining outsiders and for a variety of personal contacts.

In Search of the Center's Coherence

The most notable cases of successful decentralization for rather large offices have been achieved with respect to governmental agencies, or at least some of their bureaus. This is true in several countries in Europe as well as in the United States. It may be related to the fact that the trends in the distribution of offices are now taken between two fires: on one hand, powerful socioeconomic factors work for more concentration within the area easily accessible for frequent personal contact; on the other hand, political pressures work for dispersal over the whole territory of a nation. One of the basic socioeconomic forces is the competitive nature of our society and perhaps of the human species altogether. Competition does not have the same importance for governmental agencies as it does for establishments that do not enjoy the monopolistic privileges of government. It is easier to send away from strategic centers bureaus that do not compete for survival with others in the same field. A competing enterprise wants to be where it can get information, personnel, and clients as good as its competitors do. Competition is an extremely potent reason for being on the spot "where the action is," to both employers and employees. The former compete for the success of their enterprises, the latter for more opportunity and success in their careers. Competition as a phenomenon is extremely difficult to reduce to model form, and even to analyze. It is certain, however, that location is an important factor in the competitive position of any activity that is part of the social and economic processes of society. Inversely, the competition among firms and people must be a factor in geographical distribution, and in the trends of concentration or dispersal. Competition between cities and within the city strengthens in fact the coherence of the urban system.

The analysis of linkages is still based on land use although it has been usually recognized, but more intuitively than systematically, that location in certain vicinities has the advantage of proximity to other establishments with which the functioning of the first establishment considered is deeply involved. This involvement may be partly a matter of the routine work of the establishment, partly a matter of personnel recruitment, partly a matter of prestige or status. This was rather well brought out as a general theory by W. T. W. Morgan (1961).[14] But it would be wrong to disregard the local environment of certain cities which may be particularly advantageous to office work if it is endowed with greater resources in terms of facilities for entertaining, lodging, servicing transient visitors, if it also offers available expert opinion on matters external to the usual routine, adding to this constellation the excitement of artistic, literary, and scientific events. All these circumstances can hardly be equally duplicated in an ever increasing number of places.

The competitive value of a given location depends therefore on more than just the categories of offices with related interests. In the transactions of large centers today there are links between establishments and activities that contribute to the quality of the community at work. The modern method of analysis has been isolating particular cases and categories instead of addressing itself to the general organization of a local manmade and fluid environment the inner wiring of which should be better understood. The centrality of a city has a certain coherence. The map of land use, a basic document, demonstrates it but it does not suffice. Taken in the conflict between forces fostering concentration and the policies of dispersal, the quaternary activities have been fighting an onslaught of chaos. The process caused a painful evolution of the central sections of large metropolises.

There is little doubt that the main international hubs of transactional activity, such as New York, Washington, London, Paris, Amsterdam, Tokyo, and Moscow, are growing so big and so complex that they appear hardly manageable. Very little is known about the way they work. In the constantly self-refining and subdividing division of labor that now affects the masses of white-collar workers, some stages of work require presence in large hubs and others could be performed elsewhere. What can be decentralized and to where are questions that have been little studied in terms of general principles. The practice has chiefly been to forbid new building for certain uses in certain zones, and this restrictive zoning or prohibitive legislation was first applied to manufactures and warehouses, then to offices. While pressure was exerted to push some employment out, incentives were provided either by the central government or by local government, and sometimes by both, to bring the moving activities to areas or places of lagging growth, or even economic decline.

It may be time to investigate the situation in cities of intermediate size (that is, with populations of between 100,000 and 1,500,000) and see how these communities work in terms of urban centrality. Such cities may be able to receive easily new industrial plants and warehouses, but it may be much more difficult for them to accommodate quaternary activities.

Many urban centers grew up owing to the presence of manufactures and did not develop substantial interwoven local networks of transactional nature. Whether such an environment would provide more than exile for quaternary establishments is a question that has seldom been examined. A few cases are known in which some large corporation headquarters tried to move out of a large transactional center to a smaller one, and most of such experiments are known to have failed. The converging moves have on the contrary been frequent and generally successful. It would seem indispensable to study now the linkages of quaternary activities in those cities of intermediate size where some networks have developed, either because of a large regional volume of industrial activity, often linked to a seaport or hub of transport function, or because a network formed around a large institution of potent transactional role, such as a great university (Oxford would be a case in point), a governmental function (such as the case of Edinburgh), and sometimes a religious (such as in Geneva) or recreational function (i.e., Nice or Miami). Some research was conducted in this respect on French provincial cities (especially by Jean Labasse and Michel Rochefort) to prepare the choice of the eight "métropoles d'équilibre."

Such an inquiry should not be restricted to the analysis of the specialized function or agency which may dominate the local situation, but it should focus on the linkages bringing about a network of interdependent activities around the original nucleus. With the support of the university, the Oxford School of Geography has started a study of the linkages of economic activities agglutinating in the city of Oxford and around it. It is hoped that parallel inquiries will be set up in other interesting medium-size cities in the United Kingdom, and later this could be compared to a sampling of West European and North American cities. Correlating the findings of such inquiries may cast some light on how much decentralization from the major hubs can be achieved in the immediate future, and also on what must be the inner structure and the coherence binding together the community of a central city.

Classifying the Factors of Interweaving

From our present yet quite inadequate knowledge of the interweaving of quaternary activities in the hubs of the greater cities, one may derive a tentative classification of the linkages not in terms of land use and physical proximity, but as categories of factors affecting functional needs of the clustering activities. Nine categories of such factors seem to be present in the large and best organized transactional centers.

1. *Accessibility* is the first prerequisite for the development of centrality. Transactional centers usually develop at major crossroads of well-traveled itineraries. In some cases an isolated seat of power may have determined the location of transactions, but these took on substantial volume and acquired a certain permanence only when adequate accessibility was provided to the isolated site. Means of access have of course varied through the ages. In the Roman Empire all roads led to Rome. In nineteenth century France the networks of highways and railways were obviously woven around Paris as the dominant center. In modern Britain the major rail lines and motorways all radiate from London. The airport has now supplied a third means of accessibility, especially important in large countries (such as the United States, Canada, the U.S.S.R., and Brazil), or for insular positions.

There are three major competing means of transport today, besides seafaring: the automobile, the train, and the airplane. The automobile has been a factor of dispersal of economic activities and has greatly congested access to central spots for large numbers of people who want to gather there, particularly at peak time. The problem of parking has been and will remain the nightmare of active urban central districts. American cities have, in most cases, generously provided for parking in the heart of the cities, increasing the cost of land in such areas and lowering the density of profitable use. The maintenance of central coherence in large transactional centers requires rapid public transit, that is, some kind of rail transit. The railway station is still an important factor of centrality in European cities. A frequent rail shuttle serving cities which want to preserve or develop a transactional network between them has proved to be essential in areas of great density of urban centers. A remarkable system of such rail connections is offered by the Trans-Europe Express (T.E.E.) trains between major European cities. The T.E.E. trains have become part of the communications and transactional network of Western Europe, and many transactions are prepared on board during the trip. The new Tokaido line between Tokyo and Osaka is another illustration of the same trend, as is the success of the Metroliner between New York and Washington. On the local scale one notices the number of cities building or expanding underground metropolitan rail systems (such as Stockholm, Milan, Paris, Toronto, Montreal, etc.). In the United States, however, the rail is badly lagging behind. Milwaukee is probably the only American city to have built a new railway station in its C.B.D. in recent years. Most of the mail in American cities is still handled through the central post office located near the railroad station; but today most of the mail travels by air, and considerable truck movement around the old post offices adds to the congestion of city streets. Plans are being made to transfer the work of post offices to the vicinity of airports.

The airport is rapidly becoming a factor of centrality. When located far from the central district, it attracts various establishments, starting with large inns and hotels equipped for conferences and specialized shopping, so that the surroundings of O'Hare Airport, for instance, begin to look like a new loosely designed central district in the suburbs of Chicago. As air traffic expands, airports are bound to attract more services and transactional activity to new locations. This may be noticed in the southern suburbs of Amsterdam, and around the London Heathrow Airport. Twenty cities, located in ten countries, generated in 1967–68 about 80 percent of all the air traffic carried by airlines in the non-Communist world. Air transport has been a factor of concentration on a smaller number of main crossroads.

2. *Information flows* are the second prerequisite of successful central-ity. This has always been the case, and the coffee house is often men-tioned as an ancestor of modern offices. Information is the basic raw material of decision making and transactions. One never has too good information for the decisions one is responsible for. The phrase of Thomas Jefferson that "knowledge is power" is certainly as true as ever. Information today does not flow only through the offices, publications, and broadcasts of the mass media, but it requires an ever-extending and subdividing network of communications. Every quaternary activity heavily depends on the availability of diverse, accurate, and up-to-date information.

Information flows crisscross at a variety of meeting points, outside formal offices: around luncheon or dinner tables, at cocktail parties, in clubs, in the lobbies of conferences, on selected golf courses, and on T.E.E. trains. Whether direct personal contact is essential for the exchange and interpretation of information is now being greatly debated. Electronic equipment to date has not succeeded in disrupting the rapidly growing need for more and more face-to-face meetings for all kinds of purposes, from simple managerial decisions to conferences of national or international experts.

The study of the possibility of transacting quaternary business by wire or over the airwaves does not appear at present to give as satisfac-tory results as does physical presence. Communication over an elec-tronic network may be satisfactory between individuals who know one another intimately and trust one another fully. Between individuals who do not have such a close relationship, communication over networks usually leads to more personal contacts. The reasons for this need of physical presence, a major factor of urban centrality, seem to be imbed-ded in human psychology and in the highly competitive character of a dynamic society.

3. *Transactional performance* is an altogether complex set of factors rather difficult to separate one from another, and to evaluate in quanti-tative fashion. It is closely related to the imperatives of competition. A board of examiners knows how to measure and grade the performance of candidates they are examining for a specific purpose. The purposes of transactions in modern economic life and in political life are quite numerous. Various conditions can be achieved to improve transactional performance in a given locale. This means providing an environment where, besides physical accessibility and the volume and quality of information, other conditions are achieved for the highest efficiency of work: the participants being kept in the best possible mood and fitness, with all the desirable equipment available. Personnel, services, and physical environment must be considered. The coincidence of so many

different conditions will obviously be difficult to achieve outside a few centers endowed with at least some of the needed assets by the past, and where the investment necessary to provide for the desired environment can be afforded. Hence the competition between cities to put together and maintain a transactional center.

4. The *labor market* is a fundamental condition for good performance. It has to be considered at different levels of personnel. The personnel of managerial and professional status is difficult to recruit and to keep outside those areas where it has traditionally gathered or to which it is now attracted by some kind of special glamour and amenities.

To perform their regular duties this upper stratum needs the assistance of a larger number and a great variety of workers at a lower salary level but quite indispensable to the good performance of the establishment. Thus, a well-organized transactional center must offer easy recruiting in a great variety of diverse occupations: from secretaries to sales clerks and restaurant waiters; from accountants and physicians to computer programmers and librarians. Modern technology and automation have accelerated the subdivision of labor in the white-collar occupations, and this process has been still further refined by the rapid expansion in the volume of information transactions require. The volume of the labor market needed at the various levels in quaternary activities will be expanding for some time; the demand is still rising faster than the supply. In a competitive situation, the larger centers can offer greater choice to the employer and more opportunity to the employee.

5. Transactional work employs rather well-paid and choosy personnel. Transactions are better performed in an environment providing *amenities and entertainment.* A center of quaternary activities is normally a large consumer of entertainment, and in competitive situations this may be an important part of the transaction. Moreover, the quality and availability of such services are part of the amenities which make the place more desirable for the workers who are the most in demand. A great variety of amenities and of entertainment services enters into the constellation of activities making up urban centrality. It does not always have to be at the doorstep of the customer, but must be within easy reach by a short trip. There are some good reasons why Covent Garden and Soho are in a central location in central London, why the Paris theater district clusters around the opera, interspersing with financial offices, and why Broadway and Times Square are in the heart of Manhattan. Entertainment is not limited, of course, to the performing arts and to catering; it involves museums, art galleries, monuments, and a variety of events. Amenities include physical as well as cultural local features.

6. *Expert consultation* and specialized services of a professional kind,

including medical services, are another constellation of factors favoring and improving the transactional environment. The need for such services illustrates well the importance of the labor market, especially at its upper level; a large volume of transactions may be expected to attract what could be called a "market of talent" in the professional field. And this links of course with the world of entertainment as well as with white-collar employment in general.

7. The *market of money and credit* involving the presence of a diversified financial community is another obvious category of linkages for any kind of transactional activity. The money market lives by information and generates more of it.

8. *Specialized shopping facilities* are another part of the amenities of the place for visitors from the outside as well as for the recruitment of labor at various levels. Office managers often report difficulties in finding good secretarial and clerical help in areas distant from good shopping facilities. There is a well-understood time budgeting involved for visitors as well as for local people in having the greater possible variety of trading services at hand near the offices.

9. Last but not least, the *educational facilities* are a factor in transactional work. When the New York Port Authority began to offer floor space in the skyscrapers of its projected World Trade Center, institutions such as the Berlitz School of Languages were among the first interested to rent space in a large agglomeration of offices specializing in international trade. The linkage is obvious. Another linkage has to do with the labor market: white-collar workers prefer a location with good educational establishments, either for the education of their children, or to promote their own competence through improved training. Moreover, a university campus usually adds to the liveliness of a city, to the quality of expert advice locally available, and to the customers of the performing arts and other amenities.

We have thus enumerated the nine major categories of interlocked factors through which one may analyze the functional linkages between the various economic activities of a large transactional community, and also the linkages that make for the clustering of each category of activities.

New and Ancient Components of Centrality

The needs and functions of centrality in the modern city are largely reminiscent of very ancient components of the central urban district. Most of the factors enumerated in our nine categories were present in Athens of Plato's and Aristotle's times. Novel elements are found in the greater variety of the means of transportation, and particularly in the disruptive influence that the automobile and the airport exert on inherited locations. Also, the greater variety of expert consultants, of specialized shopping, the much greater role of higher education and of the amenities for the majority of the labor force are new considerations and components of centrality.

The need for security in a large agglomeration, including the security of the transactional activities, is an essential aspect of "urbanity" and it has been too often disregarded until the present wave of criminality began sweeping the streets. What is particularly new and would have been fiercely resented by the political philosophers of classical Greece is the much greater role assumed in the activities of the city by visitors from the outside, usually coming from other cities to perform transactions. The function of receiving these transients, without whose presence a great deal of the transactional activity would lapse or migrate to some other place, causes a certain unbalance in the organization and the coherence of a community. The movement of the outsiders is not included in the usual counts, but it is essential to the routine of the modern central urban district.

It is significant that offices and quaternary activities are beginning to be carefully studied in the more developed countries, but the process of urban evolution will not be understood and attended to by limiting investigations to land use and employment. The central city today is a more complex, interwoven body than that. A city undergoes in its evolution erosion in some parts, fluidity, transfers, and sedimentation in others. It must be looked upon as a process with some physical features, but the dynamism of it is animated by abstract transactions, by an interwoven network of linkages binding together in that place a variety of transactional activities. Too often we avoid the analysis of these interwoven activities, which are the crux of the matter, in the vague hope that new machinery or a wonderful technology will sometime tomorrow undo the knots and simplify our work. In the meanwhile, if the city expresses our society, it also contains it, and the mismanagement and misunderstanding of the urban process gravely add to the ills of society.

Notes

1. Max Weber, *The City,* trans. D. Martindale and G. Newurth (New York, 1966).

2. Délégation générale au district de la région de Paris, *Schéma directeur d'amenagement et urbanisme de la région de Paris,* 1965.

3. Jean Gottmann, *Megalopolis* (New York, 1961), 576–80.

4. Edgar M. Hoover and Raymond Vernon, *Anatomy of a Metropolis* (Cambridge, Mass., 1959).

5. S. M. Robbins and N. E. Terleckyj, *Money Metropolis* (Cambridge, Mass., 1966).

6. Gottmann, *Megalopolis,* chapters 10 and 11.

7. Jean Gottmann, "Why the Skyscraper," *Geographical Review* 56 (April 1966), 190–212.

8. William Goodwin, "The Management Centers in the U.S.," *Geographical Review* 55 (January 1965), 1–16.

9. John Goddard, "Multivariate Analysis of Office Location Patterns in the City Centre: A London Example," *Regional Studies* 2 (1968), 69–85.

10. P. W. Daniels, "Office Decentralization from London: Policy and Practice," *Regional Studies* 3 (1969), 171–78.

11. Peter Cowan et al., *The Office: A Facet of Urban Growth* (London, 1969).

12. Ibid., 262.

13. R. A. Varley, "A Thesis at University College of Wales," Aberystwyth, 1968.

14. W. T. W. Morgan, "A Functional Approach to the Study of Office Distribution," *Tijdschrift voor Economische en Sociale Geographie* 52 (1961), 207–10.

Three

Capital Cities

The city that is a political capital has always attracted special attention. The capital is by definition a seat of power and a place of decision-making processes that affect the lives and the future of the nation ruled, and that may influence trends and events beyond its borders. Capitals differ from other cities: the capital function secures strong and lasting centrality; it calls for a special *hosting environment* to provide what is required for the safe and efficient performance of the functions of government and decision-making characteristic of the place.

The Attributes of Political Centrality

That hosting environment is rather complex; the capital will tend to create for and around the seats of power a certain kind of built environment, singularly endowed, for instance, with monumentality, stressing

The chapter that follows combines two articles. "Capital Cities" is reprinted from *Ekistics*, 299, March/April 1983 88–93. "The Role of Capital Cities" is reprinted from *Ekistics*, 264, November 1977, 240–43.

status and ritual, a trait that will increase with duration. The capital's social environment will also be very special due to the congregation there, ex officio, of certain categories of workers: civil servants, diplomats, lobbyists, news reporters, and, of course, politicians, who are not to be found in similar numbers in other than capital cities. The volume of decision-making sessions influencing various regions is bound to attract to a capital many visitors coming there to transact business, often repeatedly, for more or less prolonged visits. These "business transients" normally come from all parts of the national territory and beyond.

This social structure inevitably causes ancillary activities to develop in the capital: services of all kinds to the government and business community, mass media activities, gathering, processing, and distributing news and diverse kinds of information. Some of these ancillary activities require extra development of the infrastructure, for instance, in the fields of transportation and communications. A capital needs good accessibility to and from all parts of the territory administered and from abroad.

As a result of the capital function, a large and diversified aggregate of labor develops, in the quaternary category of occupations. The political personnel normally form only a part of that labor force. Economic and cultural functions ancillary to the government activities are important components and may come to form a majority in the capital. The diversification process is spurred on by the growth of budgetary expenditures and also by the constant widening of the area controlled or at least regulated by government decisions and legislative texts. The role of the government in the economic, social, and cultural life of most nations has considerably increased in the last century in almost all fields of human activity, through direct or indirect intervention. Although some signs of a rollback of government spending and interference may recently be detected in several countries, all the fields concerned are constantly under discussion in parliamentary assemblies, so that the capital's decision-making range can hardly be restricted. The capital's population will also emphasize the diversity of the nation as it will come from all its regions. Crowds of the discontented may also converge there in the hope of sharing in the privileges of power.

The expansion of the role of government and its attraction for the underprivileged have led to rapid urban growth in capital cities. The longstanding conflict of interest between the central seat of power and the outlying districts and smaller centers of the country has been sharpened and broadened. Center-periphery geographical conflicts have multiplied on the map of almost every nation. Decentralization has become a password, sometimes leading to a preference for federal constitutional structures or to devolution reforms. The former have proliferated throughout the world, though they have not resulted in the same sorts of relationships between central authorities located in the federal capital and the regional, state, cantonal, or provincial types of governments, distributed through the capitals of the component units of the federation. These relationships, though well established, are weak, allowing for a large delegation of authority to the constituent units, such as is the case in Switzerland between the cantons and the confederal government in Bern.

One might like to classify the United States in the category of "weak centralization." This may have applied in the nineteenth century; but, since 1920, the American federal government has steadily and considerably increased its weight within the national system and in international relations. The present image of Washington, D.C., testifies to its past and to the recent evolution.

Political centrality builds up gradually, in slow fashion. This is particularly true in democratic nations which resent all forms of tyranny. Large new capitals may arise in autocratic regimes that strangle challenges within their realm—and look strong and powerful. Thus Peter the Great could impose on Russia the supremacy of his new city of St. Petersburg. His successors developed it so successfully that, even after the city lost its capital function, it remained second only to Moscow in the Soviet Union. The tradition of autocratic government in Iran powerfully established the centrality of Teheran in less than a century. The authoritarianism of colonial governors in the provinces of the Spanish empire left little possibility of displacing the political center away from the established capitals in the republics of Spanish America. The powerful centralization achieved in Edo by the Tokugawa Shogunate prepared for the dominance of Tokyo from the Meiji era onwards.

To assess the real centrality of a capital, numerical data are helpful, but only when examined in the context of the national system which centers on the capital. The constant conflict, built into any political system, that opposes the capital's centrality to the condition of the rest of the territory must not be underestimated. The traditional analysis of capital cities begins with a look at their location in geographical terms. In recent times, a relocation of the seat of power has been carried out in several countries and has been discussed in many more. The reasons behind such moves shed interesting light on what is expected from capital cities.

Location and Relocation

The geographical position of the capital on the map of its national territory varies enormously. To draw a general characterization will inevitably lead to inadequate approximations. A first look at the political map of the world suggests the following observations: in most cases the location of the capital is either rather central or very peripheral; the peripheral locations are usually linked to convenient seaport positions; the central locations appear to reflect advantages of access to and from all parts of the territory; peripheral maritime positions often occur in nations that have been colonies of overseas powers in the past.

This last category is not negligible, especially in our time. The number of members of the United Nations Organization almost tripled between 1946 and 1982 (from about 55 to over 150). Even among the members of the U.N. in 1946, about one-half had become independent states within the preceding 200 years. However, coastal locations (by definition peripheral) also exist in countries that have not known colonial domination, for example: London, Lisbon, Rome, Stockholm, Copenhagen, and Tokyo. Also, in past centuries, Constantinople and St. Petersburg were great capitals of mighty empires. A capital city is necessarily a *hinge* in the relations between its country and the outside world. No government would easily surrender the conduct of foreign affairs to another agency; when such a situation occurs, for instance in Monaco, the state concerned is not considered really sovereign. Direct access to sea navigation has for ages been a considerable advantage in the conduct of foreign policy and the gathering of information from abroad. The move of a Russian capital from Moscow, a central inland location, to a seaboard position at St. Petersburg symbolized in practical fashion the "opening up" of Russia to external influences and its desire to expand on the seas. Similar considerations may have influenced the decision of Emperor Meiji, in 1868, to move the capital of Japan from the inland position of Kyoto to the seaport of Tokyo, which was already endowed with a strong political centrality.

The position of the capital reflects many practical and also symbolical, actually *iconographic,* elements in the selection of its chosen place. A statistical survey would, however, show that geographical centrality competes rather successfully today with coastal peripheral positions.

No political capital has lasted longer as the head of a powerful state than Constantinople-Istanbul, for 1,600 years capital of three successive empires (the Roman, the Byzantine, and the Ottoman), from its establishment as the "New Rome" by Constantine the Great (330) to its dethroning by Kemal Ataturk in favor of Ankara as the capital of Turkey (1923). Constantine chose the site on the Bosphorus officially because he had been so instructed by divine revelation in a dream. The imperial vision, much discussed by historians, may have also reflected careful planning, as is suggested by the Oxford classicist Sir John Myres (in his paper "The Marmara Region," published in *Geographical History* in *Greek Lands* [Oxford, 1953]):

If the New Rome was to defend the empire as a whole, it must be as near as possible, not only to the Danube frontier and to the northwestern trunk-road, by which Aquileia and Milan were to give and receive reinforcements, but to the Euphrates frontier as well. If it was to be a great center of population, it must be fed; so it must stand on the seaboard, within reach of the corn of Egypt, as well as any which might still come from the steppe ports. It must be able to protect these supplies in transit as well as to stop sea raiders out of the north. . . . In case of accidents to resources from overseas, it must have local supplies, and a local reserve of men; so it must command the Thracian cornlands and highlands, as Lysimachia and Adrianople had done, but without the risk of isolation which hampered both of these. . . . It must be essentially Greek for it was to dominate the sentiments as well as the interests of the Greeks.

Political, military, economic, and cultural factors combined in the decision on the location of a capital in the past. Similar considerations operate today with, however, a lesser emphasis on the military, at a time when planes and rockets can strike anywhere from afar, and even on regional economics, at a time of easier long-range traffic and transportation, in a better equipped and policed world. The complexity of the equation remains nevertheless great. It is important to observe the various balances the New Rome needed to achieve, illustrated by the repeated use of "as well as" in successive sentences. The capital is not only a hinge between the country it governs and the outside, but a *pluralistic hinge*, articulating the various sections, networks, and groups of interest within the territory. Constantinople was to be a hinge between Europe and Asia, Mediterranean and Pont, Romans and Greeks, land and sea power. That was probably why it remained for so long a great capital under very different regimes.

The concept of *hinge* may be very useful in understanding capital cities, in terms of both location and centrality. Nineteenth-century new capitals suggest either a historical hinge, linking the present to a great past, as in Rome and Athens, or a sociocultural hinge, linking two parts of a nation that have different cultures and social structures, whose daily cooperation contains a potential conflict of long duration. Such were Washington, between North and South in the eastern United States; Tokyo, between West and East in Japan, and Stockholm, between North and South in Sweden. Certainly, Brussels has been a hinge between the Flemish and Walloon sections of Belgium, and Ottawa between the two large provinces and contrasted populations of Ontario and Quebec in Canada. Even the rather central position of Paris, in the midst of the Paris Basin, had the connotation of a hinge when, in 987, Hugues Capet chose it to be the capital of France: not only was it at the confluence of rivers linking the various provinces of the Basin, but it was also a strong city that had stopped the progress of the Norse inland along the Seine—a hinge between French and Norman lands. In the equation of the Polish capital since the seventeenth century, Warsaw has also looked like a hinge between the various regions of the country. At this point, however, the element of geographical centrality appears to dominate over the concept of the hinge.

Indeed, many capitals are, and have long been, located well inland, rather centrally within the territory. This largely resulted from long historical backgrounds that vary from nation to nation. The more successful powers have generally added to their territories, annexing land at the periphery. Such a process obviously indicated a highly central position for a successful capital. It may occasionally have been reversed at some time by political events. Thus Vienna first commanded the Ostmark, an eastern marchland of the Holy Roman Germanic empire. By conquest eastward it acquired a central position in the eighteenth century German empire, the dismantling of which after 1919 left it in a peripheral position as the capital of a much shrunken Austria, but also as a hinge between East and West in Central Europe.

Since World War I, a number of capital cities have been relocated, and for very diverse reasons. Despite this diversity, the general trend has been overwhelmingly inward, to more central positions. To appreciate this common trend in very different cases, it may suffice to list the removal of the Soviet capital to Moscow, of the Turkish to Ankara, of the Brazilian to Brasilia, of the Pakistani to Islamabad, and of the Nigerian to Abuja. Perhaps a common denominator in all such cases was a turning of the nation inwards, towards its own reconstruction, away from foreign influences and foreign pursuits. No doubt such thoughts were instrumental in each decision, though with varying dosages. But, with the exception of Moscow, they involved the development of new cities or the considerable expansion of small ones, moving the capital away from some large bustling metropolis. They endeavored something new, central, more specialized, in the political function of the capital.

Political Stability Versus Urban Growth

The idea of moving the capital to a new, virgin location and perforce a smaller, specialized city is not new. Certainly, St. Petersburg and Washington, D.C. testify to it. But there are many more ancient precedents, Constantinople among others, and even Megalopolis in the central Peloponnesus, conceived in the fourth century B.C. by Epaminondas as a new town to be the capital of a federation of Greek states, located in a central position to unite North and South, Athens and Sparta. Megalopolis failed rapidly as a capital; Constantinople lasted sixteen centuries as an heir and rival to Rome. In the background of all such moves either recent or ancient, one discerns, repeatedly, a flight from large metropolises, from well-established seats of power, from bustling centers of business. The belief seems well entrenched in the human mind that the political process needs stability and security and that it may be safer, more virtuous, and more efficient in a well-planned sort of political ivory tower.

This attitude is well documented in theology and in political philosophy. In the Bible and in Plato examples of it recur and I have quoted them in several articles. A permanent conflict in politics has opposed the large growing metropolis and the central government of the country. This is an important matter in our days of rapid urbanization and large-scale "metropolitanization." It is expected that, by the year 2000, a clear majority of humankind will live in large metropolises. Perhaps it will also be a world very difficult to govern.

As one examines the long record of the past, one hears the spokesmen for large urban communities asking for more autonomy and freedom. In his excellent book *Ancient Mesopotamia* (Chicago, 1964), Leo Oppenheim mentioned a petition presented by inhabitants of Babylon to Assurbanipal (seventh century B.C.) in which "it is asserted quite pointedly that even a dog is free when he enters the city of Babylon." It needed a large metropolis to challenge a powerful king; but the commercial and cultural activities of a metropolis, especially when it is also a political capital, require some freedom of behavior, of the circulation of information and of traveling, and the guarantee that business freely transacted will be respected and not interfered with in an autocratic fashion. Medieval history is filled with constant conflicts, negotiations, and agreements between rulers and large, rich cities. Many rulers seem to have been so scared of these that they kept nomadizing, with their courts, from castle to castle in small towns or rural sites. The capital city hardly functioned in a feudal context. The political evolution that led to modern democracy starts in Western Europe with the internal party strifes in the autonomous cities of Italy and Flanders. The history of London at different periods could well illustrate the role which the frequent conflicts between the city and the crown played in the process that forged the British system of government.

The case of Paris deserves a special mention: it is often given as the classical example of early and strict governmental centralization, as the seat of strongly unifying authorities, whether monarchic or republican. In fact, the French capital was in almost constant opposition to its rulers. The Middle Ages saw recurrent struggles of academic or merchant elements in the population with the King's *gens d'armes;* grouped on the Left Bank (that is, outside the isle where the royal palace and the cathedral stood), the students and masters of the colleges, having fought kings and bishops, obtained from Rome the charter that gave autonomy and self-government to the University of Paris under the distant authority of the Holy See. On the Right Bank, the Prévôt des Marchands usually led the opposition and, in the fourteenth century, the court moved from the island to the Louvre on the Right Bank, not only to direct the defense against attacks from Normandy, but also to supervise better the merchants' business; the fortress of Bastille reinforced this supervision to the East. However, in the sixteenth century, the court was seldom in the capital and wandered between royal castles on the Loire, St. Germain, and Fontainebleau. Henri IV had great difficulty in obtaining the allegiance of Paris and only the strong administration of Richelieu succeeded in keeping the national government in the capital city.

The return of the king and court to Paris did not survive Richelieu for long. Under the regency of the Queen Mother and the government of Cardinal Mazarin, the civil war of the Fronde agitated Paris for years. The infant king, Louis XIV, had disturbing memories of the crowds around the palace, once even invading his bedroom at night. As he came of age, he spent as little time as possible in the capital and avoided sleeping there. The castle of St. Germain-en-Laye became the main royal residence from 1661, until the new town and great palace of Versailles were made ready to receive the court in 1683. For formal audiences, the king came to the Louvre, and the route of his twenty years commuting between St. Germain and the Louvre has become nowadays the main axis of the expansion westward of the central business district. That major axis of suburban planning, via Neuilly, La Défense, and Nanterre, follows a royal route which expressed Louis XIV's fear of his great capital.

The building of Versailles, planned as a new suburban seat of the court and government, twelve kilometers from Paris, marked an obvious will to separate the big city and the center of political power, that could not be entrusted to the turbulent metropolis. This arrangement lasted a century. One of the first acts of the Revolution of 1789 was to bring the king and court back from Versailles into the city. To make the central city safer for the government after the troubles of 1848, the Second Empire supported the huge urban renewal directed by Haussmann. The metropolis continued growing. The republican governments of the twentieth century tried repeatedly to enforce decentralization policies and stop the growth of the Paris region, so often accused of sucking the sap of the national system. Today the Paris metropolitan region accounts for about one-fifth of the nation. This is not an exceptional proportion: similar situations of the conurbations of the capitals exist in many other countries, for example, the United Kingdom, Denmark, Austria, Ireland, Greece, Japan, Argentina, Uruguay, Chile, Peru, Colombia, Costa Rica, Mexico, and Nicaragua.

It is rather common, in fact, for the capital to be the largest city in the country. With modern urban growth, this situation tends to become a rule in centralized nations, but in federal structures it is usually not the case. The United States has set the fashion of capital cities of moderate size, away from the main metropolis. Washington was set in the District of Columbia, not only as a hinge between North and South, but also to locate the federal government away from the great American cities of New York and Philadelphia, which had vied for the role of capital. Even on the level of the individual American states, capitals have often been situated in rather small towns: Albany for New York, Harrisburg for Pennsylvania, Annapolis for Maryland, Austin for Texas, and Madison for Wisconsin. These cities have all grown but on a more modest scale than the major metropolises in their state.

Canada, with Ottawa, has followed the American model; and the choice of Bonn for West Germany probably follows a similar concept. The Netherlands have, for several centuries, adopted another, seldom applied, solution: their statutory capital has been Amsterdam, the great metropolis, but the government and parliament have been at The Hague, the old seat of the counts of Holland. In the dense urbanization of the Randstadt Holland, The Hague may look, on the European scale, like a suburb of Amsterdam. It is, however, a substantial agglomeration of about half a million people. To avoid a city-crown conflict, The Hague was never given city status; legally it remains only a "village," which echoes Henrikson's description of Washington.

Recently the vogue of new capitals has been spreading: carefully planned, specialized cities established in central locations at a distance from the major growing conurbations. Thus, Ottawa, Ankara, Canberra, Pretoria, Brasilia, Islamabad, Abuja. Several kinds of considerations dictated the decision in each case as well as the choice of the site. Often it was the desire to create an active growth point in a central location, in the midst of a little-developed section of national territory. It must be recognized, however, that a dislike of the environment of a great, bustling, turbulent, cosmopolitan metropolis as the seat of the national government has, in every case, been one of the determining factors. This distrust is not altogether prejudice or inherited tradition. The political fear of bigness in cities remains one of the stumbling blocks to better urban planning, even in the more advanced nations. There is something inherent in the large metropolis that causes a conflict to arise in the markets and the streets with the normal viewpoints of national politics. Certainly this is partly because the successful metropolis, especially if it is also the capital, tends to assume too much authority towards the rest of the country, to attract too many of the desirable functions, and also shows too much independence through reliance on its foreign and distant relations. It may also be partly due to the greater familiarity with the machinery of power that living in the same community breeds among the citizenry, giving it a sense of responsibility and authority which other cities may lack.

Old and New: The Search for the Optimum

Capital cities have rather frequently been on the move. In China, Japan, and some other countries, this used to be the custom in ancient times. Each ruler or dynasty preferred a new seat of power, perhaps as a symbol of the passing of authority from the preceding establishment. New capitals have sprung up and old ones, once demoted, have had varied destinies. In a few cases, the capital function has been returned to an old place that it had deserted for centuries. Rome and Moscow are cases in point. Both, however, had continued to play a signal role after they had been deprived of their political capital function.

At a memorable discussion on capital cities at the Società Geografica Italiana in Rome in 1981, the distinguished Italian scholar and statesman, Francesco Compagna, asked the question: "And what of the former capitals? Has their fate been studied?" He was thinking, of course, of his city of Naples, and also of many other Italian cities: Venice, Milan, Turin, Florence. . . . The case of Italy in this respect is special, but it is not unique, and evokes other lands with a scattering of former capitals: Germany and India among others.

As the search proceeds for the optimum hosting environment of a capital, new capital cities arise, causing past capitals to multiply. As one scans the historical record and the present map, one realizes that, on the whole, past capitals have survived the moving out of government institutions fairly well. Most of them have remained notable cities with a substantial economic centrality. In some cases cities that enjoyed the powerful capital status for a prolonged period inherited from it the function of a religious center. Although the temporal authority seemed lost, a spiritual authority maintained political significance for the place. Rome, Jerusalem, Constantinople, and Moscow are famous examples from the past, and there are others, such as Ghardaïa, in the Sahara, heir to the short-lived Ibadite empire. Still, the main road to survival of past capitals has been through their economic activities. In contrast, some failed capitals, especially those of short duration, have barely survived as villages: thus Megalopolis of Epaminondas, politically artificial even if centrally located.

In 1967, having lectured on the city as a political phenomenon at University College London, I heard a memorable comment from Lord Holford, the great British planner, who chaired the session: what I had said of Louis XIV's attitudes to Paris and Versailles had reminded Holford of the instructions he received from President J. Kubitschek, of Brazil, when working on the committee which selected the plan for Brasilia. Brazilian politicians, said Kubitschek, did not feel at ease in Rio de Janeiro, which was too cosmopolitan, a city penetrated by foreign interests and too linked with ventures abroad; they needed a new capital, inland, where they would "feel at home." Surely a similar feeling strongly influenced Ataturk's decision to move the capital to Ankara; while it was just the contrary, to combat the inward-turned spirit of the Moscovite establishment, that drove Tzar Peter the Great to build St. Petersburg. In each case there certainly was also a will to create a new well-endowed growth point, and to erect a lasting monument to one's own rule; still the deep desire to get away from an established, little-controllable metropolis was probably decisive, as it had been in the building of Versailles.

Capital cities reflect the political life of their nations and the personalities of the leaders. As circumstances change, the search goes on for the optimum hosting environment. The twentieth century has seen a very large number of cities around the world achieving the status of political capitals of independent nations. Many of these nations have been recently formed political units, resulting from the whims of history and colonial rule. Their capitals were bound to be, to a large extent, "artificial" in the sense that they were produced by external influences rather than by a slow, secular process of internal selection and evolution. It is noteworthy that, in most cases, the nations achieving independence preferred to keep as their capital the city where the colonial administration had been centered. Continuity prevailed in this respect amidst the change.

Partly this may be a compliment to the flair of the past governors who seem to have set the seat of their administration in the right place. That place may have already been a historic center which benefited through the years from the centrality it enjoyed under the colonial regime. Partly, these decisions were influenced by the existence in those cities of a hosting environment fitted for the exercise of authority, for decision making, concerning that territory. Preparation for this was more in terms of the built environment but also to some extent of the social environment. In fact, as one looks back over some fifty years, capital cities have moved much less than one might have expected.

Still, decisions to build new specialized cities as capitals for countries with federative constitutions have been much admired. Long discussions have also taken place and plans have been drawn up for Brasilia-type new capitals in unified and centralized nations, such as Japan. There is always a desire to decentralize very large metropolitan systems that are also political capitals. The idea of taking out the capital function springs naturally to the fore, and it may be reinforced by an obvious vogue of brand-new capitals. The question then arises again: Is there an optimum pattern and environment of a capital? The answer hinges on a more general problem: Does the political governmental process operate better, in a safer and more stable fashion, in an ivory tower specially conceived for the purpose or in close contact with a lively metropolis? The answers to these two questions remain hotly disputed. No doubt the daily life and the bustle of the metropolis are an unsettling factor, bound to disturb the serenity which, in principle, ought to prevail in the exercise of authority. On the other hand, the ivory tower circumstances may remove, or at least delay and blur, the knowledge of the daily problems of a fast changing world, whose solution or alleviation form a major task of the government. It has often been argued that the specialized new capital, even if in an isolated location, is no longer an ivory tower owing to modern communications technology. Indeed, the airplane and the progress of telecommunications have overcome most of the previously isolating effects of distance. Brasilia was designed in the shape of an airplane to remind us all of the new circumstances of the era, and air shuttles keep it much closer to major metropolitan centers than would have been possible in the past. Telephone, telex, and television work in the same direction. Still it is a much quieter place than Rio de Janeiro. Brasilia is a very young city. The vitality and size of Brazil have caused it to grow fast, and it will certainly develop further. Nevertheless, it is not a happy or really lively place. Should the capital reflect the tone of the nation or not?

Brazil is a very original country. Its culture and behavior are clearly different from those of other South American states, which have received more Spanish inheritance. It is also a vast, complex, and diversified country. Perhaps it needs the symbol of the airplane to keep it together and progressing. A capital city must be, first of all, adapted to the culture and expectations of the country it governs. Generalizations in this field are bound to be frail. Perhaps the safest deduction from all that precedes is that the human species has always been divided and hesitant on this issue. It has wanted the capital city to work well as a hinge and yet still to enjoy the philosophical advantages of the ivory tower.

Basically, humankind is a highly experimental species. It likes to try new solutions. In an age of rapid and massive urbanization, the fashion has arisen of putting governments into specially designed, somewhat secluded places, equipped with the tools of modern technology. There is excitement in the experiment; there is also a deep-seated fear of the uncontrollable big city.

In the context of this age-old dilemma concerning the location of government, I was fortunate to observe in 1946–47 the curious experiment of the procedure that led to the choice of the permanent headquarters of the United Nations. The invitation to settle in the United States being accepted, the U.N. was offered a variety of possible sites after its first temporary and most unsatisfactory quarters at Lake Success, in Long Island. The possible permanent sites were scattered from the East to the West coasts, some in suburban locations, some in a rural territory with specially designed new buildings to house assemblies, offices, and personnel. The choice appeared very difficult to make. Suddenly the offer was made of a derelict piece of land near the heart of Manhattan, at Forty-second Street on the East River. It was quickly accepted and with pleasure by a large majority. There was some apprehension about New York City; but there was even more apprehension about a rural secluded place. Most people who work in governments seem ultimately to prefer the big city, even though they may not feel at home there. Should the capital be a home to relax in? It hardly ever was for the personnel of politics.

Primate and Capital Cities

An increasing number of cities are acquiring the status and function of political capitals. This is the result of a great political partitioning of the world: there are not only many more independent countries but a larger number of these have adopted federal or regionalized constitutional systems. National or regional capitals are mainly seats of governments whose competence extends over a territory of some size. The area of territory is not, in fact, of decisive importance in determining the actual role of the "capital function." Singapore, for instance, is a rather small island and the city which is its capital occupies a good part of it. But the city's population is large; its economic and political activities, by their diversity, intensity, and the far-reaching systems of relations make it an important capital, despite the smallness of the country as a whole.

The emergence of one particularly large and commanding city in every country was documented in 1939.[1] Such primate cities were often but not necessarily the political capital; there were notable exceptions, such as New York, Zurich, Calcutta, and others. In a few cases the seat of government had been transferred from a primate city to a much smaller place for the specific purpose of divorcing the two. Such separation has long existed in the Netherlands, where Amsterdam, a primate metropolis, remains constitutionally the capital, but the seat of the government, except for a few solemn acts, is located at The Hague.

Specialized Capital Cities

Choices of smaller cities as federal capitals have been more frequent since 1800, often as a compromise between rival large cities or conflicting regional interests, thus: Washington, Bern, Ottawa, Canberra, Pretoria, New Delhi, and more recently Bonn.

A somewhat different set of considerations determined Kemal Ataturk's decision in 1922 to move the Turkish capital from Istanbul, the primate city, to a geographically more central location at Ankara. Ataturk presided over a new national and republican Turkey, which had lost its empire. While Istanbul symbolized a peripheral and cosmopolitan development, Ankara was the symbol of an inward-turning nation, concentrating its endeavors towards the development of its own territory and personality. In a way Ankara pointed to a national reform almost opposite to what Peter the Great had attempted two centuries earlier, when opening up Russia to the outside and moving the capital from Moscow to the new city of Sankt-Petersburg on the Baltic. Curiously, Lenin, seeking to eliminate Western influence in the Soviet Union, moved the capital back to Moscow after the 1917 Revolution.

The spectacular decision by Brazil to transfer its federal capital from Rio de Janeiro to the centrally located and carefully planned new city of Brasilia was due to combined reasons which included the desire to avoid the rivalry of great cities (Rio and São Paulo), the will to turn national policies towards the development of an immense and empty interior, and the hope that such a central and isolated location would free the political process from the pressures and lobbies of the large business center of "cosmopolitan" Rio de Janeiro. If the move to Brasilia could in many ways be explained by considerations similar to those associated with the choices of Washington, New Delhi, and Ankara, it is most closely akin to the last. The main imperatives were to spur on the development of the interior and to get away from the international and merchant character of Rio, which politicians from the interior such as President J. Kubitschek deeply distrusted.

The distrust of the turbulence and power of the organized interests in a large commercial and industrial metropolis has long been deeply ingrained in the political process, especially of democratic systems. Representatives of the people who live outside the primate city are naturally suspicious of the wealth, greed, ambitions, and adventurous spirit of individuals and organizations normally concentrated in great, bustling economic centers with far-flung networks of interests. They seem strange and evil to the quieter, more localized, provincial approach which usually predominates among the political representatives of a nation. The Bible provides a clear illustration of this attitude in the representations made to King Rehoboam against continuing his father Solomon's costly expansionist and cosmopolitan policies, which made Jerusalem such a great capital, and in the revolt of the ten tribes that followed (1 Kings 12, and 2 Chron. 10). Plato in his *Laws* wanted in an ideal *polis* the population gathered inside the territory and screened from foreign and maritime influence and involvement by a small corps of specially trained civil servants. His theory was that a high degree of isolation would foster better and more stable policies.[2] Both Ataturk and Kubitschek applied Platonic political philosophy, perhaps without knowing it, in the choice of Ankara and Brasilia.

There is something inherent in the large growing metropolis that causes a conflict to arise with the normal viewpoint of national politics. Partly this is because the successful metropolis tends to assume too much authority towards the rest of the country, to attract too many of the desirable functions, and to show too much independence through reliance on its foreign and distant associations. Partly it is because of the suspicion and fear of the foreign interests and their associates so obviously concentrated in the primate city.

One of the essential functions of government is, nevertheless, to deal with foreign relations, and foreign trade, and to supervise the networks linking the country with the outside. In the modern era, the networks of relationships between nations and between cities have proliferated in all directions. A capital city cannot avoid serving as a hub for the interplay between these external networks and the internal economic and political structure of the country. The greater political partitioning of the world, the increasing division of labor between various regions, the growing intricacy and interweaving of foreign trade and international financing all concur to make political systems of the inward-turned Plato or Tokugawa variety rather unlikely in modern capitals. In such circumstances the very dynamics of capital cities would have to adapt to new mechanisms. If the seat of the government is kept isolated, highly specialized, and separated from the center where the major transactional movement occurs, the political capital may develop slowly and remain relatively small. It will not escape some foreign presence and some international intercourse, at least, owing to the existence of a diplomatic corps.

A capital city may, however, leave to another, larger metropolis the role of economic capital. Such a duality of capital functions may in some cases be inherited from the past, as in the Netherlands, Italy, the United States, Canada, Switzerland, Morocco, and Israel, among others. Or it may be a recent and more complex relationship, such as in Turkey, Brazil, or West Germany (the latter two counting a plurality of "economic capitals"). In fact, all such situations cause some political functions to be exercised in the economic capitals and some economic institutions and transactions to develop in the political capitals. A more frequent occurrence is still the coincidence of both functions in a primate city which is then the real capital.

The Growth and Wealth of Athens

An interesting analysis of the recent growth of such a primate capital city is to be found in the book on Athens by the French geographer Guy Burgel.[3] Burgel shows that the growth and wealth of Athens cannot be explained either by geographical location or by the industries in the city and its vicinity. The explanation, as he sees it, lies in the capital function of Athens.

Its wealth appears based much more on consumption than on production, its dynamism supported by acquired wealth rather than by the advantages of undisputed location. . . . The observer cannot simply understand the budgets of either the conurbation or of its inhabitants, so disproportionate are the resources to the expenditure. . . . Its mode of growth makes Athens representative of a new generation of urban centers. . . . Artificially recreated in 1835 by a foreigner-king, eager to establish his prestige and authority on a historic site, Athens is a Brasilia that has succeeded.

Dr. Burgel surveys diverse paradoxes in the present vitality and development of Athens. Basically he explains that the growth mechanism is due to the capital function which succeeded in concentrating the political, economic, and social direction of Greece. He compares Athens to the two other capitals of Mediterranean peninsular countries: Rome and Madrid. Both grew rapidly in the last twenty years, achieving a population size similar to the Athenian, that is, close to three million. Rome has recently grown faster than Milan, and Madrid faster than Barcelona. The capital function is indeed an important factor in the redistribution of urban weights around the Mediterranean.

In the case of Athens, Dr. Burgel may have underestimated the contribution to the Greek capital of the networks provided by the Greek Diaspora. This is difficult to survey with precision but is certainly an important component in the Greek capital's equation. Similarly, the world crossroads function plays an even greater part in the dynamism of Rome, as shown by Ludwick Straszewicz, the Polish geographer, in his comparative study of great European capitals: London, Moscow, Paris, and Rome.[4] In Rome, the spiritual and cultural external networks compensate for the absence of the economic capital function which is still located in Milan.

Roles for Capitals

The modern role of a capital may, therefore, be assessed by combining a plurality of factors. If an equation to determine a capital's role could be worked out, it would consist of at least three categories of factors. A first category would provide measurements of the national or provincial entity administered from the capital: area of territory, size of population, variety and volume of local resources, wealth of the people, rate of growth, and so on. A second category of factors would outline the networks of outside relations of the political entity concerned. A capital is by definition the place where major decisions are taken which relate the political entity governed and its inhabitants, resources, and institutions to the world beyond its boundaries. The capital is a crossroads where sets of internal and external relationships and networks interlock and interact.

The third category of factors would express the extent of control or intervention that governmental authorities in the capital exercise over the people, resources, and activities within the territory: what portion of the domestic product is gathered by taxation and redistributed through the budget; how much legislative and judicial interference into the people's lives is allowed by the local regime; are the institutions in the capital endowed with temporal authority only or with functions giving spiritual guidance and cultural direction to the community as well? The degree of governmental control over the production, trade, or services in the territory governed is of considerable portent, especially through its consequences for the size of the bureaucratic personnel and the variety of business transacted.

An equation of the "capital role," incorporating and relating all the factors that may be included in all three categories, would vary greatly, depending on the specific case. It would also change frequently in a time of instability. The present era is characterized by a rapid evolution of technology, of economic and social circumstances, which is bound to cause substantial changes in capital cities in most cases.

The role of government in stabilizing poles of urban growth is, however, an old and permanent factor of urbanization. The "castle" and the "temple" are the oldest architectural and locational symbols of urban centrality. These still are of paramount influence in shaping, supporting, and stabilizing the internal structure of central cities which can claim a castle and temple function. The castle must be interpreted as the seat of political power; nowadays, one may wonder whether the high towers housing headquarters of large corporations or strong professional organizations could not be assimilated to the castle function. In modern times the power of private concerns managing far-flung networks extends far into the administration of political as well as economic affairs: such concerns may be multinationals providing goods or services, large banks or insurance companies, or even labor unions and professional organizations.

The temple function is subject to more specific interpretations: it deals with spiritual rather than temporal authority. Despite the decreasing role of religion *stricto sensu* in the social and economic life of individuals, the political weight of religious beliefs and organizations remains considerable throughout the world. The presence of a cathedral no longer signifies as much activity, authority, and transactions as it did in the Christian world prior to the eighteenth century. But who could doubt that the presence of the Mormon Temple in Salt Lake City, capital of Utah, and of the headquarters of Christian Science and of a Roman Catholic Archbishopric in Boston, capital of Massachusetts, still contribute substantially to the vitality of these two cities.

The temple or castle functions of the past have bequeathed some modern versions of spiritual influence to many cities in which they used to be important. These are still measurable in the form of academic authority or of cultural pilgrimage, and both these categories of activities produce economic spin-offs for the locality. The case of Boston reminds us that the former capital of American Puritanism has retained not only its role as a center of historical pilgrimage but also its immense national and international cultural, especially academic, influence. Education and the advancement of culture used to be closely related to religious authority in Christian and Moslem countries. Most universities began in medieval Europe in the shadow and under the protection of a cathedral or abbey. They succeeded especially well in places where they could also claim the patronage of a strong castle. The early histories of Paris, Montpellier, Bologna, or Oxford, among many others, testify to this rule. Some modern centers of political pilgrimage, which also attract offices of international political organizations, owe their role to a tradition of religious authority: Rome, Jerusalem, and Geneva are outstanding examples.

The twentieth century has enormously expanded the impact of government and of private large-scale management. Administrative interference in economic, social, and cultural activities increases every day. These trends develop both in totalitarian countries under communist regimes and in capitalist democracies because all need more planning, more provision and regulation of services on a vast geographical scale (whether national or regional), and more redistribution of the collectively generated wealth to obtain welfare and some economic protection for the individual.

The rapid advances of technology and automation may have relieved the constraints on human labor by the necessity of producing goods. However, the complexity of the ensuing processes increased the need for governmental intervention. In the pre-industrial age, for instance, most of the services to transport people and messages could be left to private initiative and enterprise; nowadays, governments find it necessary to regulate, and in many countries to operate, the transport of passengers, and the operation of the post office and of the telecommunication networks. Hence the rise of employment by governments and the greater transactional activity in and around governmental offices, so obvious in cities endowed with a capital function.

The expansion of the regulatory role of government is the foundation of the growth of capital cities as centers of employment and of economic activity. This is not simply a corollary of the rising numbers of jobs in government employment: large sectors of this personnel must be broadly deployed throughout the territory, as is the case for postal carriers and police officers. But government activities cannot develop without constant participation by representatives of those concerned. The famous 200-year-old slogan, "no taxation without representation," has not lost any of its timeliness. Participation through some sort of representation is accepted in most political regimes and increasingly so. Thus government activity generates a generous spin-off of related activities in major centers: it results in the continuous or recurrent presence in these cities of large numbers of active persons who may be officially resident there or elsewhere, and who may officially be employed there or elsewhere, but who spend time and perform an important part of their work in transactions at such places.

Transactional Crossroads

Modern capitals experience a dynamism which cannot be adequately measured any longer by the usual data on population and employment. A capital is a transactional crossroads catering to the problems and needs of vast areas from where transients come to the capital, in more or less regular and recurrent fashion, to transact diversified business or gather information. The recent evolution of Paris could not be understood without allowing for such currents.[5] The problems of London, Paris, or New York, among many other great cities, must be seen in the light of a new urban geography that adapts to the trends of the contemporary world towards a predominantly white-collar society, processing information, and seeking amenities and excitement while engaging in complex and tiresome abstract transactions.[6]

The capital city assumes among transactional centers a particularly active role. Arnold Toynbee in his *Cities on the Move* rightly stressed the role of capitals as melting pots and powder kegs, but the modern evolution is even more complex.[7] The governmental function fosters the endowment of capitals with amenities of various kinds, with rituals and touristic attractions. The commanding operations of political, economic, and cultural affairs necessitate the gathering and processing of masses of information. In the present mutation of mankind's styles of life and modes of work, a capital city develops a special quality of attraction for people as a place either to live in or to visit. And the number of cities exercising at least in some specialized or regionalized way a role of capital is certainly increasing. The intensity and complexity of the functions concentrated in the large capitals breed decentralization and delegation of authority to smaller centers. It may be worthwhile to attempt a classification of the emerging categories of capitals around the globe. The notion of capital city is not simple nowadays and such a list of categories may well be long and difficult to draw up.

With the modern evolution of employment and of society, the function of the capital city increases in weight as a factor in the selection of growth centers. It also improves the way in which the community looks at itself. The web of capitals becomes the foundation of the shaping networks of transactional cities.

Notes

1. Mark Jefferson, "The Primate City," *Geographical Review* (1939).
2. Plato, *Laws* 4.704–5.737.
3. Guy Burgel, *Athenes, étude de la croissance d'une capitale mediterranéenne* (Paris, 1975).
4. Ludwick Straszewicz, *Wielikie Stolice Europy* (Warsaw, 1974).
5. Jean Gottmann, "Paris Transformed," *Geographical Journal* (March 1976): 132–35.
6. I shall not elaborate here these trends with which I dealt already in previous publications (see especially *Megalopolis* [New York, 1961], chapter 11, "The White-Collar Revolution") and in several articles in *Ekistics*, especially "Urban Centrality and the Interweaving of Quaternary Activities," *Ekistics* 174 (May 1970): 322–31 (see chapter 2 of present volume), and "The Evolution of Urban Centrality," *Ekistics* 233 (April 1975): 220–28.
7. Arnold Toynbee, *Cities on the Move* (London, 1970). See also Jean Gottmann, "The Growing City as a Social and Political Process," in *Transactions of the Bartlett Society* 5 (1966–67): 11–46 (see chapter 6 of present volume).

Four

The Study of
Former Capitals

Reflecting on the category of past capitals raises many interesting problems.[1] No one would doubt that such cities exist and that they must have specific characteristics; but how to define "former capital"? There could be many borderline cases. Would discussing the loss of capital status throw light on what is the proper function of a capital? How much of this function is or isn't removed when a city loses the title of "capital"? The whole issue of the nature of "centrality" in modern cities may be clarified thereby, for the capital is a center par excellence though many cities are great centers without being political capitals.

Where are those past capitals? Does their geographical distribution help us to understand the stability, or lack of it, characterizing certain cultures? Or could the frequent moving of capitals be fully explained by some historical inheritance? Once the title and the functions of capital are lost, does decline necessarily set in? Or could there be evolutive compensation? The study of former capitals appears potentially rich in stimulating lessons. One could not answer so many questions in a brief

Reprinted from *Ekistics*, 314/315, Sept./Oct.–Nov./Dec. 1985, 541–46.

essay, but let us try to outline a few guidelines for the study of former capitals.

What Is a Former Capital?

A capital city is the seat of central government of a separate political unit. Normally such a unit should be a "state," that is, a territory politically constituted in a way that makes it obviously different from its neighbors. It is therefore vested with a certain degree of sovereignty recognized by other states. In federal unions such as the United States, Brazil, India, or West Germany there is a federal capital plus one capital per constituent state. Thus Albany, New York, or São Paulo must be considered capitals in the latter more regional category: government institutions and processes are located in those cities.

A former capital is a city which has enjoyed the status of capital for a period in the past, and has lost it. The loss is clear in most cases, especially in unitary political systems. It may be more disputable in federal systems: for instance, West Berlin may still be endowed with capital status because it constitutes by itself a *Land* of the Federal Republic of Germany. East Berlin is the national capital of the German Democratic Republic (East Germany). The capital status of either of the two Berlins is of course much diminished as against what the united Berlin had been, the imperial capital of the strongly centralized Germany of the past. Still Berlin is not a former capital. Neither could Hamburg be considered one, although the amount of autonomy and sovereignty that free city now enjoys as a *Land* of West Germany is much diminished in comparison with what its political powers might have been when Hamburg was a member of the Hanseatic League and a free city of the Holy Roman Germanic empire. The category of former capitals need not be extended unduly; in the contemporary world it is numerous enough: Istanbul, Leningrad, Cordoba, Nancy, Pau, Naples, Venice, Turin, Kyoto, Nanking, and even Edinburgh are obvious examples among others.

A few national constitutions recognize a plurality of capitals in the same state. This is usually an inheritance from a historical evolution which has removed the actual seat of most governmental institutions from cities which are past capitals but has not removed the constitutional title and dignity from these cities. Such is the case of Morocco, where normally the seat of government is Rabat, but owing to tradition, Fez, Meknes, Marrakesh, and Tangiers all keep the title of capital, and occasionally the king comes to reside in one or another of these cities. Another variant is found in the Netherlands, of which Amsterdam is the statutory capital where certain solemn acts must be performed, but The

Hague is the seat of the court, government, and parliament. The Hague however is not even classified as a city, but is considered a "village" despite its population of half a million. The Hague used to be the seat and capital of the counts of Holland during the feudal era. Should it be termed therefore a "former" capital even when it is the seat of political institutions and of decision-making processes which precisely characterize national capitals in other nations? We shall not do so; history and geography abound in curious, self-contradictory situations. But the Dutch situation suggests another question: How sovereign and lasting should a city's capital function have been in the past to justify its being recognized as a former capital?

This question hints at many difficulties in the way of a clear-cut definition of capital city. In modern times we have become accustomed to a certain stability of the location for the capital function and to a clear definition of what the national state is. This simplicity, however, may have been illusory. Both concepts result from a picture of political organization that emerged in Europe and the Americas during the nineteenth century. The remaking of the world map after World War I, continued in the aftermath of World War II, gave to many the impression of the whole planet being almost totally covered with independent national states, each with its capital. There are today some 160 such recognized states, twice as many as around 1950. There are at least a dozen more not recognized by the United Nations. The proliferation of nation-states, of varying size, strength, and cultural or economic development, rapidly brought about doubts as to their viability as full-fledged partners of the international community. Indeed, around 1960 the opinion could be voiced in influential American reports that "while everybody was becoming independent, nobody was really sovereign any more." Others wrote about the decline or even demise of that national state. Capitals of great standing were being demoted; new ones were being built. A number of the newly formed national states, especially those physically constituted on archipelagos of scattered islands, experience difficulties in ascertaining that the cities designated as their capitals function in practice effectively as dominant national centers.

The difficulties and doubts experienced in an era of accelerated change, of momentous transition, owing to the political and economic restructuring of the world system, underscore the complexity of the centrality a capital must possess in order to function as it ideally should. To obtain this result in a city, it is not enough to install there the institutions of central government, including the parliament and the highest courts of law, and to gather around them the attendant activities such as the diplomatic corps and the ancillary services (which include entertainment, adequate transport facilities, etc.). A striking example of the hosting environment of the political process is provided at present by the case of Brasilia, the new monumental city in the heartland of Brazil, where the Brazilian national government gradually moved since 1960 from Rio de Janeiro. In terms of planning capitals and creation of new towns, Brasilia has been a spectacular event, watched with attention all around the world. Backed by strong political will and by the resources of a vast, rapidly developing nation, Brasilia may be considered a success as an endeavor at new capital building: its population rose from 140,000 in 1960 to 1.3 million in 1980; its monumental government buildings are widely admired; it has become a place of pilgrimage for architects and planners; it has been imitated in other countries that decided to decentralize from their main metropolis and to transfer the government to a geographically more central location.

But what has happened in Rio de Janeiro, the former national capital of Brazil? The city's population still increased from 4 million by 1966 to 5.5 million in 1980, adding in 15 years more than the total population of Brasilia. Its outlying suburbs continue to grow, and several new monumental buildings, including a new cathedral, have been erected in the last 20 years. It remains the seat of many leading economic establishments, and of major Brazilian offices of foreign firms which have not gone to São Paulo, the largest city and industrial center in Brazil. Most linkages with the outside world, especially outside South America, operate from or through Rio de Janeiro. The hosting environment of transactional activities has remained very lively. The former capital continues to be the major hinge between Brazil and the outside. This is especially obvious in cultural terms, despite the active competition of São Paulo. Most international conferences meeting in Brazil take place in Rio; in fact, it is the only Brazilian city that has the facilities and personnel to accommodate them.

One may observe that Brasilia is a very young capital on the scale of history, even for the New World. It is still being built up, in a central but yet little developed area. Moving all the institutions and related services of the government of a large and rather centralized nation takes time. Rio de Janeiro in the meanwhile keeps various functions inherited from its past capital status. It may well be that former capitals can profit from their heritage, and it may be enlightening to try to explore what that inheritance bequeaths.

The Inheritance and the Orbit

The political power located in a capital city demonstrates its predominance in several ways which are bound to leave an imprint on the city:

it erects large, impressive buildings and monuments; it gathers, to the extent it can manage it, the instruments of control of the national or imperial orbit. These instruments are of many sorts: economic, juridical, religious, cultural (that is, educational, scientific, professional). Because so many decisions are made and business of all kinds transacted there, the capital will attract artists, lobbyists, lawyers, experts, and a great many visitors seeking a decision to be made, an award of some kind, or special bits of information. Personnel experienced in transactional work will be attracted there. A good network of means of access from the outside will be provided.

The size and scope of the concentration of buildings, people, and wealth and the volume of transactions depend of course on the orbit over which the capital exerts authority, and also on the strength of the authority that the government located there may exercise. The orbit — that is, the geographical area gravitating around the capital and under its dominance — is an essential component of the capital's role and function and of the heritage that may be left to the city after the seat of political authority is moved away from it. The orbit is often multiple, encompassing several fields of variable design, especially in a capital that has endured for a long time and for periods extended its control over large spaces.

In several parts of the world the custom existed in the past for every sovereign of importance, king, or emperor, or every dynasty to move the seat of power to another city, probably in order to make a lasting mark on the land. Thus many new cities were created or older ones were endowed with palaces, fortresses, temples, and a new aura. In this tradition capitals moved often in ancient Egypt, in China, in Japan—and even in some parts of Europe. The idea of the stability of the capital and boundaries of a state seems to have been generally adopted only since the Renaissance and in Western Europe. Even there it was not a strict rule. The location of the capital was a whim of the sovereign, though the sovereign always wanted his capital to be impressive, respected, and a symbol of his power, and therefore it was usually reasonable and convenient to locate in a large and central place.

When a capital was moved it usually left behind a rather large city endowed with impressive buildings, a good network of access, and an aura of dominance. The scope of this inheritance would be proportional to the size of the orbit, and to the duration and centralization of the authority exercised by the sovereign who had been located there, though in each case some variation could be observed. Certain capitals were thoroughly destroyed when taken by foreign conquerors: some of these cities live only in literature and popular memory, such as Troy; some just fell into disuse and ruins, like Persepolis and Delos; others weathered the storm, or even several destructions and, being repeatedly reborn, functioned as former capitals, often places of pilgrimage, sometimes to become capitals again. The fate of Jerusalem is a case in point. Other great capitals have disappeared to be succeeded by great cities which were at times capitals in the same general vicinity; thus Baghdad may be considered a successor to Babylon and Tunis a successor to Carthage.

The locale of a city with a history of having been a brilliant capital often acquires a symbolic value for those who cherish the memory or keep a sentimental attachment to that past period in history. In many parts of the world fallen capitals of dissolved realms survive as religious centers, holy cities of some sects, places of pilgrimage and worship. This is often the case around the Mediterranean. The French geographer Jean Despois observed that the small town of Ghardaía, one of the gates of the Algerian Sahara and the main center of the Mozabite sect, had been the capital of a short-lived Ibadite empire. He believed this sort of transfer of dominance from the temporal to the spiritual level was a frequent occurrence in the Near East. Jerusalem is a city endowed with such a religious aura since the days of King David and Solomon, for 3,000 years. In a very different part of the world, Kyoto, the former imperial capital of Japan, remains a center of worship and pilgrimage owing to the incredible congregation of various temples in the city, although the main Shinto shrines are located elsewhere.

The most extraordinary inheritance is certainly that of Rome. No other city in ancient times, not even Babylon, had established a comparable political dominion with as vast an orbit. The Roman Empire at the beginning of the Christian Era extended over the whole *orbis terrarum* around the Mediterranean; beyond its limits was little known wilderness, especially in Europe and Africa. In Asia, Rome's predominance was less obvious and recognizably limited, for China, India, and the Parthians lived separate political lives. Still, Roman settlements existed far to the East, certainly in India, while no autonomous Indian or Chinese settlements seem to have existed in Roman lands. The strict military control, the elaborate system of laws, the road network, and a careful and spectacular urbanism, creating many new urban centers, integrated the Roman orbit into a political, economic, and cultural structure that remained a much admired and envied model for ages to come. The principles of Roman law continue to influence jurisprudence around the world. The ancient buildings of Rome—its arches, its baths, its temple, the Pantheon, the Colosseum, the Capitol, the Forum—supplied vocabulary and design to innumerable cities wanting to assert their role as capital or metropolis. The name of Rome became a symbol designating a great capital city endowed with magnificence. Thus Arles, a Roman colony and seat of provincial government, was called the "Rome of Gaul." When the imperial capital was transferred by Constantine the Great to his new city of Constantinople, on the Bosphorus, it was called the new or "Second Rome." When Constantinople was taken by the Turks and became for almost 500 years the capital of the Ottoman Empire, another vast orbit, though never the equivalent of the empire of the Caesars, other capitals vied for the title of the "Third Rome," especially Vienna and Moscow, and even Tirnovo!

Did Rome lose its capital status with the transfer of the imperial government to Constantinople? It was still referred to by many texts as the capital of the western part of the empire but it was soon overrun by tribes and armies from the North. The Western Empire fell to pieces, especially when the Arab expansion burst over North Africa and Spain. Still, when Charlemagne in 800 decided to restore the Empire of the Occident he went to Rome to be crowned emperor. By that time the bishop of Rome, the pope, had already ascertained his primacy in Christendom as the successor to St. Peter. Rivalry with the patriarchate of Constantinople led the Church of Rome into theological debate and to a schism that separated the Eastern Orthodox churches from Roman Catholic supremacy. One can see, however, an early shift of Rome's dominance from the temporal field, which was lost in 330, to the spiritual.

Constantinople may claim to have been a temporal capital of large political orbits (from 330 to 1922) longer than Rome or indeed any other city. It was also during all that period a religious capital, Christian or Moslem. Its patriarch is still the head of the Eastern Orthodox churches. Could one say that Rome was a former capital from the fourth century until it became again the political capital of a united Italy in 1871? The answer will certainly be affirmative if one would interpret the definition of former capitals as cities that have lost the role of hosting a government that makes independent and sovereign political decisions. On the other hand, however, the Germanic emperors in the West ruled the Holy Roman Germanic empire, and seats of power often migrated. Could it be held that Rome remained an imperial capital in title, as Amsterdam is the statutory capital of the Netherlands, while the real Dutch government is located at The Hague? The Germanic empire was a complicated assemblage of states of diverse sizes, feudal in origin, some of them ruled by kings, some by princes or bishops. When in the 1640s, at the Treaties of Westphalia concluding the Thirty Years' War, it was agreed that every state would have the religion of its reigning sovereign, Germany appeared constituted of more than 300 such states. The political map of Italy was no less complicated. Cities having lost the capital function are very numerous in these countries.

During the centuries when the status of Rome as a capital or not was rather indefinite, it was overrun many times by armies of various powers and made dependent on one or another distant sovereign. For a relatively brief period (about 75 years) the papacy even moved from Rome to Avignon under French pressure. But except for that period of "the captivity of Avignon," Rome remained the seat of the papacy, of the supreme pontiff of the Roman Catholic church. Even when the temporal authority of the pope was reduced to very little indeed, his spiritual authority extended over a vast orbit, a substantial proportion of human kind. Should we consider that Rome lasted as a capital, either temporal or spiritual, for all this time, more than 2,200 years? Or should we accept the point of view that while remaining a great spiritual center, it functioned as a former capital for 15 of those 22 centuries? The answer is not clear, for in several long eras spiritual questions dominated the political life of Europe, and much was then decided in Rome. Still it would seem to us that Rome could not be recognized at any time as a capital of, say, Hispanic America, even though the policy and instructions from the Vatican may often have played a decisive part in the life and legislation of those distant countries.

Spiritual authority appears to be inherited frequently by former capitals from past political grandeur. The geographical extent of this authority may or may not be related to the former political orbit. Moscow may be taken as another example: for two centuries it was a former capital, having lost the imperial role to St. Petersburg (now Leningrad), though its patriarchate remained dominant for Russian orthodoxy.

The importance of the religious role assumed and maintained by certain places results of course from networks of communications and established hierarchies which enable the capital to function, and they are seldom erased by the migration of the government elsewhere. That is why former capitals usually remain metropolises of importance and active centers of trade and cultural relations. The famous saying "all roads lead to Rome" also applies to other, much smaller orbits. One may summarize by stressing that the inheritance from a capital past bequeaths buildings, the status of past glory, and a cultural or spiritual personnel which often make the place a symbolic center.

It is important to point out that the competent work force seldom entirely disappears from a place with the moving out of the governmental institutions. These will usually take along at least part of their work force, but never all of it. Moreover, the government attracts to its vicinity a large volume of transactions between the public and the private sectors which are represented by numbers of qualified people in various professions and at all levels of society. Thus a reigning sovereign used to be surrounded by a court, and that attracted large numbers of lords and ladies from the realm and from abroad, each of whom was accompanied by staff. In this manner the capital's population was built up in days of yore. The varied transactional activities of the metropolis may not disappear when the capital function moves away. The three very different cases of Istanbul (formerly Constantinople), Leningrad (formerly St. Petersburg), and Rio de Janeiro, all of which lost their national capital function in the twentieth century, testify in the 1980s to the survival in the former capitals (with formerly vast orbits) of a strong transactional inheritance, making these cities still great crossroads of international connections.

The Transactional Vocation and the Hinge Function

Transactions develop in a city because the city is by definition a crossroads and in many respects functions as a hinge. First, it is a hinge between the various demands of the region around it and the services that may be supplied by its own inhabitants and institutions to the countryside. This is true not only for the distribution of goods but also for the performance of such indispensable services as the administration of justice, health care at a specialized level, better education, and varied professional advice, often including financial and insurance matters. Second, the city acts as a hinge between the surrounding country and the outside world because most of the means of transport and communications cross within it or at its gates, and because it is equipped to receive outsiders, entertain them, act as a broker for transmission of news, and for commercial or contractual transactions. Third, the city shelters a continuous hinge operation linking together all the various institutions and interests located in or visiting the place.

The "multiple hinge" function has enormously expanded in recent years the number of people it employs, the floor space it occupies, and the ancillary services it requires. This expansion is due to two reasons: first, the growth of what has been called the "white-collar" or "information society" as the automation of manual work and the progress of technology spawns new variants and specializations in a subdividing division of labor; second, the improvement in transport and communications, which has developed networks of trade, travel, social relationships, and economic and cultural linkages around the world. What some people like to describe as a "shrinking" of the world into one vast integrated system quickly develops and multiplies the transactional work needed by the operation of the hinges, and the personnel it needs.

Now these mechanisms are at work in every city, but they achieve a special size, diversity, and stability in national capitals. In the capital the internal political and the diplomatic international hinges are added to the others, and these may be expected to perform a larger volume of transactions in the national capital than in the other cities of that nation. This last quantitative relationship is not always true; it is difficult to generalize in urban geography. In nations of federal structure, noncapitals may have a larger volume of nongovernmental transactions than the total volume observed in those nations' federal capitals. Such certainly is the case for New York City versus Washington, D.C.; Toronto versus Ottawa in Canada; Zurich versus Bern in Switzerland; and surely Rio de Janeiro and São Paulo versus Brasilia in Brazil; and four out of these five great transactional metropolises cannot be called "former capitals." However, in most nations the capitals are clearly the main transactional centers, and they often continue to concentrate transactional work despite policies and endeavors aiming at decentralization. As a federal capital lasts, it gradually builds up its hinges. The former capitals inherit a high ability for transactional work and often maintain, even if readapted, a good deal of the hinge function. This is how there are so many important regional centers, which even have an international role, in Italy, Spain, or Germany: they have received with their inheritance from the past an acquired capital of skill, knowledge, and abstract linkages which they usually manage to transmit from one generation to the next. The buildings bequeathed by the past presence of a sovereign, the lords of his court, and the institutions of government also constitute a valuable capital, particularly in our era that values the conservation of works of art and monuments, and brings large crowds of tourists to visit them. Some of the great buildings can be reused for new purposes: splendid old residences now shelter museums, banks, or schools. The use changes but the concerns of the occupiers remain transactional. Italy has well reused in such fashion many of the palazzos in Venice, Milan, Florence, Naples, and even Urbino.

It is significant that I first heard the problem of former capitals raised at a session of the Società Geografica Italiana held in a magnificent Roman villa above the Forum. And it was voiced by Professor Francesco Compagna, heir to a distinguished Neapolitan lineage, and then deputy in Parliament for Naples and a minister in the Italian national government. For Italy is covered with a net of beautiful and often declining cities, many of them former capitals of orbits that greatly varied in area and duration. But Naples was undoubtedly an important capital and a leading transactional center in Europe for centuries. Still, around 1800 Naples was capital of a kingdom and one of the four largest cities in the Western world (the three others being London, Paris, and Constantinople). When the Rothschild brothers scattered from Frankfurt, they went to London, Paris, Vienna, and Naples. But in the 1980s the decline of

Naples was patent despite the efforts to revive and develop the Italian Mezzogiorno, of which it was by far the greatest city and the real hinge. One must reflect on the inheritance of the former capitals: it brings some benefits but much frustration and some resentment. A federal structure may help to alleviate the situation; the capitals of past states would remain in charge of a certain regional level of government, and the federal capital would concentrate less of the urban resources than in a centralized national structure.

Would the advantages of the inheritance make it possible to overcome the downgrading of the former capital? The lessons of recent history may suggest that it is easier to overcome the loss of the capital function if the event is followed by a long period of economic expansion and prosperity for the whole region, and it also may depend on the size of the orbit and the volume of transactional activities, but no such rule could be shown to apply generally. Naples and Munich, for instance, lost their regal capital status at about the same time in history. Their evolutions since have been very different. Although Naples was much bigger and richer than Munich in the early nineteenth century, Munich has fared much better since. True, the German economy as a whole fared much better than the Italian, and West Germany adopted a federal system after World War II. Still, even in the very successful case of Munich a certain element of frustration may be detected that has marked its politics in the twentieth century. Such frustration may be noticed occasionally in a city even as prosperous and privileged as Edinburgh.

Conclusion: Lessons for Urban Evolution

This brief chapter has only sketchily hinted at some of the lessons that could be drawn from a fuller study of former capitals. The study would be difficult. It would require some agreement on the definition of the category and also a consensus on what cities may still be considered present capitals, though not seats of national governments, especially in federal nations. Even if the definitions accepted greatly limit the number of cases to be examined, the lessons would be worthwhile. And should special attention be given to regional level capitals of states within a federation if they are also former national capitals, such as Rio de Janeiro or West Berlin?

An analysis of the history and present status of former capitals yields, it seems, valuable indications as to the nature of *urban centrality*, of the factors developing or affecting it, of the resilience of the city as a center. No doubt certain characteristics of the population and of its leadership may be found determinant in most cases. Comparative data on all such situations, trends, and relationships may teach us to understand better what helps cities to rise or fall, to be happier or to be frustrated. The evolution must be examined on several levels: economic, political, social, cultural.

The conclusions that may be drawn would also help us to understand what the presence of government brings to a city, to what extent the additional hinge functions this presence entails, stimulates, or weighs upon local life. Here again the answer seems to depend on the kind of government it is and on its behavior. Gathering data on what happens when the government leaves may be illuminating.

The more one asks questions and tries to answer them, the more new questions arise. This is of course the destiny of all serious research. Still one learns in the process. Planning new cities, moving capitals, helping "peripheral" centers—all these endeavors will be helped by a better knowledge of the fate of former capitals. The transactional inheritance would be, it seems, an especially timely matter to investigate: in the growth and spread of white-collar work and of transactional activities in modern society, what forces pull towards concentration next to political authority? And what possibilities are there of redistribution among noncapital cities?[2]

Notes

1. Jacqueline Tyrwhitt was very interested in the function and destiny of capital cities and wanted to devote one or several issues of *Ekistics* to this subject. Such an issue was finally put together (no. 299). She was still working on it in her last days, with her usual devotion to the tasks she undertook, despite pain and fatigue. On her last visit to Oxford, when she was dining at the High Table at Hertford College, I mentioned to her the question suggested to me by an Italian friend, of *former* capitals. Certainly there was a category of such cities, and many of them, at present around the world. "What an excellent subject!" Jacky exclaimed. The idea stimulated her; she felt we should do something about it. Indeed it now seems befitting to devote to former capitals a paper dedicated to her memory.

2. All these themes appear to be clearly involved in the study of former capitals. It has been stimulating for this writer to evoke them. One wishes Jacqueline Tyrwhitt would be among us to spur on the study and the debate.

Part Three   **City and
Metropolis**

So great was the pressure of all the people and all the activities seeking for a place in the cities along the seaboard or immediately back of it that the small areas first defined as "urban territory" had to be constantly expanded, and in this process of growth some of the functions originally carried on in the major cities had to be transferred elsewhere. Sometimes the shift was to new cities that would soon rival the older centers in size and prosperity (Washington grew thus as a center of government, and Baltimore as a port and industrial city). In other cases it was to suburbs, many of which were later absorbed by the legal extension of the central city's territory and some of which grew to become substantial cities in their own right, though they remained, at least in some respects, satellites of the larger metropolis from which they had sprung up. At a later stage certain categories of homes, plants, or stores that had been restricted to the well-defined bounds of urbanized districts became scattered farther away from original nuclei, dispersed in such loose order that vast areas became *de facto* suburbs, with their populations having no *raison d'être* for its existing distribution but its ties with a not-too-distant "downtown."

The process has taken on increasing complexity in the twentieth century. Urbanization in Megalopolis has covered an entire section of the country instead of being restricted to small areas within that section. "Downtown" businesses, such as department stores, warehouses, or fashionable restaurants, have scattered outside the cities, as have residences, characteristic of "uptown" city areas. Thus the urban region has acquired a nebulous, quasi-colloidal structure, with new patterns of land use. The result has been called "the exploding metropolis," a product of "the modern urban revolution." . . . The processes of city growth and suburban scattering began in Megalopolis two centuries ago, making it a *frontier* or pioneer area in these developments and an important element in American history.

Megalopolis,
"How the Cities Grew and the Suburbs Scattered"

Five

Economics, Esthetics, and Ethics in Modern Urbanization

Power and Prestige in the City

For many thousands of years the majority of humankind lived in the rural countryside and worked at making the soil yield the raw materials necessary to feed and occupy everybody. Only a minority inhabited cities — densely built-up small areas, set aside from the "open country" as separate entities, endowed with a set of laws and regulations peculiarly their own. Walls, ramparts, or at least legal lines enclosed them. In some cases city people may have engaged in farming outside the walls; they may have drawn most of their income from agricultural revenues. But the city was more typically specialized in trade, manufacture, administration, and in large gatherings for religious, political, recreational, or commercial purposes. These specially *urban* functions carried power, and with power, prestige. For whether it was a temple, a market, a tribunal, or a king's residence that originally determined the city's growth on a given site, a city was always a seat of some kind of power. A scholarly international meeting recently held in Chicago to examine the

Reprinted from *Ekistics,* April 1963, 197–204.

origins of the urban process in ancient times published its proceedings under the title: *The City Invincible*. Indeed, the city was a place from which the open country was dominated, where wealth was gathered, the locus of authority and responsibility. It claimed a long, lasting future of dominance.

Change affects much more than the attitude of the rural population towards the modern urban centers. It modifies the very structure of the city, the means and the aims of those who plan, build, and govern cities. Architects and urbanists used to be concerned mainly with beauty and prestige: their job was to build churches and castles, fortresses and ramparts. Because all these buildings housed prestigious and respected functions and people, they had to be spectacular, to impress the outsider, the people passing by. A certain kind of beauty, of esthetics, was indeed one of the buildings' functions. It may have been functional to decorate and overstress the esthetic features. This past of architecture and urbanism has brought us an extraordinary artistic heritage, in fact most of the world's marvels. A great art thus evolved, going through many styles, schools, and stages.

The people of our century are more intent than ever on preserving the monuments of the past, on treasuring and admiring the art and techniques of architectural and urbanistic beauty. Every city retains, for the various aspects of community life, an urgent need of spectacular buildings, the materials, design, and appearance of which give expression to the beauty, dignity, and authority of the functions performed within and to the virtues of the owner, whether private or public, individual or corporate. But this is no longer the main market for the talents of the architect, urbanist, and builder. Those talents and endeavors are also and increasingly to be exercised for a completely different market of mass consumption, mass transportation, mass production, for the daily use of the rank and file as much as and perhaps more than for the use of those who hold power and prestige. And still we all want the city to be beautiful, as well as comfortable and accessible to all. The urbanization of the world carries with it social progress: a more urbane way of life for the vast majority of the people, more comfort, better education, more leisure, and better taste. Two centuries ago people craved more happiness for all; now we talk of the opportunity for excellence. Our social and political ethics require the greatest possible equality in distribution of benefits. Are such requirements consistent with esthetic demands inherited from a very different past, and with the economic mechanisms of the time?

These are not purely academic questions. The solutions provided are molding the environment of our generation and the next. Their discussion has already aroused strong feelings; for the appearance and structure of cities reach much deeper than just matters of habit, comfort, and landscape. As a seat of prestige and power in the midst of the open country, the city was a symbol of high moral values. Here religion was administered, government managed, trade transacted, all functions requiring that moral principles be elaborated and upheld there—for how could society survive and progress be made without such guarantees? But it was also well known that as loci of power and wealth the cities offered to the less virtuous the broad opportunity and frequent temptation of lax moral conduct in business or in private life. Many an angry voice cried out against the city's vices, condemning it to an apocalyptic downfall. Such castigations and prophecies are repeatedly found in the Bible, directed at Nineveh and Babylon, Jerusalem and Rome. Long would be the list of famous outbursts against one city or another in more recent times. Still every voice so raised to condemn a city or a group of cities would also announce some new, clean, shining, saintly city to come, which would replace the corruption of the day. The behavior of the city folks and the morality of the city fathers are potent factors in the general esthetic feeling about the city. Operations of urban renewal that beautify a city miss their aim in terms of power and prestige if they pay little attention to the deep moral and ethical instincts easily aroused in the urban population.

The New Volume of the City

Our very concept of the city has been exploded by the massive expansion of modern urbanization. A city which, with its suburbs, gathered a million people or more in a densely built-up area was an infrequent occurrence as recently as half a century ago. The world outside the United States counted at least seventy-two cities of more than a million population by 1960; if the concept of metropolitan area (or of the British conurbation) were adopted more generally, the figure would be above one hundred. Breaking out of the old bounds, walls, boulevards, or administrative limits which set it apart, the city has massively invaded the open country, though parts of the countryside may have kept their rural appearance. The growth in size of population has also meant a spectacular growth in area for the modern metropolis.

Modern urbanization increases city volume, or size, in several dimensions: to expansion in area and in population is usually added an expansion in the variety of economic activities performed. This last results both from the mass of the urban or metropolitan system itself and from the ever-deepening and developing division of labor, the intricacies of which are bound to multiply as the size of the market increases. Fifty years ago most small and medium-size cities in industrialized countries were "specialized": each lived from one special product or service supplied to the outside. There were mill towns, developed around one plant: a textile or steel mill, for instance. There were company towns built and controlled by a corporation to house a plant or two and the workers. There were university towns, cities that were political capitals, or fishing ports, or market towns, or military strongholds. It is becoming increasingly difficult in the better developed countries to find cities of some size which have remained so specialized. One can occasionally see a factory standing almost alone near a small village and draining its labor force from a radius of a dozen or more miles, but a community the size of a city will usually combine several functions, a whole collection of interrelated economic activities.

At the same time, a new classification has been evolving, applying mainly in larger metropolitan areas: central city, satellite city, dormitory town, manufacturing city. Also, we believe that a category of "brains towns" is forming out of university towns to which further activities of an intellectual kind—research, mass media, and so on—are attracted. The enormous scale of modern urbanization multiplies the metropolitan centers around which entire constellations of towns are developing. For increases in population, area, and diversity proceed together, one pulling the other, and the whole process shapes urban districts of great variety and of such size as to become sections in the national state.

The Rhythm of Growth

Many countries are concerned about the rate of their economic growth. In the 1950s and the 1960s growth over most of the world just reflected a certain rhythm of urbanization. Expansion of manufacturing is, of course, a stimulant of urban growth; but it is also a product of the great demand for equipment entailed by urban and suburban expansion, and the demand for consumer nondurable goods generated by the hordes that find better pay and a higher standard of living in the cities. A three-fold process spurs on the growth of urban pursuits. The United States has experienced this process for some time. Another great power, the United Kingdom, is also well experienced in it. In both countries rural farm population is below one-tenth of the nation, and still lives well largely because of the subsidies that the other nine-tenths can well afford to give the farmers. But other nations are just undergoing now, and at a pace quickened by the "population explosion," what the United States and Britain have already experienced and studied for about a century.

One could perhaps try to demonstrate, by manipulating loads of statistical data, that the ease with which high rates of growth are maintained or increased in many lands is due mainly to their rapid urbanization, while many of the difficulties the British and American economies have recently experienced in maintaining such high national growth rates may be attributable to the relative saturation of their earlier developed urban areas. So many forces are at work in the vast and tangled economic mechanisms of Britain and the United States, so many ties now link them to the world beyond their borders, that any easy "monolithic" explanation such as their more advanced stage in the process of urbanization would fail to meet the challenge. It is true nevertheless that, as urbanization accelerated its rhythm in so many other countries, the American economy began to look older than many rejuvenated countries of the Old World.

In Western Europe the cities are beginning to grow by leaps and bounds everywhere. Even in the relatively stagnant economies of Spain and Portugal, many cities and medium-size towns now offer the image of rapid expansion and much new construction, especially on the periphery. Lisbon is extending long tentacles along the estuary of the Tagus River, both on its south and north banks, and another suburban area stretches along the electrified railway to Sintra. Portugal has only some ten million inhabitants, but it is estimated that one million of them are surplus labor on the farms, and ought to be transferred to urban activities; presumably they would then soon adopt urban or suburban residences. In France, which has almost five times the population of Portugal, one may well expect a flow of several million people, probably close to five million—also one-tenth of the nation—toward the larger urban agglomerations.

These trends are not limited to Western Europe and North America. They are just as urgent and often more marked in the countries dominated by communist regimes, and in the underdeveloped lands of Asia, Africa, and South America. This worldwide massive trend towards urbanization at an accelerated pace adds to the difficulty and in fact to the novelty of the problem: a rhythm of economic growth is needed which will match a situation that has seldom if ever been encountered in the past, and the volume of needs to be provided for is absolutely without precedent. This is certainly true for the world taken as a whole. Individual countries may find that Britain at some time since the Industrial Revolution, or more likely the United States in the past half-century, has been in somewhat similar circumstances. This is often realized, though dimly, by the top management in business and government in various countries. The American example is thus often studied and occasionally imitated. But the world is today in a great hurry; much more must be provided per head of population to modern city folks than was the case some fifty or even thirty years ago: they ask for more space, more comfort, more educational services, and more services of all kinds. Shortages are now discovered in space to build residences, in green areas to serve as parks or for seasonal recreation, not to speak of shortages of parking space and even of space on the roads themselves to accommodate traffic. Other problems arise in the field of the financial means to sustain the expansion and provide the equipment desired. The economics of urbanizing at this rhythm and with such volume are novel indeed; they were so considered a few years ago even in the United States.

Urbanization alters a country's modes of living and working: not only the residential pattern but most of the economic structure as well. Land use and occupational distribution evolve accordingly, recreational habits are deeply modified, and transportation needs are completely reshaped. The study of Megalopolis has shown how a new order in the organization of space is being painstakingly elaborated in one of the older urbanized areas of the Western world, the biggest and in many respects, the most advanced in its degree of urbanization, but one also where growth is proceeding relatively slowly compared to the present pace in smaller areas of more recent urbanization. Many of the trends and problems of Megalopolis foreshadow what is in store for other areas. But Megalopolis had several important advantages in its endeavors to cope with the necessities and hardships of urban growth: its great concentration of wealth, its long experience in big-city problems, its skill in managing credit. These attributes are not found in every large metropolis, and most large metropolises are much less developed, making it much more difficult to finance urban growth at the present rhythm.

To the authorities in charge of financial matters in areas undergoing rapid and massive urbanization, every day brings dilemmas. The limited funds available seem needed for many urgent tasks. Priorities have to be established. Choices of priority can be made according to various considerations: in some cases economy will be the overriding factor and urban growth may be stifled thereby; in other cases the feeling for beauty and for the esthetic prestige desired will orient spending towards spectacular buildings and avenues, restricting expenditures for the comfort of the masses. In still other cases, and under the pressure of urgent need, available funds will be appropriated for cheaper kinds of housing and rapid transit.

Usually, an expanding urban center will give some attention to all these and other considerations. The emphasis on prestige will be limited, however, by moral and political principles: it would not seem ethical for a growing community that needs more and better housing, public recreation space, schools, roads, public transportation, and so many other services for the masses to spend a large proportion of its means for beautification alone. The esthetics of a city are of course an important part of its cultural capital. The city beautiful is a more pleasant place for work, leisure, and study; urban esthetics is one of the ethical requirements of the good modern city, but it is only one of them. The city fathers, and all the experts working for them, including the urban planners and architects, must also consider the other ethical requirements: avoiding blight and dirt, decreasing pollution of water, air, and sidewalks, as well as supplying adequate housing to all, managing transportation to save time and avoid strain for the users, and providing satisfactory schools and parks. Whether the problems of urban and metropolitan expansion are approached from one angle or another, the same basic difficulties of satisfying all the needs at the same time remain to be solved.

Thus, economic considerations may be influenced by ethical principles, and both will be found in the way of plans for better esthetics. However, the art of the architect and urbanist was long oriented towards an esthetic demand which could largely disregard economic questions because it built for power and prestige. This kind of art and the professions devoted to it must adapt to the needs of the time; many architectural journals have been debating the matter. Architects are thoughtfully reassessing their role in modern society. The mass, volume, rhythm, and intensity of modern urbanization require a competence most architects have never had, because they did not need it. Urbanization today is an enormous and intricate process quite different from the mere techniques of designing, constructing, and distributing buildings within a given perimeter. Ethical and economic factors seem overwhelming. It is obvious, however, that esthetics must not be swept under by the huge demand for more urban areas.

Old Patterns and New Shapes

Many arts seemed to emancipate themselves from the geometric rules of past tradition and to evolve towards algebra. The trend towards abstraction was gradually effacing the geographical variety still apparent in the arts of yesterday. But architecture, urbanism, and landscaping can hardly adopt the "abstract" approach. They are rooted to a given compartment of geographical space, and to the laws of geometry and gravitation. True, building materials and methods can now be easily transported from one corner of the world to another; the same shapes can be made livable in any climate with modern air conditioning and lighting; comfort may be achieved indoors whatever the outdoor environment, and if the necessary equipment is produced in large enough series, the costs of such standardized architectural methods could be made palatable. Such delocalization and standardization of the basic decor of life are hardly acceptable. Although a great deal of uniformity is creeping into the modern way of life in all parts of the world under the name of modernization, westernization, or Americanization, every nation and every region wants to assert its own individuality, its personality, in some way that expresses the national or even local traditions, history, culture, environment.

Urban patterns will remain many and diverse despite all the technological, economic, and cultural forces promoting uniformity and standardization. Partly the variety of urban geography will be an inheritance from the past: conservation is increasingly in fashion, for natural as well as human-made landscapes. Every community now wants to preserve its own heritage, which for its members, especially if they grew up there, is an important part of the esthetic framework of life. Thus old sections in cities which may have been badly blighted for a period are being restored to their former elegance as residential areas or historical monuments.

Modern urbanism has been fed with a few basic patterns inherited often from a much older period than Ebenezer Howard's. A few forms seem constantly to recur in the plans that architects and city planners have drawn over the ages. One pattern is the orthogonal grid, in which cities are laid out as checkerboards with regularly spaced streets intersecting at right angles. Thus did the ancient Greeks build Miletus: Vitruvius taught that cities be built that way. The French medieval architects used this pattern for the *bastides* or fortified towns of Languedoc, and for some other cases. The Spanish kings ordered new towns in their American possession to follow this pattern; and William Penn applied it in his plan for Philadelphia. In the twentieth century this simple geometric plan came to be known as an "American" pattern.

Another old pattern visualized the city as a circular thing; the main arteries within the city were to be concentric circles intersected by avenues radiating from the center towards the city gates. Ancient Carthage may have been so planned originally, and archeologists have found the ruins of several circular cities in India and Iran. The primary reason for adopting the circle may have been very simple: cities needed the protection of a wall or of fortifications in old times, and the circle being the shortest perimeter for a given area, this principle of geometry made it economical to build circular ramparts around an area of a given size. Where the topography or some other local consideration made the perfect circle inadvisable, an oval or elliptic shape was often adopted.

Thus, imperfect circular forms developed and multiplied. Paris is the most famous example, with its concentric belts of boulevards that replaced the successive quasi-circular lines of ramparts. Many other circular cities are found throughout Europe and Asia; the perfect wheel was fashionable for small new towns in the sixteenth and seventeenth centuries in northern Italy, the Low Countries, and elsewhere. In northeastern France the small town of Rocroi, which grew little after 1700, still offers a plan in the form of a perfect wheel.

There are only a few classical shapes in geometry; the circle and the quadrangle are the two main patterns, and to repeat them came naturally to designers of cities. But too much geometric consistency causes monotony in the landscape. Although great vistas opened by large and long avenues have an inspiring beauty, linear design can get tiresome. The ellipse is a third solution, more difficult to repeat many times, but a pattern that can be associated with either the circle or the quadrangle by juxtaposition to obtain variety within some geometric orderliness. The number of forms found in the physical world is, after all, rather limited, and geometry was ironed out to achieve order and beauty as well as maneuverability among human-made shapes. Modern urbanization has so sped up the creation of new urbanized and suburbanized areas that the styles have not been renewed as promptly as the landscapes. The modern metropolis has taken on a nebulous, somewhat disorderly structure. Fractions of it have been planned, not yet the ensemble. Whether metropolitan governments can operate successfully before some general theory is at least proposed for the organization of these vast spaces and the coordination of their various parts, is a question that a few responsible people are beginning to ask on both sides of the northern Atlantic.

The Emergence of New Patterns

In most countries other than the United States the larger metropolitan growths have developed around the national capital. So it was with London, Paris, Moscow, Tokyo, Vienna, Mexico City, Buenos Aires, and on a smaller scale with Amsterdam, The Hague, Brussels, Copenhagen, Madrid, Athens, Warsaw, Budapest, and so on. This made the capital's problems national concerns, attended to by the qualified institutions in the central government. Such situations have not always led to happy solutions. In recent times, in the case of both Paris and Moscow, the central government disapproved of too rapid growth and tried to stifle or control it; these efforts in both cases proved unable to check the influx of population, and the restrictive measures only contributed to worse congestion, especially in housing. No case can be cited of an authority having successfully planned rapid expansion of a wide urbanized region. Perhaps the planning by the Dutch government of the distribution of people and industries in Holland is the closest a policy of national control has come to successfully providing for the people's needs while preserving the esthetics of the landscape. But as a rule, metropolitan growth is proceeding in rather disorderly fashion, creating new, nebulous structures on the maps.

The general appearance of disorder largely results from the existence of contiguous communities, each with its own problems and tastes, applying certain regulations which do not have to be coordinated with what goes on in other parts of the same urban or metropolitan system. If a coordinating authority came into being it would know how to tackle in the best interests of the local people's welfare such *technical* problems as water and air pollution, water and energy supply, sewerage, child education and recreation, and perhaps public transportation. But in the general design of land use and in the architectural methods to be applied, it seems doubtful that the coordinators could follow established principles. For too much has been said recently in purely emotional and negative fashion about urban sprawl, and too little about what an urban community should be. Utopian writers of yesterday have also contributed more apocalyptic visions of what, alas, the great cities were going to be than suggestions of how people might avoid or control the threats of the future. Perhaps the way out of what looks too much like a dark bottleneck is to ask ourselves if in the present liberal disorderliness patterns are not emerging that could serve as anchors for the new thinking and drawing needed.

The first characteristic of the modern city is its tendency towards *dispersal*. The residences are scattering in the much described suburban sprawl; the manufacturing plants and wholesalers' warehouses are also scattering to a much greater extent than was envisioned even twenty years ago. This trend has been made possible by the new facilities in transportation and communications and by the full equipment with such facilities of vast areas in several parts of the world. Manufacturing can now afford to be suburban or interurban without special difficulties: the plant will be supplied and serviced with the same ease, perhaps with even more ease, as the access to it will be less congested all day long and as space for expansion can be provided ahead of time at reasonable cost. Retail trade and various special services will also scatter to keep closer to their customers. Retail trade, wholesale warehousing, manufacturing plants, and residences for the labor of these establishments need no longer be concentrated. A manufacturing plant duly automated employs fewer people for greater production and is less dependent than factories used to be on proximity to a vast labor market. All those economic activities which were the very functions of the agglomerated urban habitat in recent centuries may now spread over large areas, much of which will remain rural in several respects, creating a scattered urban landscape.

Considerable variation appears from nation to nation as to what are the preferred locations within a large metropolitan area for the various sections of the population. Young couples in the middle-income brackets with children prefer to move out to suburbia and even exurbia in the United States; they prefer to stick to the center of large cities in France; they prefer peripheral locations in England. In fact, as one studies the differences in modes of suburban transportation, in credit for and taxation on housing, and the availability of it, in greater London and greater Paris, one realizes that the "fashions" of suburbanization in the former and clinging to the central nucleus in the latter are essentially dictated by sordid economics and very little the result of "patterns of culture." National policies of credit and taxation on one hand, the organization of the metropolitan transportation network on the other, are essential controls anywhere of the existing pattern of land use and housing distribution. Changes in the economic status of the population and in the housing market will quickly modify the map of any metropolis.

Esthetics for the Masses and for Vast Spaces

It is often argued that neither the Dutch nor the Swiss cities have reached a size comparable to that of urban areas of the great American cities, or of Paris, London, or Tokyo. But no reason prevents a big center from applying rules of health, zoning, and transportation similar to those of somewhat smaller urban centers. The greater cities may have to build higher on the average than the medium-size ones, but high-rise buildings have an accepted esthetic of their own. If disposed adequately they may offer a much finer spectacle than the ordinary small town: enough space must be kept open and green in between the high blocks to give variety of view and to let the skyline be admired from several angles. An impressive skyline is as beautiful a sight as a range of hills, as newcomers to New York City often remark. At night the lights of the city built in height offer views of great beauty; this kind of architectural esthetics is already exploited by photographers with some success. A new art is growing out of modern architecture: the use of a building's inside lighting to decorate the landscape around it. The views on winter evenings along Central Park or Park Avenue in New York demonstrate how the great city achieves fairy esthetics of its own through the activities going on within the high structures. The Seagram Building opened a new chapter in that art of modern architects in coordinating the colors of the lighting with the materials of which a building is made or covered.

In the countries where it develops, modern urbanization creates economic expansion, and as we already know, a good deal of it. If adequately oriented in terms of credit, taxation, zoning, and general understanding of the forthcoming economic evolution of the area concerned, urban and metropolitan growth cannot help producing prosperity and a rising standard of living in the city and around it. Not every district will benefit equally, not every individual will get what he or she wants out of it, but general improvement and social progress will ensue. The esthetics are not in opposition to the ethics of urban planning and redevelopment; they both can be managed in such a way as to yield handsome economic and social benefits.

What will be needed to attain such results is primarily a teaching and acceptance (first of all by the professions directly involved) of an esthetic for the masses and of esthetic rules for designing and organizing vast spaces. With the concept of the city itself, the artistic ideas of architecture and planning must break out of the narrow confines of their traditional domain. Today an ugly or blighted district is not the basic problem; any large city always has had and will have such spots. It is their repetition over a large area or in too close succession that must be prevented. The monotony of the city is an enemy to be fought by imaginative variety in the design of large areas; a particular style can be adopted for one district but ought to be avoided for twelve contiguous districts. One of the most difficult problems—where to find nourishment for the imagination—may be helped by inspiration taken in the patterns of space distribution in famous parks, gardens, and palaces of past centuries. Big blocks of apartment buildings could be shaped along the lines of the Louvre, with courts and gardens inside the large A-shaped structure, or on the plan of the Escorial with wide green space around it. Garden design of the Le Nôtre school seems to have inspired L'Enfant for Washington and Haussmann for Paris; more of this tradition could be applied to the vast spaces of the modern metropolis.

The decision to keep much space open and green within the city may be the hardest to make for those concerned with land economics: such "waste" of expensive real estate! But restrictions against building on that space will favor the extension of the city in area, and therefore increase the value of more land at a distance. Last but not least, the provision of such greenery will make the city lighter, sunnier, a more healthful and pleasanter place to live in or to visit. The welfare of the people is well worth such a contribution in terms of land, at a time when leisure is assuming a larger role in the average person's schedule.

A good deal of land inside a city could be secured for green belts and avenues, even for small parks, if most of the transportation were channeled underground. The proliferation of the automobile has already chased underground whatever used to be on rails in the large cities (the streetcars, elevated railroads, and some of the longer-range railways); it has also caused a whole subterranean life to develop for pedestrians along networks of corridors under very active crossroads (as under the Rockefeller Center and Grand Central Station areas in Manhattan, the Opera Square in Vienna, and other places). It might even be preferable to reserve the ground level to pedestrians and keep cars as well as buses and trains in tunnels. A trend in that direction started over fifty years ago; it could well be accelerated. The general gains in cleaner air, less noise, and safer and better traffic movement in the more congested districts can hardly be disputed. The costs here again would hardly be too great, as the techniques of tunneling are rapidly progressing. The Swiss, Italians, and French are now in a great fever of tunneling under lofty mountain ranges, river estuaries, and even arms of the sea. If it pays to build tunnels several miles long under high mountains to shorten the road from Paris to Madrid, or Geneva to Turin, how much more and in how many respects should it pay to build such devices to save traffic congestion on the ground in the heart of New York, London, or Paris!

In this century of the common man and of mass production, the better city planning too often remains still specialized in the expression of prestige and power. Small areas are artistically planned and designed where such prestigious institutions are located, as are gathered in the Lincoln Center for the Performing Arts, or the United Nations headquarters in Manhattan, and in the Golden Triangle of Pittsburgh. New national capitals are beautifully planned and built: our century has produced Canberra, Pretoria, Ankara, New Delhi, and, last but not least, Brasilia, with as much concern for esthetics as was the case with Versailles in the 1660s. What a contrast between the splendor of the new capital cities and the drab monotony of the "new towns" or "Levittowns"! The spirit of our time should be able to produce exciting schemes and cities for common use too, on a grand scale and with diversity.

The professions of city planner and architect should certainly not renounce their artistic formation; but their training needs to include some competence in many fields they rather despised in the past: the financing of the construction and of its management; the economics of the area they will plan or build; the geography of a wider region around it; the social needs and habits of the users. Great architects of the past practiced such universality, despite the high status and wealth of their clients. Today all this needs to be taught in every good school of architecture, in a way that would not conflict, but harmonize with esthetics.

To imagine what we want to build we must be familiar, of course, with the whole legacy of the past: neither techniques nor esthetics can be invented all anew, and the number of possible forms and patterns in the physical world being limited, some repetition is unavoidable. But we have modified our environment, increased our power to mold materials, and we should be able to do as well as, and sometimes better than, the masters of preceding ages. The volume and rhythm of modern urbanization and the ethics of our time make it easier now to apply all our growing economic means to achieve better and more beautiful cities.

Six

The Growing City as a Social and Political Process

City Form and Function in a Changing Society

So much has been initiated and achieved in the field of urban studies and planning in Britain, and particularly by Londoners, in this century that one feels humble coming from abroad to comment on such matters here. This choice of topic, especially by a geographer, may well surprise architects and planners. I recall my first visit to the University of London, to do some research with a fellowship from the Sorbonne in the autumn of 1938: I was at that time invited by Professor Eva Taylor, who contributed so much to historical geography, to attend the lectures given at Birkbeck College by a visiting French geographer of the generation of my teachers, Professor Raoul Blanchard of the University of Grenoble. He spoke on the multi-storied farmhouses of the Alps of Savoie. His were lectures in geography, though their subject may seem more architectural than what I am talking about today.

The difference between the topics of Raoul Blanchard and myself reflects the change that has occurred in these past thirty years in the

Reprinted from *Transactions of the Bartlett Society*, 5, 1966–67, 11–46.

scale and in the nature of the professional concerns of both architects and geographers. The change is due to the rapid evolution and the fluidity of society in this century. Our professions have in common a certain interest in the study of the environment. In the first half of the twentieth century environmental analysis focused mainly on local conditions; this outlook has been rapidly broadening in recent years. The geographers have been essentially studying the environment; the architects and planners have been making it, particularly in its material framework. This is leading to a new and fruitful interdisciplinary endeavor in which both geographers and architects feel a duty to help prescribe for the improvement of the urban environment which has been increasingly suffering from diverse and serious ills. While in the past we may have been satisfied with a somewhat descriptive or anatomical analysis, we are now getting into a sort of physiology or even medicine of our cities and in this process the study of environment acquires a more scientific attire.

As this modern method is taking shape, the many factors at work in the complex process of urban growth have been determined, defined, and classified. Basically, I submit, four major categories of factors have emerged: the technological, the economic, the social, and the political. The first two categories are well recognized and are the object of much research and of an abundant literature. The last two categories have attracted less attention and are less well understood as yet; still, the social and political components in the process of urban growth are commanding elements which need to be brought into the limelight. Hence my choice of the subjects for these lectures: perhaps we might start thus together something towards the improvement of our approach to the city's ills and their treatment.

The Fluidity of Society and the City's Form

It was only recently that the growth of cities all around the world, and particularly in the countries of more advanced economy, was related to the fluidity of modern society. Once the relationship had been observed, many of the characteristics of the social processes were ascribed to the migration towards the cities, to the conditions of living in higher densities, and to the other features of the urban frame. Although some of the trends in urban life could be explained by the new material framework in which people from rural areas had come to live, the deeper relationship between the fluidity of society and the form of the city seems rooted in a rather inverse process: a rapidly changing society, uprooted by the liberating influence of technological and economic progress, was modifying its habitat both in terms of distribution over the land and in terms of ways of life. The new geographical distribution of population, especially in industrialized countries, gathered most of the people in urban agglomerations which expanded considerably in area as a result. In a few cases vast urban districts developed around brand-new cities; much more often they grew around the nuclei of older, existing large cities. This urban growth produced a sort of dispersal of the city as it used to be known in the past. It was no longer a small area, tightly built up, that could be designated just by a dot on the map. It now expanded, shaping a less dense formation of much larger area; and as neighboring cities grew one towards the other, conurbations, metropolitan regions, and even wider urbanized regions had to be indicated as larger patches on the maps.

As the number of city dwellers increased rapidly, and as their standard of living, time available for recreation, and general mobility all increased together, the space consumed per capita rapidly swelled. Let us remember that in 1800 there were only seven cities in the world counting half a million inhabitants or more; by 1900 there were 42 cities of about that size or larger, and today these are more than 200. In 1800 also the Industrial Revolution had just begun to pile up manufacturing plants and large warehouses in and around a few cities. Public parks were still exceptional, and most city dwellers were satisfied with the right to take a stroll on a few occasions in the parks or gardens of some royal or princely mansion located in or near the city. By now our wasteful and affluent society has multiplied by a large coefficient the space needed by the average city dweller, at least in the North Atlantic world, for lodging, work, shopping, indoor and outdoor recreational activities, and cultural pursuits. No wonder the form of the city has been changing so fast, and particularly expanding, sprawling in an unforeseen and chaotic fashion.

It is however noteworthy that in recent years most of this growth and urban sprawl developed in a few selected areas in each of the well-developed countries. In the study *Megalopolis*, I described the vast urbanized region, stretching on the northeastern seaboard of the United States from southern New Hampshire down to northern Virginia, that is, from greater Boston to greater Washington, with New York City in its center. In this area, broadly delimited between the Atlantic shores and the first ranges of the Appalachians, about 40 million people now live on some 53,500 square miles, that is, one-fifth of the American nation on 1.8 percent of the land area of the conterminous United States. This kind of megalopolitan growth may look like an extraordinary sprawl around a few large cities, the oldest in America, but it also indicates great concentration of population on a small fraction of the land.

Similar megalopolitan concentrations, though of somewhat smaller size, may be observed in a few other regions of the well-developed parts of the world: in and around London, in the urban district of Paris, in the Amsterdam-Ruhr-Calais triangle of northwest Europe, in the Tokaido region of Japan, in southern California, and so on. Indeed, something resembling a general rule may be formulated: in most countries 15 percent to 30 percent of the total population is now gathered on less than 5 percent of the land area around some large metropolis. Such a "law" is already true in every well-developed country, and it is becoming increasingly so in many developing nations.

This in-gathering of the people in a few selected spots of the well-developed world contradicts somewhat the frequently encountered assertion that the modern city is sprawling all over the landscape, devouring entire countries, and will soon engulf continents from coast to coast. This kind of thinking is rather common today among certain schools of planners and sociologists in America, and it is also being heard in Europe. It must be realized, of course, that such prospects remain extremely remote. Even if the urban sprawl goes on devouring as much new land in the United States as it did during the 1950s (that is, at an estimated rate of a million acres a year), it will take about 1,000 years to stretch across the continent from New York to Los Angeles. In fact, more land sees its population being thinned out by contemporary trends than there is land on which population thickens substantially. This has been true for some time in the United States; it is also true in many European countries, even in this era of rapid demographic growth.

This indisputable and increasing concentration of population in a few chosen areas within most countries has been going on for some time and has accelerated in the last quarter of a century, despite many endeavors of local or national policies to stem the tide and keep the people where they were, and also despite an obvious and much advertised lack of facilities in the major conurbations receiving the migrants to house them comfortably. If people chose to keep on congregating in areas which had hardly been made hospitable for most of them, it was not because the city's form and equipment pulled them in but because something else, bigger and deeper, induced this trend. The growing urbanization of society in our time is a deep social process, which may be better understood as one analyzes the changing functions of the city.

The Changing Social Structure and the City's Functions

The functions of the city may be defined at any time in history as those activities which were carried out in places of densely agglomerated population which had set themselves aside from the surrounding countryside and organized a self-governing community. This self-governing characteristic was from the earlier stages of urban agglomeration an important feature. The population of the city may accept in certain circumstances that its government be headed by officials appointed by an authority established outside the city's limits; but these limits still demarcate the city as a governmental unit different from the environing area. We shall return later to a fuller analysis of the political aspects of the urban phenomenon; it is, however, significant that the city was a separate governmental entity: it had to administer and protect a set of economic activities and interests, as well as some special functions, which needed a sizable agglomerated population in a well-policed, that is, safe, location.

Traditionally the city's functions were symbolized by the temple, the castle, the market, and the stores; these meant the locus of administration, transactions, warehousing and redistribution of goods, and the celebration of collective rites. Some castles, temples, markets, and warehouses may have been located at isolated spots in the open country; when several of them came to locate and last one next to the other, if the place was not already in a city, a city arose around the place. We recognize these functions in the early stages of Jerusalem and Athens, Paris and London, Copenhagen and Ispahan, Moscow and Tokyo, Boston and Mexico City. In some cases a single function was responsible for the birth and early growth of a city: the economic function was by far the most prolific in this respect, although the political function has also been very important, whether for strategic reasons (fortresses) or for governmental needs (administration of justice, etc.).

The production of goods was not necessarily a basic function of the city. As a rule, agriculture and mining were not located within city limits; manufacturing always existed in the cities as well as in the villages, and in many regions was also found dispersed on many farms. It was the new technical developments of the Industrial Revolution that concentrated manufactures, since the eighteenth century, in large or medium-size cities. For some two hundred years urban growth has been largely due to clustering manufacturing plants and warehouses. The manufacture and storage of goods in this period needed locations well serviced by rail and water transportation, provided with an abundant labor supply and efficiently policed. Where labor was scarce or access difficult, costs of production and handling were bound to rise more easily than in more central places. My generation still grew up in the belief that manufacturing industries and wholesale trade were the essential functions of the city.

The twentieth century has been changing this rapidly. The technological evolution, spurred on largely by the social trends which make for

more organized and more expensive labor in the large centers, constantly reduces the number of hands employed in producing a given
quantity of goods. Started in agriculture, this trend is well known in mining and now is rapidly gaining in the manufacturing and handling of
most industrial goods. Mechanization, automation, rationalization of production tend to reduce employment in production work, while expanding the quantities and the variety of products obtained. The wider the
market the more profitable is the use of more automated techniques of
production and transportation.

Curiously enough, the United States was the first industrialized country to find that a majority of its labor force was employed in the services
(which happened in the middle 1950s) and a little later in white-collar
work (which has been true for a few years now). Despite the vast,
almost plethoric agricultural, mining, and manufacturing production of
the United States, the majority of employed Americans are not engaged
in production work. Perhaps it is not *despite* but *because of* the huge size
of the American market, of the high standard of living, and of the rapid
social evolution of the majority of the American population that such
technological results have been achieved there first. Western Europe,
and even Japan to some extent, are following on the same path: employment in agricultural and mining production is declining now in the countries of advanced economy; employment in manufacturing production,
transportation, and wholesale trade is still increasing in absolute numbers, but less rapidly than total nonagricultural employment. In the
United States, from 1950 to 1965, the number of production workers
employed in manufacturing remained rather stabilized in the vicinity of
13 million, while nonagricultural employment added some 13 million
other jobs, a few of them in construction, but most of them in the services and also in the white-collar sector of the personnel of manufacturing corporations.

This trend may develop or lag in the various parts of the world with
varied rhythms; there is little doubt that in the long range it announces
the general picture of future employment: less people occupied with producing and handling goods, and more in the services and the white-
collar occupations. Two immediate consequences can be drawn for our
perspectives of forthcoming urban growth: on one hand, manufacturing
and warehousing plants may now leave central city locations to scatter
along well-serviced arteries of traffic in otherwise rural territory; on the
other hand, growing employment in qualified services agglomerates
larger masses of white-collar workers in central cities, particularly in
some of them better fitted for the kinds of activities that need grouping.
The result of these two corollaries of the evolution of the labor force is a
divorce between the geographical distribution of urban growth and

industrial location. The mutation of the Industrial Revolution itself now brings to the city a new set of white-collar activities, modifying once more the essence of the city's functions and the requirements of the urban environment.

It may appear that the removal away from the urban centers of the apparatus of industrial production simply restores the system of the city's functions to its ancient contents, and to some extent it is true. The era of association between urban growth and a "black country" landscape is over; even the association between urban growth and masses of blue-collar workers is being disrupted. The urban landscape and society of the nineteenth century do not fit the needs and the means of the second half of the twentieth. The intellectual inheritance my generation received is outdated, but it is difficult to shake it off. I was brought up reading such British authors as H. G. Wells and Patrick Geddes, who spoke extremely well of the future of the cities but underestimated the speed of both technological and social change. Wells forecast around the year 2100 enormous cities full of a hard-laboring proletariat in blue overalls; Geddes still held the map of coal deposits as the main factor in the location and spread of urbanization. What we project ahead of us is too often what we understood yesterday the world to be. Among the accelerated rhythms of the twentieth century such projections are bound to produce grave errors. The Royal Navy had already shifted to petroleum fuels when Geddes still insisted on the determinant factor of coal for urban growth. The early generation of robots was already in use when, around 1900, Wells predicted the massive blue-collar city. It is very difficult indeed to visualize a society liberated from hard physical work and even from the bother of the actual production of ordinary, mass-consumed goods. We know, however, that we are headed that way and, barring an unforeseeable catastrophe, the countries of advanced economy are rapidly concentrating their manpower in nonmanual work.

The technological progress making these trends irreversible appears as both a cause and an effect of the fluidity of contemporary social structure. It must be recognized that the foundations of economic and social power have been shifting considerably in Western Europe and in North America for quite some time, and that the consequences of these shifts are becoming obvious: ownership of land and of the physical equipment of the land (such as means of transportation, tools of production, housing, etc.) makes less and less for the actual power and prosperity of individuals; this property is increasingly held by institutions or in some collective form. It is regulated and its use is controlled by an involved system of laws and regulations restricting the free operations of individual owners. The distinguished American economist Adolf

A. Berle rightly entitled one of his books *Power without Property,* and in a pamphlet written with the Rev. Father Paul P. Harbrecht, S.J., compared the functioning of large modern corporations to the monastic orders of the Middle Ages. This means a great change versus the economy and society of past centuries. New currents within society are creating this extraordinary fluidity which scares many people, including many scholars. The evolution of the city reflects all these currents. It is the large modern city that trains and gathers the personnel of those new economic activities in which employment is expanding so fast, and which may be called the *quaternary* activities. In this category, which must be differentiated from the tertiary economic activities in Colin Clark's well-known classification, we shall *not* include transportation and wholesale and retail trades, but only specialized services requiring adequate training and responsibility, such as the management of public and private affairs, research and higher education, banking, insurance and other financial professions, and an ever-increasing variety of professional and technical services. Certain activities often classified as manufacturing belong in the quaternary sector: thus the research laboratories and administrative offices of industrial corporations, the editorial staffs of newspapers and publishing houses, and so on. These are the sectors of employment that need to be close to one another, as they all depend on their proximity to two "markets": the market of *information* in a great variety of fields and the market of highly qualified manpower.

The quaternary employment was always very important by its functions, but numerically it was negligible until recently. Now, it is already substantial, corresponding to several million jobs in Britain and probably close to ten million in the United States. Precise statistics cannot yet be offered, because the standard classifications presently in use in most of the advanced countries for labor statistics permit only vague approximations of the whole range of quaternary employment. Still, it is significant that in 1965, "professional and scientific services" employed 2,471,000 people in the United Kingdom; about 370,000 people on the nonindustrial whole-time staff in the civil service seemed to fit into the quaternary category. The "administrative, technical and clerical workers in manufacturing industries" represented 35.4 percent of all employees in the chemical and allied industries, 30.3 percent in engineering and electrical goods, and 23.5 percent in all manufacturing industries in Great Britain, which amounted to 2,096,000 in 1965. Just these three categories of the standard classification brings a total of almost five million jobs. Part of this total may include menial jobs requiring little actual training and responsibility; however, the activities involved are of a quaternary nature. And we did not yet count the employment in finance, insurance and banking. . . . There is no doubt that the quaternary represents a substantial part of the total labor force. Most important is that it groups the faster expanding sectors of employment, and this is true not only in the United States and Canada, in Great Britain and France, but in most European countries and also in Japan.

The future large cities will be agglomerating mainly white-collar non-manual workers occupied in quaternary activities. These activities need to be close to one another, and their growth feeds the rise of the larger metropolis where the major functions are not purely industrial. The city must realize and recognize the change and adapt itself to be the locus of the activities and habitat of better educated, more demanding populations. In a way we may sum it up by saying that the functions characteristic of the Agora and Acropolis in Athens, of the Forum in ancient Rome, and also of the academy, the stadium, and the theater section of the ancient cities take over once more in the city of the late twentieth century, putting an end to the dark, smoky, manufacturing city of the Industrial Revolution. But such a description would not be entirely satisfactory; for the newly rising urban civilization, the ancient forms and functions are not adequate any more.

Agglomeration and Communications

As resources that bring prosperity and authority are becoming increasingly dematerialized and essentially abstract and organizational, it is the social quality of the individual that becomes important. The lord of the land, isolated in his castle amid the acres he owns, is no longer a power in modern society. The important person is one who controls many channels of communication, and who participates in many transactions involving vast organizations. To achieve such a status or just to achieve active participation in a social system in which most of the decisive work increasingly consists of abstract transactions, which in turn direct the flow of production and distribution, one must be in a hub, in a "nodal" or "central" place where communication constantly is maintained with many others. The locus of this exchange of communication, of information, and ultimately of transaction, is the city and usually the large city.

The agglomeration that goes on in the growing cities is largely due, therefore, to the growing need for more communication between all those engaged in the various economic activities of today. The rapidity of the technological progress, economic change, and political evolution concur in fostering an imperious need for more contacts, more exchange of ideas, data, and other information to run business efficiently. Obviously the quaternary activities are intertwined and interdependent: government needs the proximity of mass media and of private management, as well as constant relations with research in various fields; management needs just as much information, research, expert advice, and the vicinity of government. All of them need well-trained, highly qualified personnel, the new supply of which comes from the universities. All the various strains of these upper levels of white-collar work congregate in a metropolis because it is in such agglomerations that they find the best conditions for their work, for discharging their duties in the most competent possible fashion.

Hence the clustering of the skyscrapers in the business districts of large cities, the agglomerations of offices architecturally expressed by the modern "skyline." It is noteworthy that the various reports prepared for better planning and control of the growth of great cities such as London, Paris, Amsterdam, or Stockholm appear to have consistently underestimated, in the recent thirty or even ten years, the growth of the "office industry." They still thought these great capitals had attracted too many factories, and, as they wanted to decentralize industry, they laid down rules and regulations against the agglomeration of manufacturing plants. Now, all the proper authorities have recognized that the essential problem is in the so-called "office industry," in the agglomeration of white-collar and quaternary jobs. This trend has proved more difficult to break up. Some doubts have arisen as to the wisdom of scattering too much the bureaus that manage most of the many pieces making the involved machinery of a national economy; this may well diminish the efficiency of the whole system.

In the interwoven activities of the modern city the university has come to play a new and essential role. It is almost symbolic to observe, in a city such as Newcastle-upon-Tyne, the growth of the campus of the young University of Newcastle in the heart of the city. The old City Hall is moving from its former location, near the river and the cathedral, to a larger modern Civic Center next to the university. In an old city, burdened with the heritage of the Industrial Revolution's outdated "black country" imprint, the central location of an expanding university can improve things a great deal, as it brings a note of rejuvenation, gaiety, a variety of cultural activities, and the promise of sustained growth in the coming years.

Newcastle is only one case among many cities which are now shifting the emphasis of their central district from manufacturing to cultural activities. This is true of a long list of medium-size cities in Western Europe, where new academic institutions have been recently established. They add to the amenities of the place for the whole population; they offer a pole of attraction for other activities in research or mass media. The university is an essential component of the evolution of our society towards quaternary or transactional structures. One of the more interesting experiments in this respect can now be observed in the American Midwest: not only do we see an impressive development of old and new campuses in large cities (perhaps still medium-size by American standards) such as Saint Louis, Milwaukee, and Memphis, but an already substantial cultural center has been created since 1947 in Carbondale, Illinois, by Southern Illinois University.

About 100 miles south of the Saint Louis metropolitan area, Carbondale is located in one of the regions of North America best endowed by nature. Within a 300-mile radius of it are found rich soils, great deposits of coal, oil, and various metallic ores. Large navigable streams converge towards this area (the Mississippi, Missouri, Ohio, Wabash, and Tennessee rivers, to mention only the major waterways), and hydroelectric power is developed on a large scale and could still be increased. In addition, a dense network of railways and highways radiate in all directions; the population center of the United States is at present situated close to Carbondale, just a little north of it. This region, richer in resources well known and better equipped than most other areas of similar size in the modern world, is, however, depopulating. Most of the counties of southern Illinois, around Carbondale, have been on the list of the Area Redevelopment Administration as eligible for subsidies from that branch of the federal government. The first county in the area to be taken off that list was the one in which Carbondale is located, as its general economic status improved owing to the growth of Southern Illinois University, which in 1966 counted 16,000 students, a faculty and staff of about 1,000 people, and employed 800 people in construction alone. Southern Illinois University had been located in Carbondale to bring higher education and an expanding new activity to a rather depressed section of the rich state of Illinois. Small cities and towns had scattered in that area, over the last century, largely due to coal mining and manufacturing plants. Carbondale itself was created in the 1890s as a rail hub for the mining area on the main line from Chicago to New Orleans of the Central Illinois Railway. It is becoming a synonym of successful academic growth in what used to be almost "Appalachia," although it is west of the mountains, and a cultural wilderness. To obviate its isolation from other great centers of communication, Southern Illinois University had to deploy great endeavors: at considerable expense it attracted a lively faculty staff, gathered a large new library (now reaching a million volumes), developed the schools dealing with the performing arts, which also contributed to brighten up the local mode of life, and improved links with the outside world by running its own airport and a fleet of some eighteen university planes! The university adds to the variety of the quaternary activities, to the recreational quality, and to the general cultural level of a city. In the growth of modern cities, even of modest size, a university is a precious asset; for large cities it becomes a "must." An interesting discussion is developing in Britain, in France, and in some parts of the United States as to the wisdom of locating universities inside the old urban nucleus rather than on the periphery, in suburban if not rural surroundings. I do not have a standard answer for all the cases I know: a lively university today has to be able to expand; locating it in crowded quarters may soon prove regrettable. Many people argue that if the "campus" must be a small city within the city, it may be as well to make it a separate city outside the large city frame, on more expendable territory. Let us, however, remember that to many old industrial cities, the centers of which are now declining, the location of the university in the center may greatly help to reverse the trend. If we recognize that communications are increasingly summing up the essence of the modern city's functions, the university appears as a vital component of a well-organized "mass media market." Thus a central district location for an expanding university ought to be welcome in such cases as Newcastle or Leeds in England, or Milwaukee and St. Louis in the American Midwest, Toronto or Montreal in Canada, Grenoble or Nice in France. It is, however, a different matter when a case the size of Paris is considered. The University of Paris, with almost 100,000 students, is an overgrown, enormous organization, large parts of which will of course remain in the traditional "Latin Quarter" district of the city or in its vicinity. But the suburban ring of Paris, which already counts over five million residents, that is, almost the population of Switzerland (a country with a half-dozen distinguished universities), cannot be left without several higher education institutions of the size, rank, and quality of universities. At present, it has been granted only two *facultés:* one for the sciences at Orsay, south of Paris, and another for the humanities at Nanterre to the northwest. That some professors of the Sorbonne openly resented such "decentralization" and "scattering" of the university function outside the central city, astonishes whoever observes the incredible crowding achieved in a university which must serve a metropolitan population of nine million plus large numbers of students attracted to it from many other parts of France and of the world.

The modern policies of decentralizing as much as possible from the "crowded" centers of the major metropolises could be well illustrated by a study of the actual role of the university in the modern city. The decentralization of manufacturing has been achieved to a substantial extent in many cities and countries. It has not stopped the rapid growth of the more successful major urban centers because there develop hubs of communications, markets of mass media based on the interwoven activities of quaternary functions. This is not a matter of size, but quite clearly of function: it is not only true of great capitals such as Paris and London, but also of Amsterdam (which is not the seat of the national government of the Netherlands) and of Stockholm, of much smaller size, and even of Zurich and Geneva, of still smaller size. Naples is a much larger city than Geneva; still, anybody who knows the two cities today will agree that the latter has infinitely more the characteristics of a great metropolis — and this is mainly due to Geneva's function as a great hub of international communication.

If agglomeration nowadays results so much from communication, is it wise or wrong to endeavor to disperse the instruments of communication? For example, is it wise or wrong to disperse managerial offices, research institutions, government agencies, news editing or dispatching, entertainment and education at the higher level, financial direction, expert advice? In our increasingly complicated world, about which the amount of available information and knowledge is rising, a constantly self-refining division of labor is bound to develop and it must expand the number and variety of quaternary jobs. The interdependence between all the specializations cannot help becoming greater. Dispersing the instruments of communication may well do more harm than good to the mode of life of the people involved. Our policies of decentralizing from the few successfully growing cities or urban regions seems to work against the evolution of labor and society. The conflict thus created between the deeper trends and the official policies makes it much more difficult to solve the problems arising at all stages in the growing cities as well as in the lagging ones.

Migration and the Scope of Opportunity

Most of the contemporary urban growth results from migration rather than natural increase of the urban population. The migration was partly caused by the mechanization and rationalization of agricultural production which reduced the number of hands needed on the farms. This push off the land was an economic factor of some importance. In the same period, the expansion of the urban economy, through the growth of employment in industry and the services, created in the cities a demand for labor. But the pull of the city, which added its strength to the push off the land to accelerate urbanization, was not merely a matter of jobs, an economic factor. In an era of social progress, the cities offered also to the mass of newcomers a broadening of the scope of opportunity which was, and probably still is, the primary mover of the whole process.

The majority of the migrants who came to the large cities from the farms, the villages, and the small towns, accepted uprooting, hard working conditions, inadequate housing, a polluted and crowded environment, and preferred it to the seemingly greener pastures they were leaving, because they had hopes of improving their lot rapidly, of rising on the social scale and achieving a better and brighter life for themselves or, if they failed in their own lifetime, then for their children. The city offered opportunities that could not be found for the majority in a small community with a much smaller amount and variety of resources. Moreover, the vast urban crowd offered an environment in which an anonymous individual could suddenly rise through merit alone. Last, but not least, the city offered the means to acquire more knowledge, a broader or better education, or at least special technical training without the local community concerning itself about what an individual would do with the newly acquired ability. In a large city or urban region, the social structure is a vast system, used to fluidity and to a certain rhythm of change. The rise or fall of a few individuals or even groups can be absorbed in the elasticity of the mass. A small community, based on the control of land or on a restricted set of resources, is bound to be more self-preserving in terms of its social structure. It has been often argued that in the large city an individual feels "depersonalized," while one's personality is more affirmed and recognized in a small town; this is certainly true, even to the extent that those who do not belong in the upper strata of the small town are known by everybody not to belong; these persons may have a hard time to achieve by merit alone a higher status to which they may aspire. Social fluidity, a striking characteristic of our time on a large scale, is certainly easier to achieve in the growing city than in a smaller and more stabilized community.

The dynamics of this modern social process of urbanization may be illustrated with quotations from two great classicists who were both interested in the social philosophy of history. Montesquieu wrote in his *Spirit of the Laws:* "He who has nothing but has a trade is not poorer than he who owns a few acres of land and must till them to subsist. The worker who gave his children his skill for heritage has endowed them with wealth which is multiplied in proportion to their number. The case is different of the man who gets his living from the acres he owns and which he divides among his children" (Book 23, Chapter 29). This remark takes on a special significance considered in the light of the gradual dematerialization of resources occurring nowadays. In 1920, the American historian Frederick Jackson Turner published his famous book *The Frontier in American History;* the volume is mainly known for its first few chapters stressing the role of the frontier advancing westward across the continent in the shaping of American national tradition, character, and society. These points had been expounded first by Turner, in the

1890s, when he was worried as to what may happen to the American tradition with the completion of the transcontinental march and the disappearance of the frontier. But in chapters 9–12 of his book, written in the 1910s, Turner stated that the massing of population in the cities, accompanied by urban and industrial growth, provided the American nation with a new frontier for the twentieth century. The spirit of the frontier consisted in his mind of reshaping the society with every generation; if such social fluidity could be kept flowing, he felt that the dynamism of the nation would be preserved. It seemed hardly possible in the 1890s, as all the vacant land seemed appropriated; but it loomed once more possible, at least for some time, as the processes of urbanization developed.

Montesquieu and Turner are two links in a long chain of thinkers who pointed out in various ways how the broadening of the scope of opportunity is an old and essential function of the growing city. This broadening function is more effective than ever in our time, and it leads also to the broadening of the city's shape. For the migration into the city increases the number of the inhabitants, and therefore either the density of occupation of the land or the area urbanized. Today, in fact, both are on the increase: the urbanized area expands on the ground as the number of inhabitants increases and as the progress of the standards of living requires also an expansion of the housing and office floor space per capita. The average density rises also in most cities, if not always in terms of population density, then in terms of density of occupation at work hours in the business districts. The form of the city is thus shifting, new additions to the old core are constantly necessary, and some economic activities are displaced or replaced; there is so much movement that the expansion makes the city itself migratory.

Because it attracts people, promising better opportunity to the less privileged, the growing city is also bound to be an arena of social mixing, a melting pot of a kind; within its bounds come to live together with the established, traditional population large numbers of newcomers alien to the local community and whose neighborhood may well be resented by the old-timers. The coexistence within the same space and community of very different categories of people often causes tensions, sometimes turmoil. The classical example today is found in the American large cities to which flows the migration of colored immigrants from rural areas, from the South or even from the West Indies, particularly Puerto Rico. This migration into the central sections of the large cities is usually considered as one of the major reasons determining the exodus of white residents, particularly of the middle-income brackets, to the suburbs. The flight to the suburbs started in many large cities in America long before the Negroes or Puerto Ricans began coming to these cities in large numbers. Suburban expansion is largely the fruit of growth altogether: it has been, however, magnified and accelerated by a desire of social segregation of residences. The same process may be observed in many other countries and does not necessarily connote racial segregation.

The famous and enormous operation of urban renewal and redevelopment conducted in Paris by Haussmann in the years 1852–67 was spurred on by concerns of a not so different nature. The first stages of the Industrial Revolution had attracted large crowds of poor people from the provinces, seeking employment and opportunity in the rapidly expanding French capital. A first period of growth in the late eighteenth century was probably instrumental in bringing about the political situation that led to the French Revolution of 1789. But the crowding of laborers in the 1830s and 1840s led to the Revolution of 1848 and the "Second Republic" replaced by Napoleon III's Second Empire in 1852. A major task of the new authoritarian régime was to establish order and ensure security for the frightened ruling classes in the capital. The Revolution of 1848 had affected several European countries and threatened the social structures of Austria and Germany, as well as France. And the publication of the Communist Manifesto added to the fright. The wide avenues, often radiating from wide circles, which Haussmann built through Paris, had an obvious strategic significance besides their esthetic quality: they were intended to help police the city, to facilitate the movement of troops in case of riots. But the enormous urban renewal thus achieved had another immediate and rather permanent consequence: the new boulevards and avenues were lined with new multistoried buildings (usually five to seven stories high, giving Paris the highest average height of buildings of any large city at the time), and the flats in these buildings were large, rather comfortable, and expensive. The clearing of the maze of narrow streets and innumerable old small houses chased out of the city of Paris towards the suburbs a large part of the poorer section of the population, particularly of the industrial workers. The "frightening mobs" had been pushed farther away from the centers of affluence and power; the industrial workers were crowded in industrial suburbs and the richer residents could enjoy an elegantly rebuilt capital, remaining in the central city, particularly in its western half.

The renewal, according to Haussmann's plan, created trends giving Paris a geography almost exactly opposite to that now developing in most large American cities: the central city is fashionable and inhabited by the more affluent part of the urban population; the suburbs are more crowded in many respects, poorer, less planned, and less well serviced. The suburbs, however, cling to the city proper. It is considered desirable to live as close to the central city as possible, but for a few small relatively fashionable locations developed in the suburban ring in post-

Haussmann times. The social and political maps of Paris offer many contrasts with those of New York and Chicago. The case of Paris was deliberately planned and easily enforced; it produced a very beautiful city amid rather ugly suburbia. The poet Baudelaire wrote in Paris, during the Haussmann renewal, a few remarkable verses that sum up also our modern urban dilemma: "Old Paris is not any longer; (the form of a city changes faster, alas, than a mortal's heart)," and he added a note about "the chaos of the lively cities." Change is most resented when it affects our esthetic or social habits. The evolution of the growing city, expressing social fluidity and change, reshapes deeply the esthetics of the cityscape. And to these emotions are added the fear and resentment of the chaotic condition fostered by rapid growth.

No wonder we have so much trouble making up our minds about the way we want our cities to function and to look. The youth of today may find it is sentenced by history to live in outdated cities. This situation could hardly be improved until we fully understood that the form, the design, and the material frame of our urban areas cannot condition or determine but must simply express the rapid evolution of our society. And these problems are compounded by those inherent to the political process of the growing cities.

The Bonds of Size and Density

A city is a large agglomeration: a certain size and a rather high density are prime requirements for a place to be a city. The concept of city, however, requires beyond the size and the density of population a personality of its own, usually embodied in the form of a unit of government. In the complexity of the contemporary very rapid growth of urban centers, this governmental unity of the community and area defined as a city is being occasionally lost; clusters of municipalities, or entire metropolitan areas, are sometimes described as vast or continuous "cities"; I am often told that what I described under the name of Megalopolis, an enormous urban region stretching from greater Boston to greater Washington, was, after all, just one big city by modern standards. These standards are changing so fast that it becomes increasingly difficult to differentiate in every sentence the central city within its governmental limits and the suburban ring or rings. Indeed, when one speaks of greater London or greater Paris as a "city," one refers to a much broader agglomeration of people and activities than used to be meant by "city" in a purely municipal sense. New institutions are taking shape which may encompass the whole "greater city area," but they do not erase the older political units. One ought to beware of confusion. It is too easily taken for granted that continuous urban sprawl will ultimately become one community: whether it achieves a unified or coordinated system of government, or remains a maze of contiguous but different uncoordinated units, makes a great deal of difference for the local population and economy.

Another and perhaps more serious set of problems arises in the relations between urban areas and central governments, because of the usual trend to underestimate the changes wrought by urbanization in the political structure of a nation. The densities achieved in the large modern urbanized regions call for substantial reforms. Mankind experiences today the greatest redistribution of its habitat and constant modifications in the densities of population grouping over the land. To resolve their daily problems and provide for their needs, the growing cities require that the available resources be redistributed according to the new relocation of needs; a new regulation of the use of resources and of the customs of neighborhood suggests considerable legislative changes and new institutions, and, to obtain such reforms, a reshuffling of the political system inherited from past centuries. In practice this means that taxes are paid and budgetary expenses appropriated according to another map than previously. To receive their share of the available resources and to plan adequately for their future in a period of growth, the cities or urbanized regions clamor for a new order in the patterns and channels of distribution of means. The response of established authorities is seldom favorable.

Density and Size of Urban Agglomerations

In the modern city, as it grows, the size of the densely urbanized area usually expands faster than the average density rises for the whole urbanized space. In fact, the residential density tends rather to decrease as against what it used to be in the cities of yesterday. This is true of the central city because of a generalized exodus of residences towards the suburban rings; it is also true of the average density of the urbanized area in the older cities which were already important and very crowded in the past. Today the average city dweller requires, and in the Western countries usually enjoys, a large acreage per capita. However, never before had such high densities spread over such wide spaces as are found now in the urban regions either of megalopolitan type or of smaller but still substantial size around a lively metropolis.

Residential density, which is population density as counted in every modern census, provides only part of the actual picture. In 1851 the city of London, with an area of one square mile, counted 185,000 inhabitants. This residential density of 185,000 per square mile was probably not unusual for the central districts of the major cities of the time. In 1961 the city kept only 4,500 residents; still during office hours on an ordinary working day, the density of occupation of that square mile was probably above the 185,000 figure of 110 years ago if one counted, besides the residents, all the people working there and those who had come to transact business. Meanwhile, the residential density of greater London, with an area of about 750 sq. miles, had reached an average of 11,000 per sq. mile for a total population of 8.2 million. In 1962, the urban agglomeration of Paris counted over 580 sq. miles about 7.3 million inhabitants, that is, an average density of 12,600. At the same time, the residential density of the eleven central *arrondissements* of the city of Paris reached over about 11 sq. miles an average of 86,300; the daytime density of occupancy of that dozen of square miles was at least double its nighttime residential density, that is, in the vicinity of 200,000 per sq. mile.

In New York City, the central borough of Manhattan had a residential density of 77,000 over about 23 sq. miles; the daytime density of occupancy was also more than double and probably close to 200,000 per sq. mile. The whole city of New York counted a population of about 8 million, with an average density of 24,700 per sq. mile; the much vaster urbanized district of New York still had a density of 7,462. Washington, D.C., counted 12,442 per sq. mile in the District of Columbia, and 5,300 in the urbanized district; in Detroit the density reached 12,000 in the city proper and 4,800 in the urbanized district; in Los Angeles the same figures stood at 5,450 and 4,736, testifying to the lack of centrality in the nebulous structure of the Californian metropolis.

The first conclusion to draw is the fact that modern urbanites are getting used to work and take some of their recreation in central districts where densities of 200,000 per sq. mile are not uncommon in daytime, and that they are also getting used to living and working in vast urbanized districts agglomerating many million inhabitants each at average densities of 5,000 and more in America, and of 10,000 and more in Europe. Similar densities to those in Europe may be observed in the major metropolitan areas of Japan. The size of the very densely occupied areas is increasing fastest and is especially significant; it results from the total number of inhabitants agglomerating around the more rapidly growing cities or in the major urban regions. The distinguished Japanese architect Kenzo Tange has suggested that as 1900 was the age of the one million inhabitants large city, 1960 was the age of the cities of 10 million size, and that year 2000 will be the age of cities of 100 million size!

Although there are already two regions in the world, fairly continuously urbanized, at least along a main axis, and grouping more than 40 million people each (the American Megalopolis and the Tokaido region from Tokyo to Kobe in Japan), and two other areas that are almost as continuous and that agglomerate about 30 million each on the two sides of the North Sea (one such megalopolitan region could be defined in England and another in a triangle, Amsterdam-Lille-the Ruhr), the very problems these agglomerations and their inner evolutions are creating indicate that the practical approach to urban growth is not so simple. Even 10 million people have increasing difficulty managing their living and working together without new institutions and laws. The political process is not prepared as yet to cope with such size of concentrations; the 40 million and beyond mark requires even more reform and innovation in the political and administrative system.

The sprawl of rather high average densities over hundreds, and soon, thousands, of square miles causes a first series of problems and creates intricate bonds of solidarity in the functioning of the many communities and diverse governmental units in the whole area. The concentration of very high daytime densities of occupancy (up to 200,000 to the sq. mile) of relatively small central districts requiring servicing of a diversified, involved, and intense kind, creates another set of problems. Both series are not independent one from another; by their size, they become national and sometimes international concerns, and cannot be dealt with on a local base exclusively. Both sets of problems may be summed up in the essential question of the trend of concentration characteristic of the present redistribution of habitat, of employment, and of the needs they entail. Our political system does not appear ready to cope with this trend, not even to accept it perhaps.

Managing the Growing Metropolitan Region

Growth in the size of the population that agglomerates in and around a successful metropolis causes expansion of the area urbanized. The suburbs sprawl around the central city as accommodation is being provided for more people and their average requirements of more floor space per capita; these space requirements increase nowadays for housing as a result of the gradual rise in the average standards of living, and they also increase for working quarters, particularly in the manufacturing industries, as a result of technology and automation. Thus, both residential and working requirements of space are rising per inhabitant at the same time as the numbers of the inhabitants. The sum total is expressed by the suburban "sprawl" so characteristic of modern metropolitan areas or "conurbations." The sprawl is a tide rising and expanding in different ways according to the various civilizations, even within the western and North Atlantic realm.

The sharpest contrast today is probably between the suburban rings of the larger American cities on the one hand and of the French on the other. In America the lower-income migrants coming to the city congregate close to the center inside the central city, while the middle-class residences move out to the suburbs. As industrial plants and warehouses also tend to move out to the periphery or even farther away, the central district remains lively only to the extent that offices and services continue to gather there and expand white-collar employment and activities. In cities where such conditions are not achieved, the old "central business district" undergoes a sad process of aging and decay. The suburbs on the other hand are almost everywhere prospering. According to the estimates of the Urban Land Institute of Washington, D.C., in 1965 the total population of the suburbs surpassed that of the central cities in the United States: the 1960 census counted 58 million inhabitants in the central cities and 55 million in the suburbs; by 1965 it was estimated that 68 million dwelt in the suburbs and only 61 million in the central cities. Although a number of the jobs in a metropolitan area also move out, following either the residences or the outward movement of industrial plants and warehouses, a large proportion of the suburban residents work in the central city. Commuting and traffic problems in general are intensified by these trends. And new conflicts of interests arise between the municipalities of the older cities, which feel impoverished and abandoned, and those of the growing suburban communities, which look for autonomous solutions to the problems caused by their own growth.

The trends of French urban expansion appear quite different. Haussmann's renewal of Paris a century ago has established a traditional pattern concentrating the middle class in the central city of Paris and pushing the underprivileged newcomers and the "working masses" out to the suburbs. Politically, this has led in Paris to a concentration of conservative votes in the central city, while the suburban ring is known as the "Red belt." Similar patterns may be observed in other large or medium-size French cities, where the central part remains that of more fashionable residences while the suburbs are in most cases inhabited by the lower income brackets. As a general rule, this is true of Lyon, Marseille, Toulouse, and Nancy, although a few local exceptions to this general rule may be found, and the annexation by some cities of their built-up periphery may have integrated what developed as a suburban ring into the central city's political community.

It remains that the opposition of interests between central city and suburbs exists in both cases; the lack of cooperation between interdependent communities causes similar difficulties in the management of metropolitan matters, even though the distribution of the social strata and tensions on the maps varies greatly from country to country. In America the racial element sharpens many of these tensions, all the more so as the differences in color correspond to the economic and social divisions. But the contrast in the evolution of the growing metropolitan areas in North America and on the Continent of Europe has much deeper roots which can be traced in the history and social structure of these two parts of the world. The transcontinental march of settlement in the United States and Canada has established a tradition of fluidity and transition in the location, form, and function of human settlement, urban as well as rural. Within the largest cities things have been migratory as growth or decline developed. As the threat of the Indians was swept away, towns were able to discard the walls or stockades a few of them originally erected for security reasons. No American city ever had (with the possible exception of Salt Lake City) a holy nucleus in its center to stabilize basic elements in its plan and activities; Washington, D.C., was designed, of course, around the Capitol and the White House, but even there a great deal of fluidity was allowed to develop around these monuments.

In the Old World the city was from its origins a sanctuary: it was the site of a castle and a temple, and these institutions gave a sacred character to a part of its central area which could hardly be referred to as "downtown" and could be displaced only under exceptional circumstances. Moreover, the city was a place of safety amid an open countryside in which there was little security in days of yore for most of the inhabitants. To function properly as a sanctuary, the city had to be strong, that is, a well-knit community in a well-defended location. The presence of the political authority and of the spiritual authority, symbolized by the castle and the temple, served as pillars of the city's strength. However, within the city itself a section was often isolated which contained the "sacred section": the imperial palaces in an inner city of Peking and in Tokyo still remind us of the tradition carried westward in the Kremlin at Moscow. In Western Europe these traditions have been less strict and more migratory; still, the central part of the city kept a greater significance for the community than has been the case in the younger nations of North America.

These considerations stress the variety of the attitudes towards the city, its function, form, plan, and evolution, from one part of the world to another. Because the city is an expression of the tradition of political organization and social structure of the people, every civilization deals with it in its own way, even though the physical problems and technological means may seem to be the same. The French, and residents of many other nations on the Continent, prefer to this day a higher density of population and activities in their central cities; the suburbs also have relatively high densities and cling to the immediate vicinity of the central place much more than they do in America. There is also more endeavor towards the preservation of sites, and it would be difficult to convince a European that cities should be eventually razed to be rebuilt a little farther for the sake of increased comfort or efficiency. In practice, European cities, of course, grow or decline, expand or retract, move to new quarters to rebuild themselves, as in other parts of the world, but urban geography is definitely more itinerant in America than in most of the countries of the Old World, probably because American society and politics are also endowed with greater fluidity.

The first way to measure this fluidity of geographical location is the residential density. In the United States even a very large metropolis may develop with average densities of about 5,000 inhabitants per sq. mile of urbanized area; in France, the average density of the département of Seine reached in 1962 30,000 per sq. mile, the highest population density in the world for an agglomeration of more than five million people. Another way to measure fluidity is by examining the flow of traffic; as the metropolitan region grows, even with a relatively low density and a relative lack of centrality, as in the case of Los Angeles, for instance, the traffic problems grow soon to be overwhelming and extremely costly to solve. The modern metropolis increasingly recognizes that the individual automobile is no more a way out of the traffic jams; its use in the large agglomerations becomes more and more regulated, costly, and even restricted. As public transit is adopted by more large cities all around the world, the need for cooperation between the various municipalities living side by side within a metropolitan area, and sometimes within urban regions made up of several metropolises and their overlapping suburban areas, comes into the limelight.

The traffic needs are only one item on a long list of physical relationships binding closely together adjoining sections of the same metropolitan system. They are all interested in services as good and inexpensive as can be provided, and these are usually easier and cheaper to establish as an integrated network for a larger number of customers. Technologically and economically a metropolitan area is the very best example of the need for integration, coordination, and overall planning, but politically and socially this has proven to be one of the toughest problems to solve. The opposition, inherited from a recent history of segregation of differentiated social elements of the population, is very much alive between the local governments in charge of the central city on the one hand and the suburban communities on the other. The barriers to progress are essentially in the minds of the people; but these are the most difficult to overcome.

The phenomenon is not new of an expanding metropolis sprawling beyond city limits. In the past, cities grew by annexing suburban rings or sectors, that is, swallowing them into their basic governmental unity. For very large cities, however, this has not always proved a simple solution. The case of London in this respect is, of course, peculiar but still significant: to the local government units of the London boroughs was superimposed first a Metropolitan Police, later a London County Council, then a Greater London Council. A two-tier system of government within a metropolitan area becomes a rather common feature. In the United States an interesting experimentation and an abundant literature have debated the matter of metropolitan government: in the American federal system, where there are normally three levels of governmental institutions (local, state, and federal), the generalization of metropolitan government would introduce a fourth tier, often in competition with the state government (where a major metropolitan area encompasses most of the population of the state) and sometimes in conflict with traditional state jurisdictions (where a metropolitan area straddles the line between two states, which is not infrequent). The matter is still debated, though in several cases, state government institutions took over some of the functions which may have otherwise gone to metropolitan instances: thus in Massachusetts for various problems of greater Boston. But some metropolitan areas voted in favor of new metropolitan institutions, and the intricacies of certain situations led to the creation of specialized agencies by compact between states, such as the agreement of New Jersey and New York State to establish the New York Port Authority; harbor and water problems have led to other such agencies on the Delaware river.

In recent years, several successive reforms have given to the urban region of Paris a three-tier system of local government under special supervision by the national authorities: the old municipal system has been as yet preserved; the departmental framework has been kept, though reshaped; instead of the former three *départements* of Seine, Seine-et-Oise and Seine-et-Marne, forming the Region or District of Paris, eight *départements* have now been set up, one of them coinciding exactly with the city of Paris; and a new level of regional government has been installed, for the whole Region of Paris, supervising and coordinating the eight *départements,* with a regional prefect at its head.

The agglomeration of people on relatively small areas of a nation's territory creates a whole series of metropolitan problems, in a few areas on a megalopolitan scale, which have already caused new institutions to arise. Metropolitan management is still extremely difficult because of the suspicion and resentment surrounding the idea of sharing in common the needs and means of a newly formed system in an area full of newcomers, of a diversity which easily frightens the established local people. The rapidly growing modern city does not seem to offer the city dwellers the basic security and stability, particularly in the social and political sense, which it used to be the function of the strong city to provide. Resistance to social fluidity determines political clashes and a new kind of instability. It interferes constantly with the elaboration of the policies, laws, and regulations which are urgently needed to solve the problems caused by rapid growth and change. This is obvious in the field of transportation and at least as much in the field of taxation. Because the various levels of government concerned could not work together reasonably, several large American cities now experience a three-tier system of taxation, New York being a case in point. The bigger the city the worse seems to be its condition.

The Bonds of Size in Politics

The large metropolis can hardly plan its future by a program calling for the annexation or consolidation of suburbs with the central city. In many cases the size of both population and area of the city would grow so big and so fast as to unbalance the existing frame of national politics. Let us imagine what would be the power within the United States of a mayor and a "city council" elected by the whole region of Megalopolis, already now a continuous chain of interlocked metropolitan areas: they would represent and administer one-fifth of the nation, some 40 million people, including the largest business interests, the largest money and mass media markets, many of the more influential centers of education, art, and culture, and even the seat of the national government. The rest of the country would find itself in a sort of colonial dependence on the regional government of a unified Megalopolis. A similar situation would arise in France if there were a mayor and a municipal council of the whole Paris Region, endowed with the same duties and responsibilities as the mayor and council of a small French town. The clash of interests between such a governmental unit and the rest of the nation would probably ruin their ability to work and live together.

Here again, as with the components of a single metropolitan area, the "conflict of interests" is not an economic one; indeed, it is rather political in nature. A large urban center is obviously dependent on the outside for agricultural and industrial supplies, for recreational space, and for a fresh supply of labor to make the city grow; last but not least, an urban economy works by supplying goods and services to markets outside the immediate vicinity. However, while the vast urban area needs the rest of the country it is located in, it also maintains usually an active network of relations with faraway areas, beyond national borders. There is more traffic, for both business and pleasure, between, say, London and Paris than between Paris and Bordeaux, more between London and New York than between New York and Atlanta. This is hardly because London is a much bigger city than either Atlanta or Bordeaux, but rather because the "cosmopolitan function" of those large national and international centers makes them more interdependent than each of them is dependent on a much smaller regional center in its own country. This is what causes resentment and suspicion in the "provinces" which do not want to be subordinated to and, in some way, "bossed" by the great national (or sometimes even regional) metropolis. Hence the famous American attitude claiming that New York City is not properly American, or the frequent condemnation in France of the growth of Paris.

The modern trends concentrating an increasing proportion of the total population and activity of the nation in one, two, or three principal urban regions may have a very good explanation, as we tried to describe it, in the social and economic process bringing about contemporary urbanization. It cannot help arousing much resentment and political opposition in the other parts of the country, where the population is thinned out or where the relative political weight of the region is on the decline. The national and international economy may profit by these processes as they develop; the majority of the individuals may obtain as a result the means to achieve higher standards of living, more comfort, and a more exciting life. But the political process in most countries affected by urbanization has been struggling against these trends, mainly against the growth of the best developing large cities.

It looks indeed as if a deep conflict develops between the successfully growing large cities and the central governments of their countries. This has systematically hindered the efforts of the cities and metropolitan areas to solve the problems of growth and to provide for their needs. Most of the countries of Europe have laws and regulations enforcing "decentralization" of economic activities from the leading urban area (or areas) which has been growing most successfully. In most cases decentralization legislation forbids new industrial plants from being built in the places of great concentration; in those countries where it was recognized that agglomeration of people and economic activities goes on more owing to the congregation of offices than plants and warehouses, decentralization of offices was also favored: thus for London, Paris, and Amsterdam. Offices or plants that agree to relocate themselves in areas where employment is rather depressed are often granted substantial advantages. In many ways these policies resemble the much older measures favoring and even subsidizing the small family farm to keep the rural farm population where it was. The aim is the same: it is to keep the small and medium towns from losing their people to the great

metropolis that attracts them. Most of the much admired regional planning now carried out in North America and Europe is just aimed at creating in the areas from where the people are leaving new activities and
better conditions of living to reverse the trend.

This is quite understandable: the existing distribution of people
fights to preserve itself. The major urban areas in the country are
endangering by their growth the existing distribution of votes,
resources, and political weights. The rapidly growing large cities never
have the majority in the legislative assemblies of their nation or state;
partly this is the result of straight arithmetic: urban population has
achieved a majority in the total population only recently and in relatively
few countries. This is partly due to careful manipulation by the politicians of the electoral maps to keep the cities, especially the fast-
growing large ones, from obtaining a commanding position in national
politics. The present debate on reapportionment of the state legislatures and of the House of Representatives in the United States illustrates very well the resistance of the political system in a democracy to
let the cities, even though they count now a majority of the people, dominate the legislative assemblies. In 1958, the then Senator John F. Ken-
nedy wrote: "The apportionment of representation in our Legislatures
and (to a lesser extent) in Congress has been either deliberately rigged
or shamefully ignored so as to deny the cities and the voters that full
and proportionate voice in government to which they are entitled" (in
the New York Times Magazine, 18 May 1958). Since then, several decisions of the United States Supreme Court have started a movement of
reapportionment which is gradually correcting the situation. As one
reads the debates and decisions of the Supreme Court, one cannot
help thinking of the English experience with the Rotten Boroughs in the
eighteenth and nineteenth centuries. Any given geographical distribution of political power is bound, of course, to try to perpetuate itself,
although the geographical substratum which brought this distribution
originally about may have been substantially modified. Besides the
understandable fear of an incumbent that he might not be reelected if
his constituency were modified or, even worse, merged with another,
there exists in all Western countries a deep-seated distrust of the political behavior of city dwellers, particularly as compared to the rural folks.
The bigger the city the more mistrust it suggests.

In the American debate on reapportionment these important factors
in the political attitudes towards urbanization came clearly to the fore.
The Supreme Court's majority decisions emphasized many times the
need to redraw the electoral districts because of the migration from
rural to urban areas. Basic principles of ethics were recalled to enforce
reapportionment: in a famous decision of 15 June 1964, Chief Justice

Earl Warren stated that "legislators represent people, not trees or acres. Legislators are elected by voters, not farms or cities or economic interests. . . . The weight of a citizen's vote cannot be made to depend on where he lives" (*Reynolds* v. *Sims*). In his dissenting opinion, Justice Potter Stewart argued: "Legislators do not represent faceless numbers. They represent people . . . with identifiable needs and interests . . . which can often be related to the geographical districting." Discussing the apportionment of the Senate of New York State, Justice Stewart remarked that electing both assemblies of the legislature on the basis of equality ("one man, one vote") required by the majority of the Court would put all parts of the state under the domination of "one megalopolis." This looked unethical to him.

In an earlier case before the Supreme Court, Justice Felix Frankfurter said in his dissenting opinion that he thought the Court would allow legislative apportionment to rely substantially on "geography, economics, urban-rural conflict, and all the other non-legal factors which have throughout our history entered into political districting" (*Baker* v. *Carr,* in 1962). The majority's decisions since have not supported this forecast. The Court seems to have laid down the law without allowing for the "non-legal factor." Perhaps it has become obvious to the majority that these nonlegal factors would be operating anyhow within the political process and that strictly legal principles had to be brought to bear for a better balance. The distrust of the urban crowds, and particularly of bigness in cities, is one of these factors, and it should be analyzed and accounted for at a time when such powerful tides of concentration make an increasing proportion of persons—soon a majority of them as we project recent trends—live in bigger and bigger urban agglomerations.

Most of the sociological analysis of modern large cities has focused on the *difficulties* of urban neighborhood: the difficulty of adapting to density for migrants from rural or small town areas; the difficulty of organizing a going concern community when made of newcomers from diverse origins; the difficulty of mixing people from adjoining but different neighborhoods, and so forth. A great deal of criticism of the conditions of urban living is certainly necessary in order to improve these conditions, as they need to and could be improved. The systematic analysis and teaching of the ills of the city must not, however, let us forget the opportunity opened up by the big city, and the virtues of the social process of contemporary urbanization.

If "geography" is occasionally mentioned by jurists among the non-legal factors of the political process, it could play a part on the positive rather than on the negative side of politics: instead of being used to demonstrate the "urban-rural conflict," geography should be used to effectively demonstrate the interdependence and, in fact, the *comple-*

mentarity of these two uses of the land and ways of life. Rural activities, and particularly agricultural production, have been flourishing since urban development proceeded at a pace and on a scale permitting the subsidy of agriculture in an effective manner. Western Europe produces more agricultural goods since it became more industrialized and more urbanized during the past hundred years. It is easier to better equip and support the farming population once it represents only one-tenth or less of the total population. The migration to the cities has considerably improved both the living standards on the remaining farms and the productivity of agricultural land. Bigger cities mean better farming and better rural living. If a number of legislative seats must be shifted in the process to newly formed urban districts, this should not be formulated as a "rural-urban conflict."

The size of growing metropolitan areas threatens the management of public affairs with a new kind of conflict of interests. If we return to the American reapportionment situation, we see that urban areas are gradually achieving a fairer representation in the legislative assemblies; but the urban and metropolitan regions are themselves divided, as we already mentioned, by a standing opposition between central cities and suburban areas. As the latter gain in residential population, they will also acquire a greater political weight which they may be enticed to use against the central cities rather than in wiser fashion on behalf of the bigger, metropolitan community. It has been pointed out that the limits of constituency are the limits of a politician's wisdom. This could be a narrow and regrettable use of political geography. The bigness of modern cities, the contrasts in the densities of land occupation, and the whole present evolution of land use command a new division of labor between regions which are different but complementary.

This principle of geographical complementarity calls for the understanding of the new bonds a world with big cities creates between central cities and suburbs, between urban and rural areas, between industry and agriculture, between residential and recreative areas, and between places of work and places of relaxation. What used to be called "town and country planning" and which is now a primary concern of the governments in all well-developed countries, aims at a geographical harmony founded not on uniformity but on a rational division of labor and the ensuing complementarity between the various regions of a country, and of a world, that must live and work together. Such a harmony can be brought about only through the political process; in recent times the political process has shown more suspicion and opposition than understanding for this evolution.

The Conflict between the Metropolis and the Central Government

At the root of the modern distrust of the political behavior of big cities one may discern an old and perhaps permanent conflict opposing the large growing metropolis and the central government of the country in which it is located. This is an important matter in our days of rapid urbanization and large-scale "metropolitanization." Historical records abound that illustrate the permanency of this conflict and it may be worthwhile to review them briefly in conclusion of this rapid outline of the social and political implications of the growing city.

As early as we can find references to such relations in ancient times we hear the spokesmen for the large growing urban community asking for more autonomy and freedom. We cited the example from ancient Mesopotamia in another paper that appears as chapter 3 in this volume. It cited the freedom of the city of Babylon in the time of an all-powerful king. Then, it needed a large metropolis to challenge a powerful king; but the commercial and cultural functions of the metropolis also required some freedom of behavior, of information, and of traveling, and the guarantee that business freely transacted will be respected and not interfered with in autocratic fashion. Medieval history is filled with constant conflicts, negotiations, and agreements between kings or emperors and large and rich cities. The political evolution that led to the modern democratic concept starts in Western Europe with the internal strifes and autonomous governments of Italian and Flemish cities. The history of London itself could well illustrate at different periods the important role the frequent conflicts between city and Crown played in the process that ironed out the British system of government.

The case of Paris was also cited in chapter 3. There was constant opposition by the city of Paris to the strong monarchs' efforts to control the capital. The building of Versailles just outside the city was an obvious will to separate geographically the big city and the center of political power. And the French Revolution brought the king and the government back. The republican governments of the twentieth century all tried to enforce centralization policies to stop the growth of the Paris Region accused of sucking out all the sap of the national system. In 1961 the government appointed a new dignitary (designated at first as Délégué Général, then after 1966 as Préfet de Région) to direct the planning and regional administration of the metropolitan region, the population of which gathered about one-fifth of the French nation.

It is noteworthy that Versailles was taken as a model by many other countries who sought to move the seat of government outside their biggest city which had traditionally been also their capital. The Dutch court was located at The Hague, at some distance from Amsterdam which remained nominally the capital of the Netherlands. Peter the Great built St. Petersburg not only to attract the Russian interests to the sea, but also, and perhaps primarily, to take the government of Russia out of Moscow in durable fashion. Washington was set in the District of Columbia not only to be between North and South but also to locate the federal government away from the largest American cities of New York and Philadelphia, which vied for the role of capital. In more recent times the vogue has been considerable of new capitals established at a distance of the major growing cities: Ankara, Canberra, Pretoria, Brasilia . . . .

In each case there have been several kinds of considerations that dictated the decision; but the dislike of the environment of the great, bustling, turbulent, cosmopolitan metropolis as the seat for the national government has been in every case one of the determining factors. This distrust is not all prejudice or inherited tradition. There is certainly more to it and it ought to be analyzed. For the political fear of the bigness in cities remains nowadays one of the stumbling blocks of better urban planning and policies even in the more advanced nations. There is in the large growing metropolis something inherent that causes a conflict to arise with the normal viewpoints of national politics. Partly this certainly is because the successful metropolis tends to assume too much authority towards the rest of the country, to attract too many of the desirable functions, and also shows too much independence through reliance on its foreign and distant relations. But in the wake of modern urbanization the impact of the social and political processes at play must be fully recognized. The growing city is indeed a social and political process itself; it should be understood and planned as such, not only as a maze of buildings, technological gadgets, and economic interests.

Perhaps a fuller understanding of this process of growth could help improve the product. In the city the container cannot be separated from the contained; it has been our purpose here to stress the dynamics of the contained in those aspects that must be expressed also in the mold of the container.

Part Four   **Megalopolis**

We may, however, wonder how much of a lesson the past and present of Megalopolis may provide for its own people and for the population of other lands.

It would certainly have immensely pleased the Founding Fathers of the cities in Megalopolis to find that the way of life and the economic organization developed there serve as a model to many other parts of the world undergoing the process of urbanization. The actual trends, however, are not quite so simple. The process of urban growth is in our time a worldwide phenomenon and a source of concern for many communities and governments. In every region this growth develops along specific lines, most of which differ from place to place; every community has its own variety of the usual problems, and its own ways and means of tackling them. These local characteristics must be respected. But to be informed of more or less similar problems in other places, and how they have been dealt with, is helpful; and what is learned in this way may be used to help solve one's own problems in one's own way.

Naturally countries faced with the questions of modern urbanization look first at the precedents set and the experiments tried in areas where leadership has been established. In our time Megalopolis is being thus studied and examined, for many of its various problems are or will be repeated, with some variance and on different scales, in most other countries. Whether the action taken concerning any of its urban and suburban problems warrants it or not, Megalopolis should know that it will be examined by many outsiders, some of whom will copy it just because of the prestige the region enjoys today, and some of whom may be inspired to improve on the techniques applied there. Whatever is done, whatever its real worth for the people involved, the example of Megalopolis will be followed more often than not. Observers travelling around the world nowadays report from most varied areas many instances of the obvious influence of American methods of coping with urban problems; and as Megalopolis remains the most impressive and largest urban system, as it is the main façade of the United States toward the outside world, it is mainly Megalopolitan examples that are impressed on so many cities and countries around the globe.

Megalopolis,
"Novus Ordo Seclorum"

Seven

How Large Can
Cities Grow?

Growth is an essential part of biological
and economic processes. It is a physical feature which seems quantitative and measurable. It has been observed, however, that many forms
of growth modify the structures and even the nature of the phenomena
within which they develop. The question has now been asked whether
cities, the largest artifacts produced by man, could and should be
allowed to grow indefinitely?

The growth of cities has been extremely rapid in the twentieth century and its momentum has accelerated since 1950. The million-size
city was a rather exceptional phenomenon and a subject of wonderment
in 1900. There are at least 150 cities with more than one million population each in the world today and both their number and average size are
on the increase. The distinguished Japanese architect and planner,
Kenzo Tange, once remarked that while the very big city of 1900 was of
a one-million size, by 1960 that size rose to ten-million, and by 2000 it
could well reach one hundred-million. Rather than individual cities,
Tange had in mind vast and continuous urbanized regions such as the

Reprinted from *Revista da Universidad de Coimbra*, 1978, 3–14.

Tokaido Megalopolis extending from Tokyo to Kobe in Japan or the Boston to Washington, D.C., Megalopolis in the United States. Both these regions accounted for some 40 million people each by 1970. A few similar megalopolitan growths may be observed in other areas of the modern world.

The question does then arise: Is there a limit to urban growth? How large could cities or urban agglomerations become, which encompass a plurality of closely connected cities and metropolitan districts? Urban concentration has always been held to exist and grow owing to people and supplies coming to it from the countryside and drawn from surpluses produced by the rural areas in that countryside, especially surpluses of food, water, and raw materials. If the number and percentage of urban population goes on increasing, how will these agglomerations support themselves? Would they keep on growing if migrations were stemmed from rural regions?

As urbanization swells up to dimensions heretofore unknown, and little expected in the past, the question of the limits to urban growth becomes a timely subject of lively debate. It is not only a discussion between optimists and pessimists, between adherents to Malthusian beliefs and champions of man's ability to develop the production of essentials. The larger agglomerations already appear unwieldy, unpleasant, and undesirable to many. Certain cities have seen their growth arrested; the concern about limits to urban growth suggests that immediate steps be taken to attempt to orient and direct urbanization by planning and regulation.

Scale and Standards of Urban Growth

United Nations statistics estimate the urban population of the globe to be 986 million, that is 33 percent of mankind in 1960, and to 1,596 million in 1975, then 39.7 percent of the world total. The increase in those fifteen years can be measured as a 62 percent growth or as an addition of 610 million people to the population of urban places. These figures call for thought: it is amazing that such massive and rapid increase of urban population was accommodated, or "digested" with relatively little trouble; it may be termed a hopeful indication that, with very little preparation or planning, such numbers could be added to agglomerated districts. On the other hand, a less optimistic view would underscore the individual suffering, the social and regional tensions this process has caused, and the dangers inherent for the future.

That future appears especially threatening as the forecast points to an urban population reaching 2,198 million by 1985, to form then 44 percent of mankind. This growth projection assumes that cities and towns, old and new, would absorb between 1975 and 1985 an additional population of 602 million, almost as many new people as in the fifteen years preceding, that is, a decennial increase of 37.7 percent. This may seem to mean a slight decrease in the rate of growth but an increase in the actual number of inhabitants added annually. Projection to the year 2000 has been attempted but may be meaningless because the difference between our present and already somewhat perimated concepts of urban and rural will be blurred by 1990, if not before, to an extent that would require a drastic overhauling of categories referring to types of settlement.

The first issue of the *U.N. Compendium of Housing Statistics* introduced in 1974 a concept of "big city" population to describe urban agglomerations of more than 500,000 inhabitants. Today, on the urban scale, anything below that level seems indeed small. In 1800 there were probably only eight cities that would qualify in that category, four of them in Europe (London, Paris, Constantinople, and Naples) and four in Asia. In 1960 the "big city" population had risen to 378 million (12.7 percent of the world population) and in 1975 to 698 million (17.4 percent). Growth was especially steep in this category of urban places. The forecast for 1985 stood at 1,063 million, that is, 21.5 percent of mankind at that time: people living in such large agglomerations then would be more numerous than the world urban population was in 1960. The rate of growth of big cities is obviously much more accelerated than that of small or medium-size ones.

The problem of urban growth must be considered in two aspects: the size of cities and the general urbanization trends. The general pattern of world urbanization varies according to the size, number, form, and distribution of cities. Size and number of agglomerations are, of course, interrelated; the bigger the cities, the smaller their number for any given total of people. When urban growth is discussed, it is the scale and density of large agglomerations that most worry our contemporaries. The major problems that appear very difficult to alleviate are found nowadays in the larger cities: congestion, pollution, high costs, mismanagement, and criminality seem to be worst in such places as New York, Chicago, London, Tokyo, São Paulo, Calcutta, which are among the largest cities on the planet. Could and should growth be limited for individual cities?

A big modern city is not in fact easy to measure in satisfactory fashion. The classic standard used is the figure of population, that is, the number of residents ascertained by census. The list of the very large cities today is headed by a group in which most units, by 1971, approximated 8 to 10 million inhabitants; this category comprises New

York, Tokyo, Shanghai, London, Paris, São Paulo, Peking, and Moscow. The largest was probably Tokyo or Shanghai; by 1980 the leadership may have gone to Mexico City or São Paulo. In fact, none of the census measurements is precise enough or fully comparable to the others: the residential census population of the city of London proper is somewhere around 4,500 while employment in that famous square mile stands at about 250,000; the 7.4 million census figure for 1971 relates to the Greater London Council area, which is the beginning stage of a metropolitan structure in local government. Similarly, the figure of 8.5 million for Paris refers to the District de la Région de Paris, another modern metropolitan governmental unit. The residential population of Paris, as a metropolitan district, has been and still is growing; but the 1975 census gave only 2.2 million residents for the central city, that is, the *Ville de Paris* which seems to have lost 600,000 residents since 1954.

The central areas of a modern metropolis are evolving fast; almost all of them are being or recently have been rebuilt and redeveloped for new uses. The redevelopment usually pushes a part of the residences out to the suburbs. This is a long-standing, general, and well-known trend. With few exceptions, it testified to a great vitality of these cities adapting to the changing demand on the services they provide. Thus the concept has developed at least in statistical terms, and in many countries also in terms of local government structure, of metropolitan areas or districts. Planning theory has constantly been inventing new terms to describe the realities of urban expansion that agglomerates in one system neighboring cities, towns, and suburban districts. *Metropolitan district,* for example, is an old term; Patrick Geddes coined around 1910 the term *conurbation* which connotes continuity in urbanization, and today the largest conurbation in the world is probably that of Tokyo–Yokohama in Japan, approaching 20 million people. But there are parts of the world where conurbations border one another and where metropolitan continuity extends over long and vast systems of a polynuclear structure. While studying the prototype of such growths in the northeast of the United States, I suggested the concept of *megalopolis* for a region stretching from greater Boston to greater Washington.

Is there any significance now if census reports indicate a stabilization or decline of the residential numbers and sometimes even in the numbers of jobs in the largest cities? Such statistical indications are rather indicative of changes in economic functions, land uses, traffic currents, and perhaps even urban styles of living and working. They do not mean growth has stopped or been reversed for all practical purposes. In fact, such an impression is usually corrected by the urban sprawl beyond city limits and even beyond metropolitan limits. The spatial extension is bound to arouse more problems in government, financing, and taxation, as it usually will increase pressure on the means of transport and will complicate procedures by straddling administrative boundaries. What other standards than residential population could be used to measure urban growth? There is, of course, an important spatial component in the concept of city, of district, or even of urban expansion. Urban places used to be many but took up very little space: a dot was the traditional manner to represent towns or cities on maps. This is increasingly recognized as inadequate. Metropolitan areas become spatial patches of some importance. On the maps of population density the darker shades describing the higher densities of urban character begin to spread in noticeable manner.

Could urban growth be measured in terms of area, on the extent of ground it covers? There has been much moaning about the vast surfaces devoured by urban and suburban sprawl. As the numbers of urban dwellers increase, more ground is naturally needed to house and service them, and for their places of work and recreation. With greater affluence or even welfare, with greater mobility and mechanization, the density of people, as they are distributed at home or at work, has been gradually lowered. Even with the density of massive high-rise apartment buildings, which have become a frequent sight in large agglomerations throughout the world, average urban densities of ground occupation are below what they used to be in the overcrowded cities of the mid-nineteenth century. Today in the Western world and in Japan urban densities of 30,000 or more per square kilometer are quite exceptional. In the 1860s the city of London proper had an average density of about 100,000 per sq. kilometer. Such situations may be found now in some cities of the less developed countries and in a few special cases of crowding imposed by political geography, such as in Hong Kong. As a general trend the densities are being lowered, at least for residential occupancy; it is the distances within urban agglomerations that are lengthening and becoming a new and serious problem of growth.

The modern city dweller tends to consume more space per capita, both on the ground and as floor space. This higher consumption cannot be satisfied, even in slums and *favelas,* without an increase in the consumption of services and at least of some materials. The richer the country the more it seems to allow its citizens to consume space for urban pursuits. The United States has led the way in dispersing its cities and expanding suburban sprawl. The more recently developed metropolitan areas, especially those of southern California and Texas, that grew up in the era of the automobile, display an especially high rate of space consumption. Many other older American cities have relatively high densities: thus New York, Chicago, even San Francisco. A remarkable trend of expanding municipal territory has recently developed, especially in the South and West of the United States, where many central cities consolidated with the counties in which they were located, or annexed large suburban belts. This was done in order to bring back into city limits the white middle-class folks who had moved out to the suburbs while the poor blacks, West Indians, or Mexicans flocked into the central cities. By annexing the suburbs the cities improved both their political balance and their municipal finances. There are now about a hundred American cities with a territory of more than 250 sq. kilometers each. While the municipal area of New York City covers 750 sq. kilometers, it extends over 1,200 sq. kilometers for Los Angeles, 1,650 for Oklahoma City, and 1,990 for Jacksonville, Florida (the latter with a population of 528,000!)

While such a huge extension of municipal territory may seem a rather extraordinary trend, the idea of great practical interdependence between a modern city and the environing countryside has been gaining very general acceptance. United Nations experts and academic geographers have been using the expression of "city-region" to express both this interdependence and the increasing penetration by city dwellers and influences of suburban districts even beyond officially recognized administrative boundaries of all sorts. The recent reform of local government in England, which gave greater power to the county councils to coordinate town and country management, is just one among many manifestations of the trend. American sociologists originated some twenty years ago the concept of *rurban* areas and populations. Now planners hint at a "rurbanization trend" in the more urbanized countries. Does this blurring of the old concepts of urban and rural mean that "urban growth" is receding or that urbanization is proceeding to devour formerly rural space?

Megalopolis and Ecumenopolis

Urbanization is basically a process in the concentration of settlement, although urban growth causes gradual diffusion around the initial nuclei. An important point in the debate on the limits of urban growth is that the concentration of population, either in a mononuclear or polynuclear pattern, usually develops in one selected region of a country, increasingly around its capital city. In the larger and better developed countries, there could be two or three such regions of agglomeration concentrating most of the urban growth.

This seems to be a fairly general rule. A review of the various countries of the world has led me to suggest that there are few exceptions to what could be termed a law of modern population distribution: in every country one or two regions can be delimited that contain 15 percent to 40 percent of the population on less than 5 percent of the area. This is the general pattern that leads in the more extreme and larger cases to megalopolitan formation. But this trend has determined in recent times another consequence; the resentment and protest of other regions which are losing population and which feel deprived of a fair share in the national system. Hence the policies of decentralization or deconcentration from the main region of urban growth, to obtain a more equal regional distribution. These policies are again very general throughout the world today; planning legislation endeavors to direct population and employment away from Amsterdam and the Randstadt in Holland, away from the Paris Region in France, from southeastern London in England, from Lisbon in Portugal, from the Rio de Janeiro–São Paulo corridor in Brazil, from the Moscow region in the U.S.S.R., from Shanghai in China, and so on.

Examples of such policies aiming at decentralizing the largest national urban growth are many. The cases of success, where central growths have actually been stemmed, are very few, and are as yet short-lived and often disputable. The general theory of the evolution of large-scale urban growth is, in fact, rather simple; it may be set in six major principles:

1. Large scale urban growth, as it proceeds, increases local costs of living, especially through rises in prices of real property, of most services, and taxes.

2. Rivalry between competing large cities is one of the factors of change but also of growth.

3. Rival cities located at short distances from one another will tend to grow one towards another and to urbanize the intervening space.

4. Central districts of major cities and of some other specialized towns tend to concentrate transactional activities of a managerial, commercial, and cultural nature.

5. The dynamics of large cities attract inflows of outsiders either in search of opportunity or in search of information and recreation. The servicing of these outsiders, who come to settle or to visit, expands the facilities and activities of the place.

6. Large-scale urban agglomerations function increasingly as a system of interconnected networks, some of these being internal and others being external and may encompass relations with distant centers. The importance of the external networks usually tends to outweigh the role and influence of the local networks.

Greater interdependence is thus created between large cities and urban agglomerations. A concert of interest develops that is bitterly resented by the country around and between the larger centers. Hence the constant pressure to limit large urban growth and, if possible, to decentralize. Hence also the interplay of forces that defeats the political endeavors to put an end to large city growth—an endeavor already advocated by Plato in his *Laws*. However, the forces opposed to concentration and centralization have often succeeded in limiting the means granted by national governments to the larger growths in their respective jurisdictions. The living conditions in larger cities may thus grow unpleasant as means of improvement are denied and the attractiveness of such places decreases. Some may actually be ruined by the process. Examples of the latter are few, but they exist; thus Delos, when, after seven centuries of greatness, that insular city—a great sanctuary of Apollo—was cut off from participation in major networks, first by the power of Rome, which Delos had opposed, and later by the spread of Christianity.

The examples of decline remain in fact exceptional. The rule is the proliferation of large cities, the number and average size of which have constantly increased. The pace of the expansion of the largest units may well taper off. Perhaps few individual cities will surpass the ten million size in resident population. The particular facet of growth can be controlled to some extent by stabilizing the areas and boundaries of local government units. It will not, however, arrest the proliferation of metropolitan systems, and in certain parts of the world, their clustering to constitute megalopolitan formations.

At present, if only clusters of metropolitan areas that agglutinate more than twenty-five million people each are recognized as "megalopolitan," seven such growths exist on our planet: the American Northeastern Megalopolis, from Boston to Washington, the study of which, first published in 1961, has served as the prototype of the concept; the Tokaido Megalopolis in Japan, from Tokyo to Kobe; the Great Lakes Megalopolis in North America, straddling the American-Canadian boundary, and extending from Quebec City to Milwaukee; the urban constellation centered on Shanghai in China; the Megalopolis of northwestern Europe, extending from Amsterdam to the Ruhr and to Lille; the Megalopolis of England, stretching from Dover to Merseyside, and the Italian Megalopolis, in the plain of the Po, extending arms along the Mediterranean shores from Genoa to Marseille and to Pisa.

To these we may soon be able to add at least two others, located on different continents: one consists of the two big nuclei growing fast one towards the other, of Rio de Janeiro and São Paulo in Brazil; another is forming in California, centered in Los Angeles, extending northwards to the San Francisco Bay area and encompassing to the south cities along both sides of the Californian-Mexican border. There may also be some formation of megalopolitan size and structure in India.

On the whole, as large urban regional systems, all the nine cases above continue expanding, even though the Boston to Washington

Megalopolis has given signs in the 1970s of reducing its rate of growth, and perhaps stabilizing. It may be a temporary slowing down of the process or a longer range trend. Urban growth appears less predictable than climatic cycles, but it has seldom taken the allure of a cycle. Other large urban centers in North America are still on the rise along the Great Lakes and the Pacific and Gulf coastlands. In fact, extrapolating from the megalopolitan phenomenon to a further, ultimate phase, the late C. A. Doxiadis has offered the concept of Ecumenopolis, immense networks of urbanized corridors extending as a frame over the continents, weaving an almost continuous and universal urban system which could be the habitat of 90 percent of future mankind even if it reaches the tens of billions.

Such a future is not impossible, although it is still very distant and many factors could intervene in the course of the process, modifying substantially the pattern of settlement. Whether such modifications will be desired and applied may be debated: excavations at the Akro-Thera archaeological site, on top of the island of Santorini, of that Greek equivalent of Pompeii buried under volcanic ashes by 1500 B.C., show that the major physical patterns of urban settlement have evolved little for 3,500 years. The technological innovations of the twentieth century may be causing radical changes still to be demonstrated. The scattering across country of fair-sized urban centers is a logical corollary of the increasing number of urban dwellers, of the growing concentration of population on the regional scale, and of the resistance to the speed and size of growth in a few "most favored" districts.

Doxiadis may have seen the Ecumenopolitan picture emerging with particular force as he studied the Great Lakes Megalopolis in the 1960s. It is a less dense, yet less congested, and certainly less resented concentration than the original Megalopolis on the Boston–New York–Washington axis. A similar schema could be proposed of a transeuropean megalopolitan belt crossing the continent from the Mediterranean to the North Sea and the Irish Sea as urbanization proceeds along the Saône-Rhône and Rhine valleys and penetrates the valleys of the Alps. We could visualize an "urbanized isthmus" from Rome (or Naples?) and Venice in the South to Amsterdam and Hamburg, jumping even over the Straits of Dover to include most of England. Such a formation may call for a new term, such as *megistopolis.*

The more the largest existing concentrations will be restricted or decentralized, the more other urban places will grow, and urban dynamics will make them follow major axes of transport between the older metropolises, sprawling around, filling in interurban spaces, unless the latter are strictly protected and further urbanization is deflected to other parts.

The choice seems to be again between concentration and dispersal. Another alternative would be to accept both to some extent, while regulating them. The latter solution will best express an ideal of planning. Raymond Unwin, in the England of the early twentieth century, preached the proliferation of new towns, each a rather small, compact community. If the new towns were to be kept at a size of about 50,000 inhabitants each, the United Kingdom would have needed a great many of them. They would have established a dense network over the country with certainly an intense traffic between them. It would have led to a rather megalopolitan final pattern, though a structured and possibly homogeneous one. The actual development was different. New towns are now built at the 200,000 size and more. Most of England is anyhow acquiring a megalopolitan, though diversified, pattern. The present large concentrations have not been planned. Several of them have been fought by their own national authorities for many generations. Urbanization proceeds with demographic increase and greater affluence, which makes individuals consume more space and more amenities. With the move of the mass of the labor force from primary occupations such as farming and mining, towards more "urban" pursuits, occupations, and lifestyles, the trend accelerates towards affluence and away from hard, compelling work on the land. Unlocked from their former base in space, people are on the move, consuming more space per capita. Indeed, it was the social evolution allowed and accelerated by technological progress that gave its momentum to urban growth. Should and could such evolution be denied to those aspiring to it in the yet less-developed and less-urbanized countries? The limits of urban growth now take on a moral and ethical content. It becomes necessary to discuss the purpose of eventual regulation.

"Ford Versus Gandhi": The Purposes of the City

In 1927 the distinguished French geographer and political scientist André Siegfried, concluded his book Les Etats-Unis D'aujourd'hui (in its American edition entitled The United States Comes of Age) with a relevant remark: the twentieth century seemed to him to be marked by a conflict between the concepts of living of Henry Ford, the automobile manufacturer, and Mahatma Gandhi, the Indian apostle of simplicity and resistance to the onslaught of technology. America, in André Siegfried's view, endeavored to save human labor but wasted material goods. Europe rather saved materials but wasted labor. Asia, as symbolized by Gandhi, went even farther to maintain that old tradition.

The basic problem involved in this "Ford versus Gandhi" dichotomy of fifty years ago is a permanent one: it reaches beyond the use of technology and questions the whole purpose of the organization of society. It is relevant to the debate on urban growth and its limits because urbanization proceeded with the gradual liberation of the individual from hard, compelling labor on the land to produce the necessities of life. The rise of cities could not have been possible without the existence of *surpluses* as against local needs, in the countryside's production of goods, and in the availability of labor. Then, and only then, could migrants and supplies flow to the cities.

It is not our intention to retrace here the vicissitudes of these trends in the past. The twentieth century, however, particularly since 1950, has seen an enormous change in that process, accelerating urban growth in all its forms. The acceleration was made possible by modern advances of technology and the way society used the new tools for mechanization, conservation, automation of production, warehousing, transport, and distribution. Never did people dream of such surpluses as are now available, though wrongly used or distributed.

The process is perhaps best understood by looking at the occupational structure and its evolution towards white-collar and "nonproduction" work. The processes of production are increasingly left to machines, chemistry, biology, physics, automata—all conceived, started, directed, and to a large extent, controlled by human activity but with fewer hands working at the production proper, first on the farms, then in the mines, and finally even in the manufactures and warehouses. It could be argued that the individual automobile, symbolized by Henry Ford's name in the 1920s, put most people at work in the provision of transport, but the distribution of bulky cargoes is still being gradually automated. The telephone and other telecommunications helped to overcome distance in the transmission of messages and improved the coordination of different services, processes, and activities.

The various functions of a city always consisted of decisions and transactions aiming at directing the activities in the surrounding territory by more or less remote control. Indeed, the purpose of the city was to manage a territory around it, administer it, ensure its security, absorb and redistribute its surpluses, and organize the provision of supplies that could not be locally produced. At its origin, the city was a stronghold for protection and a transactional center. It was also the site for collective rituals, securing and satisfying the spiritual aspirations of the people to whom that city ministered. These functions are again becoming the essential activities of urban agglomerations. The manufacturing function was strongly concentrated in cities only by the Industrial Revolution, begun in Western Europe two centuries ago. In this respect the "Ford versus Gandhi" debate was a culmination of the effects of that

Industrial Revolution. The technological advances of the last fifty years have taken us, at least in the more developed and urbanized countries, beyond that stage. Manufactures are now leaving the more crowded urban areas. They will employ decreasing proportions of the labor force as improved techniques are more generally applied.

The purpose of the city becomes gradually clarified. Understanding this purpose should help define and delimit urban growth. People come to the city in the hope of achieving a better life in which they will be liberated from the time-consuming and physically straining aspects of production work, a type of work that also rivets them to one place. The freedom to move around, to have more time to use as they please, to use also their own strength as they please, rather than as directed, in order to survive—these are basic freedoms, and the city seems to be the place where they might be achieved, for a happy few in the past, for the large mass of the citizens in the future. The revolution of expectations heralded by modern urbanization, using properly the potential of recent advances of science and technology, bestows on our time and on the present generations immense responsibility and opportunity.

Mankind is changing its patterns of habitat but expects, in so doing, to achieve a fundamental improvement of the human condition. The limits of urban growth begin to take shape before us. The exploding cities will keep on growing for some time. There can be neither sense nor justice in attempting to deny to those who wish to come to large cities the hope of opportunity such relocation connotes. Even if the demographic increase tapers off as parents realize that their protection and support in the future do not require numerous families any longer, the numbers to be accommodated will be enormous, and the physical expansion of urbanization will have to be satisfied.

There is little doubt that technologically the resources can be provided in terms of building materials, energy, food, and even amenities, on the condition of organizing society to accept and provide for expansion instead of resisting it. What will be the size of cities does not fundamentally matter if life in them remains pleasant. If smaller-size cities proliferate on the land, their dispersal will get denser, form metropolitan clusters and, in some parts, megalopolitan systems. The present Megalopolis in North America or in Japan grew up from the scattered but not too distant cities of the nineteenth century, which were of modest size. Essential needs will be the prevention of waste to save materials and reduce pollution, and a fairer, more equal distribution of goods, services, and amenities. Individual consumption may have to be regulated and, in some countries, restricted by other means than cost. The uncontrolled use of the individual automobile will have to be challenged. The exuberant wasting of space either by suburban sprawl or by the generalization of second homes (there are some 2 million *résidences secondaires* in France, a nation of 53 million people) will also have to be regulated.

The urban community as a unit of social organization has also been undergoing rapid transformation. Whether some shape of geographical neighborhood will remain as a basic cell of society or whether new forms of association will arise remains an open question. The metropolis can, as it long did, preserve community life in the framework of neighborhoods, in town *villages, quartiers,* or *boroughs.* The main threats to the urban social structures are not a matter of size but of mobility of the population. It is that increasing mobility which causes urban mixes to grow more diverse, exotic, and ethnically divided. It is mobility also that causes large cities to hold in routine fashion larger numbers of transients and of *transhumant bourgeois,* who have more than one home and more than one place in which they acquire rooted interests.

Whether modern urban growth can be fully directed and, in some ways, limited has often been doubted. It is probably by modifying and regulating some of the behavior of urban dwellers that most could be achieved. The process of change will proceed with a strong quantum of chaos. Future historians may be able to describe it as systematic, even orderly, creation.

Bibliography

Doxiadis, C. A. and J. G. Papaioannou. *Ecumenopolis, the Inevitable City of the Future.* Athens: 1974.
Gottmann, Jean. *Megalopolis.* New York: The Twentieth Century Fund, 1961.
——, "Megalopolitan Systems Around the World." *Ekistics* no. 243 (1976): 109–13.
——, "Urbanization and Employment." *Town Planning Review* (July 1978).
McNee, Robert B. *A Primer of Economic Geography.* New York: Random House, 1971.
Toynbee, Arnold. *Cities on the Move.* London: Oxford University Press, 1970.

Eight

Megalopolitan Systems around the World

This chapter will focus on the Great Lakes Megalopolis, the vast complex of metropolitan and urbanized areas that straddles the boundary between Canada and the United States and winds around the network of waterways and water spaces of the St. Lawrence and the Great Lakes. To give an idea of the scope of the concept and of the related problems, it may be envisaged as extending from the city of Quebec in the East to the metropolitan area of Milwaukee in the West, including along that axis such great agglomerations as Montreal, Ottawa, Toronto, Detroit, Buffalo, Cleveland, and Chicago, to mention only a few major nuclei. Measured on this scale, the Great Lakes Megalopolis is probably the largest in area of the present megalopolitan systems.

The concept of megalopolis applies to very large polynuclear urbanized systems endowed with enough continuity and internal interconnections for each of them to be considered a system in itself. A megalopolis must also be separated by less urbanized broad spaces from any other large urban network that it does not encompass. In most cases the

Reprinted from *Ekistics*, 243, February 1976, 109–13.

density of population, of urban activities, and of interweaving internal networks within a megalopolitan region is such as to make it substantially different from surrounding areas that do not possess the same mass and density of population and a comparable intensity of urbanization.

Before we can list the existing megalopolitan systems, it is necessary to agree on a minimum size for the phenomenon. A number of works published on the concept and occurrences of megalopolis set a concentration of 10 million inhabitants within the area as the minimum size. This is much below the figure I have long advocated and would still prefer to propose; I would set the minimum at 25 million. If we accept this figure, the list of megalopolitan systems will be much shorter and every case will be endowed with certain characteristics which I believe are common to the whole lot and basic to the concept. There are, indeed, six cases of such, over 25 million each, megalopolitan occurrences in the present world: first, the American Northeastern Megalopolis, the study of which has served as the prototype of the concept; the Great Lakes Megalopolis, described by C. A. Doxiadis and by Alexander Leman; the Tokaido Megalopolis in Japan, which has been carefully studied under the direction of Eiichi Isomura; the megalopolis in England which has been identified and analyzed by the team directed by Peter Hall; the megalopolis of northwestern Europe, extending from Amsterdam to the Ruhr and to the French northern industrial conglomeration, described by I. B. F. Kormoss and now being studied by an international team at The Hague; and a sixth case of which we yet know relatively little, the Urban Constellation in Mainland China centered on Shanghai.

To these six cases we may soon be able to add three others, located on different continents. In each of these cases, the different parts seem to be coalescing fast enough to be considered megalopolitan systems in their own right, and the populations of each seem close to my proposed minimum of 25 million inhabitants. One case consists of two big nuclei that are growing fast and are being linked by a narrow corridor, that is, the Rio de Janeiro–São Paulo complex in Brazil; another, differently shaped megalopolis is forming in northern Italy, centered on the Milan-Turin-Genoa triangle and extending arms along the Mediterranean seashore southward to Pisa and Florence and westward to Marseille and Avignon. The third case will probably be in California, centered on Los Angeles, extending northward to the San Francisco Bay area and encompassing urban centers along both sides of the Californian-Mexican border. There may also be some formation of megalopolitan size and structure in India, but I have as yet no clear information on that part of the world.

If we lower the minimum size of population to 10 million, the number of megalopolitan systems would rise rapidly and in a disputable fashion. On the one hand, many mononuclear urban agglomerations could be identified at about the 10 million size, for instance, around Paris, Buenos Aires, Calcutta, Bombay, and perhaps Moscow. On the other hand, by accepting the 10 million gauge, we would be justified in breaking up the larger megalopolitan systems, some of which could then be considered independently of the adjacent and interconnected parts, so that greater New York would be considered a megalopolis on its own, as would be London, with its southeastern crown; the Ruhr-Cologne complex, the Tokyo-Yokohama and Osaka-Kobe metropolitan regions, and so on. The Great Lakes Megalopolis could then be dissected into several sections, each in the 10 to 15 million size: one around Chicago and Milwaukee, another in the Detroit-Cleveland sector, and still another in Canada from Hamilton to Quebec. The general view of the interconnected vaster system would be lost. The important idea to keep in mind is that megalopolis is *not* simply an overgrown metropolitan area. It is not only another step on the quantitative scale. It is a phenomenon of specific qualities of a different nature.

Hinges of Development

The megalopolitan systems have arisen along *polynuclear,* rather elongated axes. Sometimes the system takes on an irregular or a triangular shape, as has happened in Europe, but there is always a major axis of traffic and communication, and the nuclei strewn along it have a national and international function. For my original American Megalopolis, I used the metaphor of the "continent's economic hinge" to describe its major function throughout history. All megalopolitan regions have been *hinges* in terms of trade and cultural, technological, and population exchanges between the countries they belonged to and the outside world they participated in. This is obviously true of the past and present functions of the systems that have grown along an axis such as Boston-New York-Washington, or Tokyo-Osaka, or London-Liverpool, or Amsterdam-Antwerp-Brussels-Cologne, or Montreal-Toronto-Detroit-Chicago.

It seems that a necessary condition of a megalopolis is a hinge articulating two or more networks, one of them a national internal network, and another an international and overseas network. Hence the importance of the seaport function of some of the major bolts forming the hinge. It may be noteworthy that of the large megalopolitan systems, the axis of only one is not directly related to a seaboard, and that is the Great Lakes Megalopolis. Still this extends along a system of navigable waterways forming an international boundary.

Water transport and peripheral location were especially important in the past, when all transport went by surface means, when ships were by far the cheapest mode of transport, and when the essential breaking points in the networks of transport and communications were located on the shores of the land masses. Water and especially sea transport still preserve some importance owing to the greater ease and lower cost of shipping large cargoes by water. A large concentration of population and industry consumes huge quantities of goods. Megalopolitan growth occurs in highly developed countries where the per capita consumption of goods and services is much larger than average. Hence the intricate web of networks to carry goods, people, and messages within and around a megalopolis. Looking at the various maps of means of transport and communications and of traffic flows around the world, one is impressed by the extent to which the existing webs enveloping our planet converge on the main hubs of the megalopolitan systems.

The convergence is increased by the part played by the hinge in the handling of an enormous volume of *transactional activities* resulting from the linkages in the networks connected by the hinge. The expansion in the volume of the transactions, and in the personnel they occupy, explains the rise of the megalopolitan system and its relations to other parts of the world. The recent evolution of technology and society, that transferred large numbers of people from the work of producing or processing material goods to work in the services producing or processing information, is largely responsible for the megalopolitan phenomenon.

Characteristics of Megalopolises

The first characteristic of a megalopolitan region is its density of settlement. The megalopolis concentrates a larger proportion of a country's population, at least one-fifth, on a small fraction of the land area. This results in relatively high densities of over 250 per sq. kilometer on the average, and a great density of nuclei of a particularly urban character— of towns and cities in which the population density is still much higher than the average in the megalopolitan region. This pattern of a thick network of towns and cities within megalopolis is a very important characteristic: it entails more proximity between the constituent parts and, therefore, a more intertwined web of relationships between a variety of distinct urban centers. The web of relationships is expressed partly in a physical infrastructure consisting of highways, railways, waterways, telephone lines, pipelines, water supply, and sewage systems crisscrossing the whole area, and partly in more fluid networks, some of them visible and measurable, such as the flows of traffic, the movement of people and goods, the flows of telephone calls, of mail, and of financial instruments. The same web includes other networks of a more abstract and rather invisible nature, such as common interests and concerns, rivalries or cooperation, exchanges of information, ar J the human relations that make for community life.

The superimposed networks of linkages help make the region more united and more intricately intertwined, creating the interdependence of the various components within the megalopolis. But this fact should not overshadow the diversity and complexity existing in the megalopolitan structure. The sizes and specializations of the various spatial components are extremely varied, as demonstrated by the diverse characteristics of the cities, towns, villages, suburban, and rural areas that form the vast system. In each sector along a megalopolitan axis that may be endowed with some greater unity because of its dependence on one or two major metropolitan centers, there is still great diversity in the land use, in the people, in the occupations and interests. No megalopolitan region is as yet completely and fully urbanized in the sense of being totally covered with buildings at a thick density. There are interstitial spaces, some reserved for recreation, some for other special uses (such as water reservoirs, for instance), some for agriculture of a specialized and usually very intensive kind, and some are wooded.

In my study of the American megalopolis, published in 1961, I reported that in the mid-1950s 48 percent of its area was under commercial forest cover. A recent inquiry made by another research project of the Twentieth Century Fund has shown in the late 1960s, within the limits I had assigned to that megalopolis, 49 percent of the total area was under forest of commercial value. In the intervening fifteen years the population in megalopolis and the suburban sprawl had substantially expanded; however, there has been apparently enough abandonment of tilled land or pastures, which were turned into woods, to cause a small increase in the total area of commercial forest. These trends will not continue forever; they reflect a complex interplay of economic and social processes. The role that forest and agricultural land play in spatial terms within the megalopolitan structure involves not only land use but various aspects of the region's way of life, its resources in terms of amenities and supplies of certain goods. This is true of Megalopolis on the American northeastern seaboard; it is also true, to an even greater extent, of the Great Lakes Megalopolis. The concept of megalopolis must include the green fringe of the densely built-up corridors. It should not be made into an image of hopeless crowding, of a hell of cement, steel, brick, and automobiles. The appearance of megalopolitan systems coincides in time and in space with societies blessed with more leisure time, more outdoor recreation, and more physical and social mobility. The spatial framework of the system incorporates the resources available in the environing areas for the needs of high density. New constraints appear, new regulations are desirable. They must be considered in the proper staging, on an adequate scale.

Evolutionary Layers

Within the urban centers, diversity has not been only one of size and site, but it has been compounded by the history of past growth which deposited several layers of economic and technological evolution one on top of another. To an earlier stage of settlement, when cities and towns were chiefly centers of administration, trade, and servicing of surrounding rural areas, a layer of industrial revolution was added, piling up manufacturing plants, warehouses, and all the attendant infrastructure. Today, it is agreed that, in the better developed regions, a third stage has set in. The instruments of heavy manufacturing are gradually moved outside the major metropolitan centers. Now offices cluster in the central business districts of most cities, attracting the institutions that service the new transactional way of life. The evolution of a large sector of the labor force towards white-collar employment and quaternary work processing various forms of information has given a new allure to many cities within megalopolis. It is certainly exploding in the landscape of central Chicago or the skylines of Montreal and Toronto, and even more so in the recent growth of the metropolitan complex of Ottawa. These trends have been recognized in most large urban agglomerations, but they originated and have taken more spectacular shape in the megalopolitan groupings.

The diversity is again increased by the variety of the population. The process of growth and concentration of so many millions of inhabitants on a relatively narrow strip of land has involved many different waves of in-migration. Migrants came into megalopolitan areas from the surrounding regions, but also, and especially because of the hinge function, many came from afar. Ethnic and linguistic pluralism must be added to the gamut of occupations, levels of income, and social variation that exist in every megalopolitan system; some of this spectrum is found even in the most homogeneous of them, which is certainly the Tokaido Megalopolis.

A megalopolitan system must be described and understood as a huge *social and economic mosaic.* This term has been, I believe, recently used and accepted in Canada to describe the national structure. It

expresses both an indisputable reality resulting from the great fluidity
and diversity of the modern world and also rare wisdom in the assessment of human organization. The megalopolitan structure is particularly
well described by the term *mosaic,* because both the land use and the
population are formed by an immense number of places of great variety
tightly put together and all interdependent. The diversity of the constituent elements remains well apparent even when one admires the
unity of the whole design.

The *mosaic* is physical, economic, and social; it is also political and
governmental. The density and fragmentation of the system causes an
extremely intricate lacework of administrative and political limits to be
woven over the megalopolitan land. This can be clearly seen on a map
of units of local government, but it also appears strikingly in the distribution of governmental and political divisions on higher levels. It is not a
simple accident that the older megalopolitan systems arose along axes
which extended across boundaries between states, whether those were
some of the original states in the American federal republic or the
national states that divided among themselves the northwestern corner
of the European continent. This political plurality may be both cause
and effect of the lively competition between the major cities along a
megalopolitan axis as they play their part in the operation of the hinge
function. Similar economic competition may have obtained between
large cities and industrial centers under the unified rule of one nation
under the conditions of a rapidly developing Industrial Revolution, especially within the geographical constraints of an insular kingdom, as at
different historical periods must have been the case in Great Britain and
in Japan. Whatever the difference in the individual cases, it remains
that the mass, density, and plurality of a megalopolitan mosaic make
such a region particularly difficult to manage by governments.

Studies of the megalopolitan phenomenon cannot get away from the
extraordinary complexity and ensuing difficulties arising in such a
region. But it is necessary to strive for solutions even in such environments. Accepting that the complexity, the diversity, and the complementarity between all the pieces of the mosaic resulted from the process of
growth and concentration, it should be possible to establish solutions
on the foundations of plurality and complementarity.

An Incubator

Modern economic theory and analysis has come to recognize that, in
the process of economic development, social stability, or change, the
social, political, and institutional trends and forces are more decisive

than the purely physical, economic, and technological factors. Any regional development of megalopolitan or submegalopolitan scale and nature cannot be understood without acknowledging a special convergence of social, political, and cultural forces. It is in these fields that the answers needed will be found or the causes will be lost. The pressures arising in megalopolitan circumstances affect both the physical environment, in its natural and human-made elements, and the people in their modes of life. Megalopolitan systems have been the framework and location in which have developed many recent trends shaping our ways of life. Megalopolis is an incubator of new trends. Change occurs there at a faster and more intensified pace than in a more stabilized and homogeneous area experiencing fewer pressures and problems.

To the characteristics of megalopolis as a hinge and a mosaic, must be added its function as an *incubator.* This function is a threat to habit and stability, because it introduces change. It compounds the difficulties of local governments and of national and international administrations. However, it is their mix of functions and their great dynamism that have made the megalopolitan regions so important in the present world and have bestowed upon them so large a share of the general direction of contemporary economic prosperity and of the general advance of civilization.

Dilemmas

The growth of megalopolitan structures and the importance they have assumed testifies to the capacity of these regions and their people to accommodate concentrated and even congested development, and to withstand the pressures these very processes cause within the system. But a few words of caution must be uttered in conclusion.

First, the pressures have reached danger level on many occasions and at times it has seemed that megalopolitan regions are becoming unmanageable.

Secondly, the size and intensity of such concentrations of wealth and power have been resented by other regions of the countries in which megalopolitan systems have arisen. The other regions claim a more equal share in the sum total of the country's population, wealth, and power. An overly large portion of these seems held in the megalopolitan areas. There is a basic ethical and political problem inherent in geographical concentration on such a scale.

Third, the resulting spatial imbalances cause concern for the future fate of the vaster spaces gradually thinned out, especially for nations with large territories.

Fourth, the very large urban structures are accused of generating an environment that crushes the individual and debases the human condition.

Finally, the concerns thus aroused, though largely political in nature, also entail moral dilemmas, and I would like to give two examples of these. In the much studied decisions on reapportionment by the United States Supreme Court, of June 15, 1964, a minority opinion opposed the strict application of the "one man, one vote" principle to both houses of the legislature of New York State, arguing that it would leave the inhabitants of large upstate areas at the mercy of the interests and decisions of a megalopolis. To this legal argument may be added a theological one. Twelve years ago in Vancouver I was asked to comment on a statement made by a bishop in that city that Vancouver's growth should be restricted because very large cities were inordinately sinful.

These concerns stem from long-standing dislike and distrust of large, dominant cities. They remind us of the ancient invectives against Nineveh, Babylon, and even Rome. In our egalitarian times flagrant inequalities in the distribution of population and of economic weights, created by modern urbanization, come under fire and suspicion. In the more congested parts of megalopolitan systems, indeed, the problems pile up and methods are not incubated fast enough to cope with them in adequate fashion.

But, if megalopolitan growth arouses so much worry and protest, how is it that it has developed on such a scale? Despite all the stress, strain, and unpleasantness it may cause, urban growth on a huge scale continues. Despite the endeavors of national and state or provincial governments to spread population and economic opportunity more evenly, the large agglomerations, as a rule, have not shown signs of dissolving. In Canada, despite warnings and measures that favor outlying territory, Vancouver has kept expanding and so has the megalopolitan area from Quebec to Windsor. In fact, during the five intercensal years from 1966 to 1971, metropolitan Toronto alone added some 205,000 inhabitants, a figure that amounts to more than the total population increase in the same period of the provinces of Alberta, Saskatchewan, and Manitoba, plus the Yukon and the Northwest Territories. As a longer-term trend, the large urban agglomerations continue to attract very large numbers of migrants, and of course they also grow because of local natural demographic increase. The peripheral hinges of the continents continue to gather activities of a transactional nature in an era of worldwide economic and political interdependence and complementarity.

Some redistribution in space is, however, occurring, either as a result of concerted planning or under the pressure of social and market forces. The formation of megalopolitan, more-or-less continuous axes and networks is in itself the product of deconcentration from the main original nuclei. Older categories of industries are gradually scattering away from the larger and more congested metropolitan centers. Some students of urban affairs even believe that the diffusion of the functions and trends that originated in megalopolitan systems disperses them rapidly to a multitude of other widely scattered towns and cities, particularly in the United States and Western Europe. In these countries, and in Canada, the migration off the farms will soon be almost completed and reduced to a trickle. Ultimately, megalopolitan systems will mainly grow through natural increase and international immigration, if allowed.

While diffusion, delegation, and decentralization are certainly developing in many respects and on a vast scale, it does not seem, however, from recent trends of migration and population change, that megalopolitan systems are doomed and dissolving. Careful observation of what happens around the world indicates that, within the framework of expanding and generalizing urbanization, the old megalopolitan structures still prosper, and that new ones arise.

Twenty years ago, the patterns of urbanization along the Great Lakes did not yet seem to be truly comparable in density and function with the Northeastern Seaboard Megalopolis. A vast chain of metropolitan regions was forming there, especially on the American side of the lakes, but with a looser structure and a specialization in manufacturing production rather than in quaternary activities. Now a rapid evolution has taken place modifying the picture, and I am much inclined, even in my strict interpretation of the megalopolitan concept, to recognize its rise here. The Canadian sector of the Great Lakes Megalopolis is probably, in the present circumstances, the most megalopolitan indeed by its rapid development of transactional activities, and by its national and international role as a hinge and as an incubator.

Megalopolis is a spectacular and fascinating phenomenon. Facts so huge and so stubborn can only be caused by the convergence of powerful and sustained forces. As a product of the twentieth century, it arose with mechanization and automation on the farms, in the mines, and lately, in the manufacturing plants. It took shape as the people of the more advanced countries obtained more freedom from constraining work, more leisure time, more means to consume goods and services, more mobility, and more education. It is not simply urban growth on a bigger scale; it is rather a new order in the organization of space and in the division of labor within society, a more diversified and complex order, allowing for more variety and freedom.

Nine

Planning and Metamorphosis in Japan

Perhaps no other country that I have vis-
ited offers in its landscapes as much an impression of chaotic development as does Japan, especially in and around cities. This is, apparently,
a result of the last hundred years, a period of very rapid evolution of the
society and economy of Japan. Before the Meiji era of modernization
and industrialization began in 1868, the Tokugawa shoguns ruled a
highly disciplined, orderly nation. In the tight-knit society, individuals,
groups, and resources were locked into their respective places, socially
and geographically; little change was allowed.

After 1868 Japan endeavored, and in many ways succeeded, in
catching up technologically and economically with the most advanced
countries of the world at a time when these were also evolving fast. To
rapid change was added the strain of rebuilding, twice in less than fifty
years, a large part of the national habitat, first because of terrible earth-
quakes, then because of terrible destruction in World War II. At every
step of the incessant process of renewal and redevelopment since 1868,
Japan surveyed the environing world and found it undergoing a "perma-

Reprinted from *Town Planning Review,* April 1980, 171–76.

nent revolution." To adapt and readapt to the shifting circumstances has been a difficult task. Nevertheless, many of the goals proposed have been attained: from an isolated, marginal nation, emerging from quasi-medieval structures, Japan has become one of the best equipped leaders of the modern economy. No wonder such a rapid metamorphosis, which is still proceeding, gives a chaotic appearance to Japanese cities. The speed and success of the transformation could not have been achieved, however, without careful and skilful policies directing the dynamics.

For twelve years now I have followed the planning and the metamorphosis of Japan. More than any other nation, the Japanese have tried to foresee the future and provide for it. The leadership of a country that has navigated stormy seas for a long and hard century has got into the habit of peering anxiously at the distant horizon. In the circumstances of Japan, economic and political policies cannot forego careful accounting for land use and population distribution. This small archipelago (372,500 square kilometers) is inhabited by some 116 million people. Despite a low rate of increase, the population grows by about a million a year. The density of 311 inhabitants per sq. kilometer (or 778 per square mile) is already very high. The pressure it exercises on the land is considerably increased by the country's topography: the islands are largely covered by mountainous ranges with steep slopes; the extent of flat land is very limited and the larger plains with the better soils surrounding the major cities (Tokyo, Osaka, Nagoya) are being rapidly urbanized. No other large nation is as short of flat space. The urban densities are among the highest recorded.

The uses of the land must change with the evolution of a society which redistributes the population and its activities. Urbanization has thinned out most rural areas and concentrated the population around the main cities, especially along the Pacific Coast and the Inland Sea. Half of the Japanese nation is today agglomerated in the Tokaido Megalopolis, which stretches along the ancient imperial road between the conurbations of Tokyo-Yokohama and Osaka-Kobe. In recent years the concentration around Tokyo has continued, creating the largest and densest conurbation in the world. Yokohama, just a small fishing town in 1880, then a leading port and the gate of the maritime silk road in the 1900s, is now the second city of Japan, overtaking the old commercial metropolis of Osaka; its rapid growth is largely due to overspill from Tokyo.

Land use planning was slow to start. The Comprehensive National Land Development Law of 1950 stipulated the need for a Land Development Plan. The first plan was adopted only in 1962; it aimed at balanced economic growth, dispersing industrial and urban development and reducing regional inequalities throughout the country. Decentralization policies like these are familiar to European planners. The laws enacted in Japan in 1962–65, in order to implement the provisions of the 1962 plan, appear to have had little impact. Concentration went on, accentuated by rapid industrial growth and skyrocketing land prices. A new Economic and Social Development Plan was formulated in 1967. This plan "attempted to deal with the problems arising from the internationalization of the economy and from the labor shortage, and to achieve stable rather than rapid economic growth by emphasizing social development."[1]

The 1967 plan was then translated into spatial terms by the New Comprehensive National Land Development Plan of 1969, which proposed to create a network of growth poles throughout the nation, helped by new large industrial complexes established in selected sites. The years 1967–69 coincided with the centennial celebration of the beginning of the Meiji era, and this prompted the Japanese leadership to look ahead once more. In 1970 the Office of the Prime Minister opened a competition for the best project planning Japan for the twenty-first century. Interdisciplinary teams were formed; they prepared carefully researched reports, competing for the award.

At the invitation of the Japan Center for Area Development Research, I took part in an international symposium which discussed nine of these reports in January 1972 in Tokyo. The reports looked forward to a new socioeconomic structure. The best thoughts of futurology had been applied. Some reports described an "information society" in which the processing of information and learning occupied most of the work force. Others discussed the role of Japan in a new regionalized redistribution of world markets; still others proposed various economic approaches to the future. On the whole the projects were more complementary than competing. They offered an interesting sample of Japanese thought about the next stage of the metamorphosis. The project of the team directed by the famous architect Kenzo Tange, proposing a detailed plan for effective integration of the whole national territory in a much expanded economy, won the Prime Minister's award.[2]

But 1970–72 turned out to be the years of emphasis on pollution, of the Minimata disease in the South of Japan, of the Stockholm U.N. Congress on Environmental Protection. Unrest developed in the cities, expressing serious dissatisfaction among the citizenry with the policies of the past. In 1972 Mr. Kakuei Tanaka became prime minister; he had written a book, *Building a New Japan,* which recommended further decentralization of urban activities through a spectacular development of the infrastructure. His book assumed continuous economic growth and stated: "The question is how the four main islands of Japan, with a total land area of only one-twenty-fifth of the United States, can afford an economy as large as to-day's US economy."[3] In 1973, however, as OPEC drastically increased the price of oil, the energy crisis arose and the no-growth philosophy spread from the West.

Although the Japanese economy steered its way rather successfully through the first stages of the new crisis, its planning policies began to shift once more, adapting to world trends. This was felt at the Nagoya Habitat Conference in March 1976, which prepared the Japanese position at the U.N. Habitat meetings in Vancouver. In late 1977 the Japanese government approved the Third Comprehensive National Land Development Plan which projected a future of economic stagnation and population stabilization, and proposed to establish regional "spheres of permanent settlement," dividing the country into some 200 such units.

How to accomplish the transition from the buoyant dynamics of the last hundred years to a period of no-growth and stabilization is now exercising the best minds in Japan. In February 1979 a symposium gathered in Tokyo to discuss the future of the metropolis; it was organized by the National Institute for Research Advancement (NIRA) and included a few foreign guests. Before the meeting we were given a report summarizing in English the work already done by NIRA in its project *Japan Toward the 21st Century.*[4]

The outline contrasted with the plans made in 1972. It assumed an "age of stalemate" and advocated a new affluence, consisting largely of nonmaterial components. It prospected the road toward a stable society, with a new welfare suited to the conditions and traditions of Japan; this involved preparing for a high proportion of aged people, developing a popular culture for leisure, with continuing education for "life-long learning." This planning does not give up entirely economic growth; it visualizes "stable growth," with a new orientation of technological progress, an emphasis on sectors of industry helping research and development, energy conservation, and the "knowledge-intensive industries" (which include mass media and advanced services to business and government). Japan would thus modify its industrial structure to iron out a new position for itself in the international division of labor.

In spatial terms such restructuring would involve many changes. The report suggests a revival of regionalism and a reform of local government with decentralization of administrative authority. Once more a better balanced regional distribution of activities is expected to be achieved. The conclusions stress a deeper evolution of the whole national culture: new, more pluralistic sets of values; more openness to the outside world, more cooperation with other nations on various levels, leading to a Japanese nation of world citizens. For a people that still likes to recall how, until recently, they "grew up without neighbours" and enjoyed splendid isolation, this program hints at profound changes and may be more difficult to achieve than even industrial dispersal. However, the experience of the past has shown the extraordinary capacity of Japan to proceed according to plan along the major lines of their metamorphosis. Much of this renewed planning still follows old tracks: dispersal of population and industry, evolution towards the information society, an international role assuming some leadership in the Pacific area, more openness to the outside. While the framework has been recast, some of the basic propositions offered by the projections of 1972 are still standing in the background of the NIRA report of 1978.

The continuity is in fact inescapable. A nation cannot ignore its geography, its history, its identity. What is admirable in the case of Japan is the willingness to accept in rapid succession the various stages of a metamorphosis, and to plan and work hard to obtain in the process a better life. In their endeavors to analyze successive situations, Japanese experts have repeatedly turned to the problems of their large cities in order to find solutions for the nation as a whole. The city remains the key to the modern organization of society. The speed and depth of the metamorphosis causes unsettlement and apparent disorder. Today the Japanese metropolis is a mosaic of diverse, contrasted components, despite frequent renewals. Even in Tokyo, sectors of old-style, traditional houses are found next to the impressive supermodern skyline of the bustling new business district of Shinjuku, developed on the site formerly occupied by city reservoirs. In many ways, Japan shows a profound respect for the will of individual citizens.

Still, the forthcoming transition will once more reshape towns and cities. This time the "software" will have to be planned more carefully than the hardware, as announced some time ago by Kenzo Tange.[5] It will bring to the fore the schools of urban and regional planning formed by such leaders as Eiichi Isomura, Masahiko Honjo, and Tange. The Japanese have traditional skills in organizing space through the manipulation of volume, form, and field of vision, so as to control the perception of landscape and of detail. The resulting experience will undoubtedly be of considerable and general value. Perhaps even more valuable will be the methods they will work out in planning the socioeconomic transformation.

Notes

1. Masahiko Honjo, *Trends in Development in Japan* (1978); a document distributed at the NIRA International Forum on the Future of the Metropolis, Tokyo, February 1979.

2. Japan Center for Area Development Research, *The Fourth International Symposium on Regional Development: Design for Japan in the 21st Century,* Tokyo, 1972.

3. Kakuei Tanaka, *Building a New Japan* (Tokyo, 1973; Japanese edition in 1972), 64–65.

4. National Institute for Research Advancement (NIRA), *Japan Toward the 21st Century* (Tokyo, August 1978); summary of a very large volume in Japanese under the same title, reporting on that project of NIRA. This document as distributed at the above-mentioned Symposium on the Future of the Metropolis, February 1979, with other papers specially prepared by various participants, especially the opening statement by Eiichi Isomura, entitled (in English): "Metropolis: The Present and Future Problems it Faces in the 21st Century."

5. Kenzo Tange, "Towards Urban Design," *The Japan Architect*, international edition of *Shinkenchiku* 46 (September 1971): 17–20. In the same issue of that publication, on pages 81–98, is summarized the prize-winning project on "Japan in the 21st Century: A Future Image of the National Land and Life," also discussed in the publication quoted in note 2 above.

Part Five   **The Transactional City**

The commercial organization of Megalopolis is certainly one of the most remarkable achievements of man's art of trade. The history of America's economic *hinge* tells an exciting story of the skill with which the traders in the seaboard cities adapted to changes taking place rapidly on the developing continent of North America as well as in turbulent overseas areas. In the seventeenth and eighteenth centuries these traders developed both maritime activities and inland penetration, harvesting the fruits of the era of great maritime discoveries. From the later eighteenth century on, the successive stages of the Industrial Revolution were used to their full advantage; transportation and manufacturing were developed in order to maintain or expand the network of trade currents focusing on the business districts in this region. In the twentieth century more changes have occurred, and the Megalopolitan traders have taken enough advantage of them, even initiating some of them, so that by midcentury they have risen to a rather commanding position in world commerce. . . .

If the various kinds of trade follow the evolution of manufacturing and scatter all over the consuming market, which itself tends toward uniformity, what advantages do the large cities offer to the commercial organization besides the crowding of consumers within small areas? The answer lies in the basic novelty of the ways and means of commerce in our time. *While the flow of materials from production to consumption becomes more and more independent of the business districts of the central cities* (except for certain goods of high value and small volume), *the management of the swelling flow of materials requires increasing employment and activity in the hubs of commerce.*

There is more *office work* involved than

ever in the management of modern distribution. Today commerce as well as manufacturing requires more negotiations, more contracting and subcontracting, more information about a constantly diversifying gamut of facts and trends. That is why the commercial organization is becoming more subdivided into specializations, why it is more than ever communications-oriented and needs more legal and technical advice, why it uses more paper, more telephone service, and finally more people, particularly great numbers of better-educated and specially trained people.

The expansion of employment in the "white-collar" professions and the increase in the use of a diversity of services are the two factors that have in recent years forced more concentration of economic activities, of the commercial or managerial categories, in the expanding downtowns and the rising lines of skyscrapers in Megalopolis. This region has been once again a pioneer in these trends. Indeed, in the 1950's it became the leading laboratory for an experiment that may perhaps be called the "white-collar revolution," succeeding the "industrial revolution" that began 200 years ago . . .

Ultimately most of Megalopolis' axial belt will be urbanized more densely than it is now, and the white-collar occupations will predominate in the labor force living and working there. The increasing ease of transportation and communications ties this vast and elongated area together better every year. The managerial and policy-making activities that still congregate there do not seem to be as easy to decentralize as production has become. The higher brackets of the communications-oriented activities seem to require three conditions that can be achieved only in a place where there is enough crowding of tertiary and quaternary occupation, these three conditions being: a large enough pool of diversified but competent labor, a large pool of various external services and skills, and easy access for personal contact. The latter condition means that a meeting could be arranged and take place within a day, possibly within half a day. With modern automobile and air transportation and telephone such meetings can easily take place between people residing or working in Washington, New York, Boston, and intermediate places. In a way, Manhattan may be favored by its position at about the midpoint on the Boston-Washington axis.

Megalopolis is just about large enough for the economic, cultural, and political function it is now assuming. If it were to grow more in length the distances might become bothersome for a smooth functioning of the system. Moreover, its position could deteriorate rapidly if any one of the three above-mentioned conditions should cease to be operative there, particularly in the main hubs of the office industry. Difficulties of physical access to the hubs could precipitate out-migration of functions vital to the region's prosperity. Loss of variety in the labor force and deterioration of the special services, or even the ever-increasing gamut of these, would seriously jeopardize the whole structure.

Since the office industry is communications-oriented, its essential raw material is *information*. Just as the small counting houses of former times have grown to be huge banks, stock exchanges, and insurance companies, so the exchange of news and the launching of rumors by chatting in the coffee houses and on the strand and the wharves have been replaced by great newspapers, publishing or broadcasting corporations, and advertising companies. Around Times Square and

Madison Avenue on the island of Manhattan there is concentrated a *mass-media market* whose impact on American life is quite comparable to that of the money market clustered around Wall Street and Rockefeller Center. Megalopolis considered as a whole appears to enjoy a strongly established dominance over the field of information and over the mass media in the United States, a dominance that does not seem to be seriously threatened despite what some employment figures may be.

Megalopolis,
"The Commercial Organization and the White-Collar Revolution"

Ten

Office Work
and the Evolution
of Cities

Cities have been much studied in the traditional aspects of planning, which are housing, land use, transport, and, more recently, recreational needs and activities. The kind of work that went on in cities and made them more or less prosperous, attractive and congested, has been rather relegated to the background. The general theory of urban growth deals with the relationship between form and function—what functions did the center perform and how did they affect urban growth. But, recently this has been overshadowed by more modern concerns about decentralization, growth poles, and quality of life.

Such shifts were understandable in an era of rapid urbanization leading to unprecedented urban and metropolitan growth, to massive concentration in selected areas and around certain centers, and to the consequent evils of congestion, pollution, lengthening commuting, and increasing blight, especially in overcrowded districts. To deal with the undesirable consequences of contemporary urban development, planning policies elaborated new geographical ethics; these aimed at a greater equalization of the distribution of the population and its activities

Reprinted from *Ekistics,* 274, January/February 1979, 4–7.

among the various regions of a national territory. Where not enough growth or even decline occurred, new growth poles should be established. Where too much concentration developed, decentralization should be carried out.

For many years now I have been mostly concerned in my own research with cases of large concentration and massive urbanization. The study of these phenomena has not been fashionable during the last fifty years. The attitude in vogue was to condemn and undo such growth and concentration. Policies favored decentralization and welcomed dispersal. However, the number and size of large urban agglomerations kept growing in most parts of the world. Where the increase of resident population figures had been stopped or even reversed in the larger cities, a great deal of activity remained, land prices surged higher, congestion barely abated.

Only very recently did the experts realize that the larger metropolises were carrying on, though with somewhat renovated functions, while most medium-size cities or new towns, toward which decentralized activities had been directed, continued to experience a variety of problems of their own kind. In the larger-size category great cities expanded peripherally and often remained crowded in their central districts, at least on work days. Medium-size cities continued to have difficulties in filling up and animating their often renewed inner districts. London, for instance, remains congested. The cost of living in central London mounts to uncomfortable levels. But in some sections of eastern London, land, especially docklands, remains fallow and blight threatens. In central Paris and New York City, the problems are somewhat different but do not correspond either to the expectations of planners and statesman. In Europe, on the whole, inner cities in provincial centers still cause concern and cry for help. Only a few provincial medium-size cities are growing well and fast; often these are communities which had previously chosen a "no-growth" policy.

What has been happening? How could the present situation be explained and improved? It now appears that the major reason for the discrepancy between past planning and the actual evolution of cities resides in a basic change of the work pursued in most cities of large or medium size. This change and its consequences for the geographical distribution of economic activity in urban territory have apparently been overlooked or long held to be inconsequential. That change consists in the shift of a rapidly increasing sector of employment from production work and the manipulation of goods to services concerned with abstract transactions, decision making, and information processing.

Some forty years ago Bertrand Russell wrote: "Work is of two kinds: first, altering the position of matter at or near the earth's surface relatively to other such matter; second, telling other people to do so. The first is unpleasant and ill paid; the second is pleasant and highly paid. The second kind is capable of indefinite expansion; there are not only those who give orders, but those who give advice as to what order should be given."[1] Several other thinkers in the 1930s began forecasting the gradual waning of the proletariat which made up the great masses of the unskilled or little-skilled work force of the past.

Studying in the late 1950s the evolution of the American megalopolis, I saw as the most significant trend incubated in that urban region the "white-collar revolution." The central city was shifting its function from manufacturing to information work, from factories and warehouses to offices which were being piled up on the rising skylines. I suggested then that, beyond the division of employment in three sectors, according to the classical classification of Colin Clark, a new *quaternary* sector ought to be recognized, made up of those occupations mainly concerned with information processing and decision making—what Bertrand Russell described as giving orders and giving advice. Indeed, this sector of work seems to be capable of "indefinite expansion" through a self-refining division of labor leading to new specializations able to analyze better, process, and generate an ever-snowballing volume of information.[2]

New Office Nodes

In practice and evidenced in the urban landscape this white-collar revolution, succeeding the old Industrial Revolution, has caused the proliferation of offices. Office work requires consultation, communication, and negotiation to produce results: hence the concentration in business districts and especially in a few selected places of the interdependent categories of quaternary workers. These places are much more numerous today than they were a generation or so ago. This is because the rapid growth of the volume and variety of office work has generated new substantial transactional nodes outside the main agglomerations determined by the location of a national capital or a dominant business community (the latter having usually inherited such a role and competence from the past, such as New York, Zurich, Geneva, Milan, or Osaka). The new, smaller centers are of regional scope or highly specialized.

How are these new "provincial" centers chosen? They seldom reflect simply a size category or a certain type of locational physical circumstance. It seemed that decentralization programs could hardly be successful unless they were established first on a clear knowledge of the factors and forces fostering agglomeration of the types of office work that expand at present, and, second, on a policy directing new establishments to places with a favorable hosting environment. The emerging role and mass of office work express deep changes in social structures.

Some of the results were published in a special issue of *Ekistics*.[3] Since 1960 the study of office location has developed as an important sector of economic geography and of urban planning.[4]

In order to find out more on the circumstances of the local hosting environment, it appeared useful to conduct detailed enquiries in a few specific cities that were developing quaternary functions or were trying hard to do so. With the help of a small grant generously awarded by the University of Oxford in 1969, it became possible to start a few such investigations in the early 1970s. Some of the results have been published elsewhere, in several countries, but in this issue of *Ekistics* the articles that follow bring to the reader the essence of a few selected case studies: Edinburgh, which may be called a capital, although not quite on a national scale, possesses many characteristics of a great nodal city despite its relatively modest size of less than a million people; Oxford, a medium-size city of about 120,000 population, but with a great cultural and historical role which gives it a particular network of external linkages; and Nantes, another intermediate-size city, the *metropole* of western France, a well-established old sea port and manufacturing center, seeking to develop quaternary functions.

The Importance of Culture

One of the obvious consequences of the shift of employment from manufacturing production to office work is the great importance of culture, and therefore education, in the newly emerging characteristics and requirements of the urban community. In the case of Oxford, the power of cultural historical inheritance, well maintained in a relatively small city, makes the part played by the university in nodal quaternary interweaving especially striking. It may not be as obvious but it is no less important in other larger, more diversified, and more complex urban structures.

Higher education is a significant sector of employment just by the number of jobs it now provides. In most nations it is an expanding field and will remain so for some time to come. Its significance is enhanced by its role in training the competent work force required for quaternary activities. The university's personnel and various agencies also provide a mass of information data and expert advice constantly exploited for their own purposes by business and government. The university is, in fact, an essential "advanced service to business," comparable in importance to the financial services; it is also a component of the hosting environment of a city that improves both the quality of work and the quality of life for all the residents. In the planning policies and other urban studies directed at the city of tomorrow, the university must be given the place and the role it deserves, and these are large and growing. In recent years, in several countries, the universities have been located away from city centers. This is probably a serious mistake and it will not benefit the harmonious development of these places. Much change has already occurred in the structure of modern employment and of modern society to which cities ought to adapt their planning. The order planning seeks to establish is now a new order, with a new set of priorities.

A study of Edinburgh by Professor Wreford Watson concurs in many ways with the lessons of the recent evolution of places as different as Oxford, New York, or Atlanta. Watson's conclusion is that the dynamics of the modern city lead to a predominance in its center of the cultural and government functions. This is increasingly so because of the kind of work that locates and aggregates in a lively city, making it central. This is decision making or information processing—producing orders and advice—plus the training of personnel to perform this work competently.

The built environment of this work, which is conducted mainly in offices, conference and lecture halls, and laboratories, consists of the city's business center, but also the university campus and other sections offering the facilities required by the way of life that office work entails. The nature of urban work and the terms of employment evolve in closely related fashion and their contemporary evolution modifies the life of cities. Besides working conditions this evolution affects the type of individual this employment requires and the interests and leisure of the work force and of their families. A recent report of the National Commission for Manpower Policy in the United States, describing *The Transformation of the Urban Economic Base,* sums it up as follows:

> To the extent that cities must re-orient to a services base, they require a workforce that is adept in the performance of clerical, managerial and professional tasks. They must place a heavier emphasis on moving people. Their firms will find a greater need to recruit personnel from distant points and a need to offer not only competitive salaries but the attraction of cultural, recreational, and educational amenities plus good housing and the assurance of a well-governed city. It follows that the critical requirements of development policy for a service-based economy are largely removed from older approaches involving simply tax incentives for industrial firms.[5]

The hosting environment of office work involves the quality of life in the city and around it, because the office work force has the time, education and means to appreciate the quality of the local environment. In fact, it has even the means to demand it, because highly qualified office workers are still in scarce supply and employers compete for them. It has taken a long time to convince employers and policymakers of the need for recasting the working conditions in cities to please not only themselves but also the staff. For some twenty years at least the present trends were obvious to the scholarly observer. For more than twenty years, the solution was just offered by the flight of residences and, to some extent, of the places of work away from the major urban centers. Yet in most of these centers office work continued to agglomerate, despite decay in the conditions of living and increasing strains within urban society.

Housing may be available in the vicinity of the large concentrations of offices but either at very high cost or in derelict circumstances. The time and costs expended on commuting increase rapidly and cause moaning in most cities of North America, Western Europe, and Japan. In this era people are not satisfied with the sort of timetable they are offered by metropolitan deconcentration into the suburban periphery. More than ever they want to travel, often long distances, for both business and pleasure. The well-documented trends of the "cities on the move" offer only a partial and unsatisfactory response to the demands of a society on the move.

The hope has long been voiced that the rapidly improving technology of communications would solve all the present hardships of office location and of residences for office workers. Everyone would be able to work at home in whatever place he or she liked. "The office may become a cottage industry," it was suggested ten years ago. For almost a century the telephone has been expected to keep the boys and girls on the farms! Later, dispersal was to be facilitated by closed-circuit television and the picture phone; and now microelectronics are offered. Human nature and even the nature of office work have deceived these prophecies. While all the devices offered have been avidly used (with the exception perhaps of the videophone), concentration of white-collar work has continued. It has even developed in an increasing number of places.[6]

Legislation decentralizing offices from the major agglomeration has now been in force for years in several countries, especially in the cases of London, Paris, and Amsterdam. Despite such regulation the large concentrations remain. One begins to understand that the great metropolis can survive decentralization because new functions develop, all involving office work and its ancillary activities. From two very different approaches, studies by Dr. Robert Cohen on the one hand and by Professors Vigarié and Mesnard on the other help us to understand the dynamics that maintain the vitality and the concentration of office activities in New York and in Paris, while also fostering other, smaller concentrations in Atlanta or Nantes (*Ekistics* [Jan./Feb. 1979]).

A recent statement by the chairman of the Location of Offices Bureau in London, an agency established to decentralize offices from greater London, says: "There has been a tremendous expansion in the office sector in London in the last fifteen years. . . . As fast as we were taking people out of London, new jobs were being created. This is because the office sector is the strongest growing sector in the economy."[7] At about the same time it was reported that the number of jobs provided in the city of London by foreign banks had risen from just over 9,000 in 1968 to almost 29,000 in October 1978. Such news must be coordinated with the announcement, late in 1977, in New York, that the American Telephone and Telegraph Company was going to build a new office skyscraper on the east side of midtown Manhattan, in order to be able to regroup under the same roof offices which had become too dispersed within the city. That such need was experienced by AT&T, which disposes of advanced telecommunications gadgetry more easily than any other organization in the world, is significant. It confirms that communications technology does not work only to scatter. It also signals that the era of office space surplus and overbuilding in Manhattan was coming to an end, as it was becoming difficult to find large blocks of office space there, despite New York's decline.

The study of offices, work, and related activities greatly helps to understand the modern evolution of cities. It may also suggest some reasons for the difficulties of urban planning and a few avenues to improve it. What our time is witnessing may be described as a renewal of urban centrality, a mutation of the functions that make a city central and its center prosperous. Failure to encourage these functions to develop centrally may cause harm to the urban system as a whole.

Notes

1. See Bertrand Russell, "In Praise of Idleness." In *Mass Leisure*, edited by Eric Larrabee and Rolf Meyersohn (New York, 1958).

2. See Jean Gottmann, *Megalopolis* (New York, 1961), especially chapter 11.

3. See "Offices and Urban Growth" (special issue), *Ekistics* (Jan./Feb. 1979).

4. There is now a considerable body of literature on office location, especially in Great Britain. Besides the publications of the Location of Offices Bureau in London, the books and articles by Dr. P. W. Daniels, of the University of Liverpool, and by Professor John Goddard, of the University of Newcastle-Upon-Tyne, are most enlightening and stimulating.

5. From Thomas Stanback, Jr., and Matthew Drennan, *The Transformation of the Urban Economic Base*, National Commission for Manpower Policy, Special Report no. 19 (Washington, D.C., February 1978).

6. See Ithiel de Sola Pool, ed., *The Social Impact of the Telephone* (Cambridge, Mass., 1977), and *The Telephone's First Century—And Beyond: Essays on the Occasion of the 100th Anniversary of Telephone Communication* (New York, 1977).

7. *The Financial Times* (20 October 1978).

Eleven

Urban Settlements
and Telecommunications

In the general discussion of the present and future of the city there are different attitudes. The two main approaches that express a broad conflict may be summarized in the dilemma: urban renaissance or urban dissolution. The city is a very complex phenomenon; the largest artifact mankind has produced. Among the students of the environment and those of society, there is a gradual realization, resented by many, that urban settlements are becoming the living and working environment of a majority of humankind. This has happened in the twentieth century with an acceleration of trends in migration, in the labor markets, and in the ways of life. These started long before 1900 but acquired much greater momentum after that date and are likely to continue in many countries into the twenty-first century.

The basic reason underlying and accelerating modern urbanization has been the evolution of technology. Certainly other factors have been involved, determining, to a large extent, the different ways in which the opportunity opened by technological advances has been used by vari-

Reprinted from *Ekistics,* 302, September/October 1983, 411–16.

ous nations. But there is general agreement on the essential role of technology, or, to use another popular image, of the several stages of the industrial revolution. Thus, the discussion of our urban civilization is very much concerned with the impact that the present state of the industrial revolution or of the technological revolution—call it what you will—may have on urban settlements. The new component of modern technology that seems to be especially relevant nowadays is usually encompassed by the term *telecommunications*. The notion includes the potential opened up for communication between people, for the transmission of messages, the gathering, storage, and even analysis of information by modern tools, produced as a result of the advances achieved in electronics, microelectronics, and all that may ensue in terms of both hardware and software. What impact will all that new technology have on society, particularly the spatial distribution of people and their activities?

The future of the cities and of the urban ways of life seems to depend to a large extent on the answer to this question. This answer, however, is still far from being clear. A number of specialists in different fields have done important research work on the possibilities opened to mankind by the various potential applications of the rapidly evolving new technology of telecommunications. Much of this research emphasized the greater ease it provided for the dispersal of settlement. It was advanced that the old urban compact forms of settlement were going to dissolve. Modern telecommunications will help all those who may so wish to engage in activities and pursue in the future a career that could be normal, without having to live in any kind of dense formation. From dispersed places one will have the possibility of adequately communicating with the rest of the world through telecommunication channels. In other words, any kind of activity may become a cottage industry. Such a possibility would apply even to those activities which have been considered as requiring a concentration of people in one place to perform them.

Certainly we have known for some time that telecommunications through television, especially with the help of satellites, can make us direct witnesses of events happening almost anywhere in the world. At the place where the event is happening, the proper equipment must be installed and properly operated to transmit the images to a broadcasting network. This sort of transmission possibility applies to any kind of information except what should be confidential. Why then should a person take the trouble of leaving a comfortable abode in order to witness more directly, that is, immediately on the spot, what can be seen without leaving the home?

What telecommunications have already considerably altered is the significance of distance in the organization of space. For the transmission of information across space, distance has become a secondary consideration. What matters most is the organization of the network installed to transmit the artifact and its technique, not the physical facts of distance and extent of space. From my home in Oxford, England, I communicate more rapidly and easily over the telephone with friends or colleagues in Tokyo or Washington than with persons I know in Oxford, who may work for me but do not have the telephone in their homes. The telephone has not been installed there because, for some reason, economic or purely psychological, they did not want it. The telephone company could perfectly well have put telephones in their houses if they had requested it. The separation to be overcome for conveying messages develops thus, not because of the intervening distance or other physical circumstances but because of the deliberate way in which networks are organized by those concerned.

This very simple rule in the use of available technology is not proper to telecommunications alone. It is valid for most applications of technology. The organization of space is man-made; it is a product of the collective will of the participants. Technology is extremely important for the understanding of the layout and functioning of urban settlements, but the way in which it is used and applied varies with people, with cultures, with individual situations and tastes. These facts may seem obvious and trite; they carry with them a first answer to the problem we have been debating: the impact of telecommunications on cities. Living and working together in compact settlements may seem unnecessary once the technology to overcome distance is well developed. However, it does not necessarily follow that the compact city has been made obsolete and that settlements will disperse throughout the countryside. It all depends on what people decide to do.

A memorable discussion of these matters took place in March 1976 at the Massachusetts Institute of Technology (MIT) on the occasion of the meeting celebrating the centennial of the first telephone call given in Boston, within the same building, by Alexander Graham Bell. The meetings, organized by MIT and sponsored by AT&T, gathered hundreds of specialists from all around the world and from all aspects of the study of telecommunications. I had the privilege of being one of the participants invited from overseas, probably because I have been one of the many scholars interested by the impact of the telephone on society and especially on urbanization.

To the question of the changes that may occur in the spatial distribution of people and their activities as a result of the advances of telecommunications, a well-informed and thoughtful partial answer was provided in his concluding speech by the distinguished physicist and science fiction writer, Arthur C. Clarke. This speech has since been printed in a volume entitled *The Telephone's First Century and Beyond,* a collection of essays that deserves more attention than it appears to have received. In his paper, Arthur C. Clarke, looking towards the twenty-first century, confirmed that the technology will be made available easily to those who choose to spend all their lives, receiving their education, obtaining a job, and working at it, in the same building. All this present running around town or the countryside could be saved. From one room the well-trained and well-equipped individual will be able to communicate with all those he wants or needs to, provided, of course, that they cooperate, that general goodwill is part of the basic assumption. Still, Clarke came to the question: Do we want that sort of way of life, all spent within the same walls?

Such could become the fate of masses of people if we decided to take the whole opportunity offered in this respect by the developing technology. Clarke even inferred (and on that point I could not agree with him) that this secluded and sedentarized way of life would not impair the career possibilities of those who may adopt it. It could be made to fit the work conditions needed by a large proportion of the labor force occupied in processing information for the forthcoming information society. In conclusion, Clarke quipped: now we can say that we know what is the aim of life! The purpose of life is processing information, but what, it may be asked, is the aim of that? "I am glad," said Clarke, "you asked the question. The symposium is over." With that he jumped off the podium, leaving the audience to face the final question.

In the matter we are examining here, it is true, like in so many other areas, that the careful analysis of the known facts arouses more problems than it solves. There is no doubt that telecommunications have reached a stage at which they offer the possibility of widely dispersing a large proportion of the population, of scattering habitat, merging place of residence and place of work. Such a pattern of very dispersed settlement would assume, of course, a proper supply of food, consumer goods, equipment, energy, all the material necessities of daily life to all those scattered homes. It would be a costly network of supply but feasible in a world of abundance. Telecommunications cannot do it all, though they may help to organize the networks of supply from centers of production and distribution, considerably reducing the personnel needed to man the producing plants and the networks of distribution. They will not eliminate centrality but, by fostering the staffing of central operation with squadrons of robots, they will again open the way to scattering the stations of most people. Then should cities as we have known them survive them? And do we still need the whole concept of urban settlements?

To attempt some serious answers, let us first consider what has been the purpose of urban settlements in the past. First of all, there was at the origin of cities and towns a matter of security, that is, physical security in times when families found it easier to defend themselves by grouping, organizing, and putting up some kind of walls around the settlement. Inside the community a defense force was organized and often a police force. A community government was set up unless a towering authority supervised and governed the town, such as a bishop, a king, or a feudal lord. Whatever the local authorities, they saw to the security within the walls and in the neighborhood; it was easier to protect a small and compact settlement than a widely scattered population. Today, this sort of security no longer seems necessary or useful. Crime and aggression roam the heart of cities as much as their surroundings and sometimes more, depending on social stratification, inner community conflicts, levels of income, and education. As to the security from external or international threats, it transcends the power of local government. The same technology that provides the means to overcome distance had made it possible to strike from afar almost any point on the earth's surface from any other point on the planet, and soon even from outside the planet, from vehicles orbiting above it. In many ways the security that the city obtained from physical ramparts seems to be truly outdated.

The defense against threats from within the community or from immediate neighbors does not seem to depend upon the density or dispersal of buildings. If the people present in the area are divided, if deep enmity and conflict arise and persist among the inhabitants, safeguards may be found in social and political reorganization, occasionally in migration, but hardly in individual isolation. Internal strife may cause a city to decline and even to be ruined; however, most great cities have, in the past, known periods of acute inner conflict and civil strife, and they have survived. The density of settlement nowadays appears less relevant to the need for physical security than used to be the case. Modern citizenry is, of course, very much affected by economic and social security. There one can only comment that telecommunications increase the malleability of the form of settlement. They may induce the thought of canceling out most of the old factors that played a role in the equations determining industrial or residential location. If such a greater freedom of choice is granted, we should return to the question: What are the purposes of urban settlement, besides the provision of security?

Urban places always had the important function of hosting diverse transactional activities. They may have been economic; market places were provided for these. They may have involved governmental decisions or legal procedures; special institutions evolved to take care of them. They may have been of a religious or sociocultural nature; in most ancient cultures social rituals were related to religious festivals and associated with temples or shrines. Gradually, more specialized services arose, such as public education or medical treatment. Cities and towns developed around some transactional institutions: a temple, a castle, a market, law courts; every city aimed generally at offering the widest possible range of transactional services. Once good accessibility and security were provided, there were obvious incentives for a variety of transactional activities to congregate at a place duly equipped to service them. Transactions that belong to apparently different categories are often in fact interrelated. One may separate in space political, economic, and cultural affairs; each of these categories of transactions operates more effectively if well informed of what happens in the two other fields. All of them need "ancillary services" which, according to Adam Smith's famous principle, will be best developed where the market is the largest. When planners or geographers speak of ancillary services they mainly think of those that provide entertainment of all kinds. This is, and has always been, an important field closely related to transactions. However, another type of ancillary service is often forgotten, which is even more important and should, in fact, be considered decisive for successful transactions. That is information, including its processing, storage, and channels of distribution.

In the modern world, with its expanding and multiplying networks of relations and a snowballing mass of bits of information produced and exchanged along these networks, the information services are fast becoming an essential component, indeed the cornerstone, of transactional decision making and of urban centrality. Surely technology could make all these information workers communicate around the world, and it does, but at a cost and at a risk. The cost is bound to increase with the probability of an immense increase in the demand for channels. The risks are threefold: a temporary failure of communications for technical reasons; a lack of privacy along the channels; the uncertainty of obtaining expert advice at the right moment just as the unexpected and therefore more valuable piece of news reaches the sorting out or dispatching center.

There must be centers for transactions, for the performance of meaningful rituals, for the processing of information. Television has had the greatest possible success as a means of entertainment. Still, millions of people strive to attend in person certain concerts, sports events, coronation ceremonies, business conventions, and international meetings of all sorts. In the last thirty years, since television has been generalized to almost every home in the United States, American cities have built more and bigger sports stadia, concert and exhibition halls, museums, and convention facilities than in any preceding half-century. Teleconferences, videophones, and similar facilities have been offered and used in major Western countries for a dozen years at least, but with only limited and rather declining success.

In these early beginnings of the information society, it has been noted repeatedly that most of the materials distributed by the various networks of communication, whether news, films, music, fashions, advertising, insurance, security quotations, or even science models, originate in a few centers that gather, process, and dispatch. Some centers are specialized, such as Zurich in financial matters, but most are multifaceted and very large cities, like New York, London, Paris, Tokyo, Moscow, Peking, Chicago, and Milan. Partly this is due to the concentration in these places of specialized institutions and of competent skillful manpower. Partly it is due to the preference of people to hold meetings there, large or small, taking advantage of the facilities existing in those places, of the opportunity to do many different things in a single trip, to conform to tradition and to fashion, and to avoid the risks involved in communicating over technological channels.

Many experts have now worked on the social impact of telecommunications, especially on the telephone and television. Among them many are geographers preoccupied with the effect of geographical distribution and especially on urban centrality. Despite all the propaganda by the technologists offering dispersal, especially places of nonmanual work, the conclusions they have reached are in agreement with mine: there may be deconcentration in some aspects, but basically, transactional activities are not likely to be scattered throughout rural territory just because technology is becoming able to overcome distance. Professors Ronald Abler, of Pennsylvania State University, Bertil Thorngren, of the Stockholm School of Economics and Dr. Michael J. Bannon, of University College Dublin agree that the relationship of telecommunications to cities is far more complex and multiple than it may seem.

The difficulty in assessing, for instance, the exact consequences of the impact of the telephone on society and on the pattern of settlement, results from the fact that the telephone is such an adaptable and unobtrusive tool. Let us consider the telephone's impact on office location: on one hand, it has freed the office from the previous necessity of locating next to the operations it directed; on the other hand, it has helped to gather offices in high densities and large concentrations in special areas. It would be difficult to visualize the rise of skylines, the agglomeration of skyscrapers, without the telephone smoothing out the functioning of such a complex and integrated system, a system which would be much more fragile and unsafe without the telephone. The thought of what the telephone has done for the skyscraper may be extended to the large city as a whole, that very involved and infinitely complex assemblage of interconnected mechanisms and networks. The telephone is only one of the many indispensable networks that enable a city to exist, but it is a great help in constantly coordinating all these systems together.

It has been pointed out that telecommunications are a great tool to foster democracy: telephone and television provide new and wonderful possibilities for participation in the political process and public activities by distant and relatively isolated individuals. The same tools could be managed by a central authority, however, to restrict and orient the information received by individuals and to direct their behavior, as George Orwell threatened in his famous *1984*. Ultimately, if the opportunity offered by telecommunications is so wide, it is and will be used in different and sometimes conflicting ways. It may propose to humankind the utopia of *fungible* space, where location could be arbitrarily decided and modified. But any response will be determined by psychological and cultural considerations, and that is why I remain convinced that the dispersal of urban settlements in a transactional era remains utopian.

To illustrate this last point may I once again mention a few personal recollections. When I worked from 1956 to 1960 at the Twentieth Century Fund in New York on my study, *Megalopolis,* an important survey of the Greater New York Metropolitan Area was conducted under the auspices of Harvard University and the Ford Foundation and directed by Professor Raymond Vernon, a distinguished Harvard economist. For a time, the list of the various volumes that were to report the findings of this survey included a title announced as "New York, the Front Office of the Nation." This volume never appeared. This was a project on which Raymond Vernon and I had agreed to cooperate and to finance jointly from our research budgets. It seemed so necessary to analyze the enormous concentration of offices of many kinds in greater New York; it gave its personality and its vitality to the vast metropolis and it obviously fulfilled an important role in the national life and international connections of the United States. For a period of two and a half years, I met Raymond Vernon regularly once a month at lunch to exchange information about the findings of our two studies. We could, of course, have discussed these matters over the telephone but he still felt it necessary to hold face-to-face meetings.

Despite the failure of the project of a book on the "front office of the nation," I learned a great deal from the endeavor. Vernon had several teams and many meetings analyzing the conglomeration of office work in New York. At a seminar of leading managers of large public agencies and private corporations, the question was discussed of face-to-face meeting versus conferences at a high level by closed circuit television.

These managers could have afforded the cost of such video conferences if they had liked the idea, but they clearly distrusted it. For, in transactions involving serious consequences and large sums of money, the element of trust is essential. It is undermined in several ways by the televised procedure. For instance, signals could be transmitted to other participants in a televised conference that could be received by some without the others who looked at the screen noticing. When a meeting takes place in a room, if a participant receives a message, the others may not know what the contents of the message are (and they may be irrelevant to the matter discussed), but it is known to all those attending who receives a message and they may draw deductions or observe any change in behavior that may ensue. This sort of checking on the partner is not possible when he appears on a screen, but stays in another setting, where things may develop that will not be visible on the screen. Similarly, two members of the televised meeting may arrange to communicate between themselves during the discussion without any knowledge of it available to others. Insecurity develops about how fair the play is, and, when serious negotiation is to proceed, the face-to-face meeting in the same room remains much more preferable.

The telephone has become an excellent means to arrange for meetings but it introduces an element of insecurity in transactions. My own inquiry, preparing my paper for the 1976 meetings on the centennial of the telephone, confirmed the decisive role of the psychological factor and of trust. The telephone was best used between persons who knew one another intimately and trusted one another fully. Even in such relationships, however, cultural variations existed: for banking and routine insurance transactions the telephone was much more accepted in New York than in London. Even in the United States government agencies, although large-scale conferences were frequently arranged over the telephone involving the simultaneous participation of 50 to 150 persons, the discussion on such occasions was kept to the level of current information and preparing the agenda for the next face-to-face conference at which the real analysis and decision making would take place.

The psychological factors at play are subtle and varied. I am reminded of a situation that developed in the 1960s in the very modern and extremely well-equipped headquarters in Europe of a large non-American multinational firm. That corporation built a large complex of buildings in a small town, close to much larger cities and in a pleasant setting, from which to direct its worldwide operations. The offices were fitted with all the gadgets possible at the time to communicate within the compound and with the outside world. Everybody working there could hold discussions on the wires with anybody else in the headquarters or abroad. The corporation, which prided itself on the efficiency of its management and good relations within the staff, came to observe, however, that trouble was brewing. Employees were getting angry, some were resigning; relations between colleagues were often strained. This had never happened before in that company. The board of directors met and worried. An American firm of management consultants was called in to advise. The consultants came, surveyed, and analyzed the situation; their report diagnosed "over-gadgeteering." Similar difficulties had been observed in large organizations that tried to use systematically the telephone and the videophone in America. Somebody felt a colleague had hung up on him too abruptly; others resented, especially while using the videophone, that attention seemed to be paid at the end of the line to things other than the conversation; all sorts of awkward remarks and suspicions spread. In conclusion, the consultants' report, recognizing that all the costly investment in the telecommunications systems in the headquarters could not be scrapped, advised the staff to have two coffee breaks in the morning and two in the afternoon, all to be taken in the lounge which thus became a meeting place to resume frequent face-to-face contacts!

I think I have now made my position clear. The isolation of the ivory tower is not the solution for transactional activity, even if the tower could be fitted with all the wonders of telecommunication technology, present and in gestation. Urban settlements will not dissolve under the impact of this technology, although they may evolve and, indeed, are evolving. For the transactional activities and new technology are rather helping concentration in urban places: first, in large urban centers, already well-established transactional crossroads; second, in a greater number of smaller centers of regional scale or highly specialized character. The specialization is to some extent helped by telecommunication development because it provides good channels for coordination between related specialists, especially those who know one another very well, and it also intensifies, when needed, relations between the smaller specialized places and the larger, more diversified metropolis. The ease of telecommunications around the world induces a larger volume and flow of information among all the centers. Transactional work grows and intensifies as a result, and some of it must then be decentralized by delegation from the leading centers to the smaller regional ones. There are many routine transactions in all these procedures that can be dealt with often on the wires or the waves.

Decentralization and specialization still carry, as a corollary, an increase in the need of meetings and of places adequately equipped for them in terms of facilities and ancillary services. We shall, therefore, not be surprised at the scale and density of large skylines in the main transactional centers. This sort of growth may be much more restricted by economic depression and shrinkage of economic activity than by the progress of telecommunications.

I do not think that in the transactional era, even with great worldwide prosperity for which we must all pray, urban settlements will dissolve. I believe they will keep on growing, though changing. A very important factor remains: human psychology. Too often it is summed up by emphasizing the yearning for rural life; getting out of the cities into a more relaxed, "greener" environment. This is an oversimplification that leads to misunderstanding. For thousands of years, those who could afford it liked to have also a country house and spend part of the time there: the Roman villas are a famous ancient example of this, but the patricians who owned them also had an abode in Rome. Today a much larger number of people can afford a second residence; one out of ten families in France for instance. The American middle-class suburbanization, also a long-standing trend, has led to much commuting. However, even in large American cities, those who can afford it have a second residence in town, even when they classify the suburban home as their major or primary residence. For work in transactional activities they still have to be in the city often, and perhaps in two or three cities recurrently, to be sure that they do not miss out on information that may be important to them. Besides the desire for knowing, human psychology brings into the equation of spatial location the element of games. The human species is playful. To play tennis on a court is more satisfying than to look at how others play on the screen. To attend a ritual on the spot has greater value than to witness it through television.

Altogether, the urban way of life has become, for a large proportion of the urban population, a more mobile, less sedentary one. All our previous analyses of the changes introduced by the advances of telecommunications in urban life in the various countries where I have looked at them have pointed out that they were not dissolving cities, but modifying them. One little realized impact of telecommunications on settlements has been to increase mobility greatly. As already noted, telecommunications are much used to prepare and arrange face-to-face meetings. They have considerably increased the human capability to overcome distance not only by transmitting messages but also by facilitating travel. Modern air and sea navigation are unthinkable without the constant use of telecommunications. Even transportation on the ground has improved, made safer and more pleasant by rail or car by various telecommunication devices.

The volume of the flows of human traffic and transit around the globe, and especially around certain parts of it, is enormous and increases every time people are given a chance to go to more places. These flows may be expected to continue swelling in the long run: for instance, it seems that the majority of humankind has not yet flown in an airplane, though there is little doubt that, given the opportunity, the overwhelming majority would like to have the experience. Only a small minority has visited such renowned places as Capri, Acapulco, or Tahiti, while it is considered a privilege to have been there. As radio transistors spread the information around, one may assume with a fair degree of accuracy that two to three billion individuals are still hoping that some day they may get there. What does this thought mean to the famous resorts to which people travel for pleasure? How much urban growth? For some thirty years now I have been occasionally visiting Williamsburg, Virginia; it used to be a small and quiet place in the 1950s. The urbanization around the old historical nucleus proceeded apace through the 1960s and 1970s. Might it become necessary some day to ration the right of access to Williamsburg, as is already the case for many national parks?

If people take so much pleasure in moving around, why should we insist on using telecommunications to keep them in one spot or as close to home base as at all possible? As we look at the growth of the business districts in the large transactional cities, we realize that the congregation of people coming there either to work or to transact business and also enjoy themselves has been a major factor pushing out towards the urban periphery the less profitable residential land uses. It has become more and more difficult to find space in the large transactional centers for the housing of the normal local population. To live in the immediate vicinity of these places of work has become the costly privilege of transactional transients and of a small fraction of the work force actually employed there. Others must commute, often long distances, hence more use of communications and of transport.

We now come in conclusion to what I consider to be a very important principle which geographers and planners have not yet analyzed and applied enough. To put it briefly: communication between people structures space—it has always been so and it will be so in the future. What has been recently changing may be called the tools used to communicate and, therefore, to structure space and settlement. Human nature is very important to consider in this process: we want to communicate as well as possible; we should like to have, as a result of communicating, the best information possible on the matters of importance to us. This has always been so; human nature is not likely to change in this respect. What may change and vary will be the use of all the versatile tools offered for communication, and the organization of space and of settlement obtained as a result.

The means of communication at the disposal of the individual have greatly changed through the ages. To begin with, to communicate, every human individual has the physical senses: vision, hearing, touch, taste. . . . Then, these are enhanced with speech. The range of these natural means of communication is very limited in space. So we extend it by displacing ourselves. Gradually we devise means of transmitting signals and messages over longer distances. The basic transmission of messages and exchange of information was done orally by traveling, assuming that at the end of the trip the language spoken was understood.

A first stage in the communication evolution came with writing and reading. This stage is still going on because literacy is still progressing around the globe. It might have seemed that, once the written message was used, it would have favored a dispersal of settlement, as less gathering may have been imperative at the places where the oral message could be heard. But archeology tells us that a great wave of urbanization in ancient history coincides with the beginning of literacy and of the recording of messages. How general and basic is this relationship between the written record and urbanization? Is there a cause and effect linkage between city and literacy? Scholars have worked on these questions without producing to my knowledge any definite answers. That there is a link, however, seems beyond doubt. To me the ancient Egyptian statue of the scribe, to be seen in the Louvre Museum, is one of the earliest symbols of the city.

Printing was another great stage of the communication evolution. The book and the journal gave an enormous momentum to the mass media. Their generalization went together with another stage of urbanization, of the use of more and bigger urban centers. Since the beginning of the nineteenth century, the stages in the skills of transmitting and recording messages crowd the world arena, giving incredible impetus to the Western civilization which originally produced all the innovations: the telegraph, photography, the telephone, the cinematograph, the phonograph, the switch, radio waves, the airplane, television. . . . Telecommunications are only part of all the technological devices helping people to communicate. Urbanization developed fast, in close linkage with the progress of communication technology, the larger metropolitan structures arising in the countries where this technology was best applied.

I shall suggest that the better the tuning we achieve in communication over vast spaces, the greater the capacity we seem to have in organizing these spaces in a more dynamic and integrated fashion. Such organization of space needs and produces more transactions among people, among regions. The larger volume and greater diversity of transactions—which means also communications—suggest more people meeting in many places and more study and discussion on the spot where all the data can be conveniently gathered. There must therefore be some kind of positive relationship between urban growth and the equipment that humankind creates to communicate. However because the equipment is better, and more cumbersome, we do not use our senses less for communication; on the contrary, I believe we use them more. The better the artifacts at our disposal, the more we still depend on our senses and judgment and the more education and skills become essential to human activities, because they provide the brain with the means to record and process.

The progress of telecommunications is a challenge to the forthcoming generations to learn more and exchange more, and they will want to do so as directly, surely, and freely as they can. The dependence on machinery gives a feeling of restricting the freedom of those who are at only one end of the line and may be cut off. The urban settlements have had such success because, rightly or wrongly, they provide a greater opportunity of choice, and therefore, of freedom.

Twelve

The Recent
Evolution
of Oxford

A vast literature could be quoted that has
described, discussed, and tried to analyze Oxford. Few cities have
achieved comparable worldwide renown over the centuries; even fewer
could claim so broad and deep an influence over Western civilization.
Fundamentally, Oxford owes its role and fame to its university and colleges. It is as a center of education, learning, and ideological debate
that this small city has made its contribution and established its reputation since the twelfth century. All the rest of its activities have been by-
products of its academic function.

Until 1914, although hailed by famous men as "the energizing source
of Empire" or "the capital of the English language," Oxford was still a
city of modest size: a few industries had located there, the Oxford University Press being probably the largest among them; it was, like Cambridge, or Heidelberg and Göttingen in Germany, a university town and
a regional market town. About 1912 a Mr. Morris, who used to provide
bicycles to the students, began assembling automobiles at a workshop
in the suburb of Cowley; in the 1920s Oxford became one of the larger

Reprinted from *Ekistics*, 274, January/February 1979, 33–36.

centers of the automobile industry in Europe. The city's population grew from 67,000 in 1921 to about 100,000 by 1945. The ancient duality of town and gown took on a new aspect: the large plants at Cowley seemed to overshadow the small compact university town; the city's socioeconomic structure was rapidly evolving towards an industrial predominance.[1]

However, since 1950 new trends have emerged. In the recent evolution of Oxford a new balance between the academic community and the industrial development has been emerging. The process is worth examining because it shows how white-collar work, mainly conducted in offices, gathers in the university town. It also conveys more general lessons as to the evolution of modern settlements.

The University as Incubator of Urban Growth

For the half century 1921–71 the automotive industry's expansion was certainly the largest factor in the growth of population, employment, and housing in Oxford. Already in the 1960s, however, the work force of the industrial plants at Cowley began to stabilize, oscillating around 25,000, while the community gathering in and around the university continued to expand.

The university's conflict of interests with the town in the past century stemmed largely from the natural impulse on the academic side to resist an expansion that threatened to engulf the city in a tide of industrial revolution. Nevertheless, the Morris Motor Works developed as a result of a local initiative. Mr. Morris had been servicing previously the academic community and the very first cars he built in artisanal fashion before 1910 had been ordered by wealthy students. The recent shift of economic development brought much more agreeable enterprises, related to education, research, and information processing.

A study by Mrs. Barbara Baird,[2] describing the interweaving of the various nonmanufacturing activities in Oxford, uses the solid data available plus the results of a sample inquiry. It demonstrates the essential role of the academic community and of the university's equipment in terms of libraries, collections, and laboratories in attracting other, related kinds of work, each of which needs at least some component of all that software and hardware.

The rapid growth of quaternary activities in Oxford partly results from the expansion of the scholarly and research work in the university and its colleges, and recently at the Oxford Polytechnic. It is very difficult to formulate statistically the actual employment these institutions represent. The first specific figure that could be put forward as to the number of people actually employed in Oxford by the university and its colleges resulted from the university's Travel and Parking Survey conducted in 1969. At that time the university and colleges employed 7,250 persons, nearly ten percent of the total employment in Oxford.[3] In the ten years that followed, this personnel is known to have been increased by additions to both the faculties membership (as witnessed by the lengthening list of Congregation members) and the technical and clerical payroll. Once the Polytechnic is added to this figure it becomes certain that the total employment of the higher education institutions at Oxford in early 1979 stands somewhere above 10,000, that is, more than one-tenth of the total employment in the urban area, now estimated to be in the vicinity of 90,000 jobs.

With the addition of the Oxford University Press and of the hospitals (the size and specializations of which are closely related to the clinical departments of the Medical School) we arrive at the periphery of strictly academic work in terms of the services provided. It is, however, a dense and substantial periphery involving several thousand persons besides those on the university payroll proper. The publishing division of the Oxford University Press, one of the largest publishers in the English language, has now concentrated most of its personnel and work in Oxford, which has meant the transfer in recent years of several hundred jobs from London.

Publishing is an important industry in Oxford, second only to the automotive. It is usually classified as manufacturing because, through printing, it produces manufactured goods, but its work belongs essentially to the office category. Oxford gathers the headquarters, besides the university press, of the Pergamon Press, another large publishing house, of Basil Blackwell's, of the Alden Press, and also of the highly specialized but large Nuffield Press, a branch of British Leyland. The importance of Oxford as a publishing center in England is second only to that of London.

The linkages of publishing with the university community are not limited to the university press. Any publisher would benefit by a location in the vicinity of the rich resources of the Oxford libraries and of the expert advice of some senior member of the university on almost any matter that might be of concern to publishing. Competent help can be recruited locally, often among the families of the dons and more generally among people attracted by the environment of Oxford.

This attraction is felt even more directly in the field of education. A constellation of numerous schools of many kinds has located in Oxford or its vicinity. It would be extremely difficult to estimate the actual employment it represents, partly because of the number of part-time jobs, some filled by postgraduate students. As Barbara Baird mentions, there is even a large school training airline pilots in the suburb of Kidlington, which has made the local airport one of the most active in Europe, by the number of takeoffs and landings counted annually. It is also significant that the Open University has found it necessary to maintain a rather large "regional" office in Oxford, although its headquarters are located at Milton-Keynes, half an hour's drive away!

A variety of specialized firms have come to Oxford to benefit from the stores of knowledge and the quality of quaternary labor found in the place. The presence of a large firm of business consultants such as Nielsen's (one of the large local employers) can easily be related to the easy access to expertise and research facilities. A similar case is that of a smaller but world-renowned firm producing scientific films which will, like publishing, be classified as a manufacturing industry, though its work is conducted mainly in offices and laboratories by highly qualified persons.

The network of outside linkages generated by the university and colleges is only hinted at, in several of its aspects, either in Barbara Baird's study or in an article by Dr. Susanne Walker.[4] It would be extremely difficult to ascertain quantitatively the flow of visitors coming to Oxford on business which involves for them some sort of office work there for periods ranging from a few hours to a few months. Academics and researchers from all parts of the world flock to this city to do some work. I shall only mention that my department, the School of Geography of the university, receives annually about 100 such visitors coming from out of town. In the whole university and its colleges one could count about 100 institutions receiving on the average similar flows of scholarly visits. A simple calculation would thus suggest that the university attracts approximately 10,000 business visitors every year, some of whom stay for prolonged periods.

This very rough estimate is probably an understatement: the Bodleian Library alone registers annually over 3,000 new readers who are not members of the university. And I do not include the movement represented by all those who come, often from afar, to attend conferences, symposia, or courses held in the various colleges in vacation time, when most of the students are away.

All these activities keep growing. This is the result of the general expansion in our time of education, research, information processing, and other forms of office employment. As Lord Annan put it recently: "From being a cottage industry, higher education had become a major calling by the seventies."[5] And those who were so educated continue to need in their occupations the contacts with the apparatus of learning to much greater degree and with a higher frequency than was ever the case. This is a crucial change in the history of human labor which brings new forces to bear on the growth of human settlements, especially those with well-established universities.

The Hosting Environment of Quaternary Work

There used to be many jokes about the future shape of mankind in an era of full mechanization and automation. As most people seemed destined to spend their lives pushing buttons or papers in offices, it was prophesied that the shape of the body would be modified with the legs and arms atrophied, while the head would expand in volume! To forestall such evolution, recent generations of office workers have taken measures to reform their way of life: never has there been more interest in participation in sports, including jogging, tennis, skiing, mountaineering, or yachting; never have people been as concerned with visiting gymnasiums, museums, exhibitions, even distant countries; never have they had as much time and means to do so en masse.

The result of these changes in modes of life, concurrent with the trends toward the expansion of office work and education, has been an unprecedented demand for amenities in the environment. It was difficult to convince a meeting of urban planners in America some fifteen years ago that planning and urban policies ought to emphasize the provision of urban amenities for the masses. I tried repeatedly to stress this in the 1960s[6] but one hardly needs to plead much for this sort of urban need nowadays, so obvious has it become.

Oxford is undoubtedly a very pleasant place to live in, especially for those desiring to take full advantage of the new modes of living. The city is exceptionally well endowed in green spaces, even in its central part. If some of these spaces are reserved for the use of special groups — as are the sport grounds of various colleges — most of them open to the public, at least for part of the day: thus the university parks, the meadows, the gardens of the colleges, and so on. A green belt tightly envelops the town, two rivers and a canal traverse it. The preservation of these green spaces in a city experiencing strong pressures from growth and multifaceted demand for other land uses would not have been possible without the influence and means of the colleges and the university and, indeed, without the need for these institutions to preserve the cadre and amenities necessary to the traditional education of their students. The pleasure that may be derived from these amenities by residents and visitors in Oxford remains a mere by-product, but it is for all the inhabitants of the place a much appreciated environmental benefit.

The architectural beauty of a vast array of buildings gathered in the city and its environs has established Oxford as one of the most admired historical cities in Europe. The diversity of styles and of the types of buildings found within a radius of two miles of Carfax is indeed exceptional. Oxford has been one of the great centers of pilgrimage for the students and historians of architecture. Those who live and work in the town or visit it often enjoy this magnificent environment as part of their daily routine. Here again the quality, continuity, and conservation of the architectural endowment has been the fruit of the endeavors of the academic community.

The education received by the white-collar workers who congregate in Oxford, besides the university, allows them to value and appreciate such amenities. An employer looking for well-qualified personnel has a better chance of attracting it to such an environment than to many others.

To the physical amenities must be added the purely cultural activities. Few towns in the world have comparable collections in their libraries and museums. The large university and the population gathered around it have brought to Oxford a remarkable diversity and density of events in the performing arts, such as theater and concerts, not to mention lectures. That is why Oxford attracts so many visitors of either scholarly or touristic inclination; that is why studies of all kinds can be pursued there in such agreeable conditions. The local government authorities were worried a few years ago when it was reported that neighboring cities, such as Swindon, seeking to attract industry and offices, advertised their location as being within a half-hour drive or so from all the amenities of Oxford. The influx of such visitors from surrounding cities and towns would create additional pressures on local public services and increase the difficulty of maintaining the daily quality of life on the city streets. Nevertheless, the attitude of neighboring communities is logical, understandable. The advantages of Oxford's hosting environment benefit a large region outside the city. The "no growth" policy adopted by the city fathers more than thirty years ago may well have benefited, in fact, the growth of the whole county and even the prosperity of adjacent areas beyond county limits.

Student life stamps the historic central section of Oxford with a youthfulness enjoyed by all the generations mixing there. University events add color and excitement, with rituals, processions, distinguished visitors. Even the trying rites of final examinations bring an element of fun and celebration, for instance, when students who have completed their finals stop traffic on High Street by erecting a barricade of empty champagne bottles in front of the austere Victorian building of the Examination Schools.

In articles assessing the future of the old university towns of Oxford and Cambridge, one reads occasionally that a factor in their favor is their location within an hour from London. This is certainly another advantage. But location within an hour from Oxford may well be an equal advantage in an era of great appreciation of the quality of life, with a greater proportion of the labor force conscious of such values and having more leisure time to enjoy them.

A Few Generalized Hints to Planning

There is no doubt that Oxford is in many respects an exceptional case. The study of its recent evolution still yields lessons of general portent for the understanding of certain processes at work in contemporary society and in human settlements.

A policy of "no growth" may help, in practice, selective expansion to develop. Resistance to expansion does not necessarily prevent some of it developing in a community organized for debate and gradual change. It is through such a process, difficult to describe, to analyze, and even to understand—because of the many contradictions it seems to generate—that evolution may be managed in controlled and wise fashion. Perhaps the recommendation so frequently cited: "Do not make little plans," conveys the wisdom of experience that teaches how little of what is proposed can actually be achieved when endeavoring to implement plans and policies.

The role of universities in the life of cities has certainly been underestimated. In an era when employment shifts to office types of work, with increased leisure time,[7] educating a competent labor force and a relaxed citizenry is largely obtained through academic institutions conscious of their function. To respond to the needs of the time most countries have increased the number and the size of their establishments of higher education. Many more cities have now such establishments and could obtain the benefits their presence can bring to the local environment if they give to these academic establishments the means to contribute to the community as they should and could, in hardware and software.

Last but not least, the town often reproaches the gown for the latter's inward-turned frame of mind, for a stifling, over-protective attitude bringing isolation to the groves of academia. There is some truth in that description: how could the teachers teach their pupils both to think for themselves and still to preserve inherited knowledge, which are fundamental tasks of better education, unless they inspire them to some introspection? The more geographers and social scientists analyze the organization of space, the more they discover that the decisive partitions are in the minds of men. Oxford has an old and strong reputation, probably somewhat deserved, for inspiring inward-turned attitudes. It has even been noticed that the architecture of the quads in the colleges seems to look inwards, turning only back walls with few openings towards the outside world. This general attitude has not prevented constant change, evolution, and frequent innovative debate. It has not prevented Oxford from maintaining its centrality for wide networks on a broad geographical scale.

Few documents demonstrate as vividly as Dr. S. Walker's article what a great crossroads the University of Oxford is and what complex and far-flung networks it maintains with the rest of the world. To some extent this picture describes an academic community more open to a broader spectrum of mankind than it was in the past. This recent evolution also reflects the changes in social, national, and international structures. The habit and propensity to introspection have not kept the academic community from adapting to the currents that move the world *extra-muros*. The model of Oxford's evolution confirms the complexity and plurality of the study of human settlements in an unsettled time.

Notes

1. My predecessor in the Professorship of Geography at Oxford, Edmund W. Gilbert, outlined the history and planning of Oxford in the first half of the twentieth century in his book *The University Town in England and West Germany,* Chicago University Department of Geography Research paper No. 71 (Chicago, 1961). A recent book on Oxford sums up the history and diversity of the city: Jan Morris, *Oxford* (Oxford University Press, revised edition, 1978). A good biography of the motor car manufacturer, Lord Nuffield, was written by P. W. S. Andrews and Elizabeth Brunner, *The Life of Lord Nuffield: A Study in Enterprise and Benevolence* (Oxford, Basil Blackwell, 1955).

2. Barbara Baird, "The Web of Economic Activities in Oxford," *Ekistics* 274 (Jan./Feb. 1979): 36–44.

3. University of Oxford, *University Travel and Parking Survey* (Oxford University Press, 1972).

4. Susanne Walker, "External Relations of Oxford: University Linkages," *Ekistics* 274 (Jan./Feb. 1979): 44–52.

5. Noel Annan in "Our age—reflections on three generations in England," in *Daedalus* (Boston, Fall 1978).

6. Among my early attempts: Jean Gottmann, "The Rising Demand for Urban Amenities," in Sam B. Warner Jr. (editor), *Planning for a Nation of Cities* (Cambridge, Mass., The MIT Press, 1966), 163–78. Since then an abundant literature has been published on leisure and amenities in cities.

7. See Jean Gottmann, "Urbanization and Employment: Towards a General Theory," in *Town Planning Review* (Liverpool, July 1978) (see chapter 14 of present volume).

Part Six   **Living in the Modern Metropolis**

Megalopolis is still attracting people . . .
Americans have always been mobile people.
It has been estimated that one American out
of five moves in an average calendar year.
Obviously there has been much migration in
and out of Megalopolis as well as within the
region. The rather special character of the
economic activities that continue to cluster
and to develop in the region, particularly in its
main hubs, has attracted certain kinds of
labor from many other parts of the country.
Included among the persons drawn to the
region are the more highly paid administrators needed for decision-making and managerial positions in private business as well as
in government, and those in such professions
as education, law, and medicine. And the
very presence of these more highly paid
groups attracts crowds of poorer immigrants
or in-migrants, in recent years chiefly the
latter—Negroes from the South and Puerto
Ricans.

Thus the highly paid staffs needed by the
governmental and managerial functions of the
region, by the financial and mass-media markets, live and work together with less-well-
paid workers and with large numbers of residents in the lower-income brackets. For the
region as a whole, however, the average family income is relatively high . . . , and Megalopolis therefore contains the greatest
concentration of wealth in the country. While
some other countries have as high an average family income, they are in general much
more sparsely populated. Nowhere else is
there as large a number of households with
relatively high average income as in the axial
belt of Megalopolis.

This attraction to the central cities of
Megalopolis of such sharply contrasted
groups of people creates various problems. It
affects land use and real estate values; the

life of children and teenagers in school and at
play; the revenue of local governments and
therefore the services they render; the established political patterns. Having served for
over 300 years as the main debarkation wharf
of crowds of immigrants, Megalopolis is
accustomed to such contrasts. The abundant
supply of cheap labor was one of the factors
that favored industrialization in the past, and
it is still a factor of economic growth, for it
helps the region to provide, at not too great a
cost, the many various services which the
people with higher incomes need and can
afford. In the past, the leadership of Megalopolis has on the whole successfully handled
the tensions and problems rooted in this
diversity. In recent times these tensions and
problems have taken somewhat new forms,
resulting partly from the kinds of people now
involved, partly from the new economic specializations that have developed, and partly
also from the very fact of greater crowding
within the region . . .

Today what we have seen in Megalopolis
can hardly be fitted into any of the orderly
patterns elaborated by theoreticians. There is
too much flow, flux, and constant change
within the region. There are too many relationships that link any given community or
area of some size to several other areas, cities, and hubs. Perhaps the best comparison
of its structure, at a time when astronomical
comparisons are in fashion, would be with
the structure of a nebula. The expression
"nebulous structure" is apt to convey the confusion spreading before us in place of the
more neatly organized systems to which we
were accustomed in the past. Some central
cities are rapidly losing their former "centrality" to become suburbs or satellites or in
some way dependencies of communities that
do not seem to have either the size or the

functions associated with the concept of "central place" and that are multiple instead of one! Downtown functions are moving out of the city's core toward the periphery and to other neighborhoods, some of which are based on their proximity to "dormitory" communities, while others grow in the shadow of large industrial establishments set up amidst a rural-looking countryside.

Megalopolis,
"Living and Working Together"

Thirteen

The Ethics
of Living
at High Densities

Modern studies of the city have con-
cerned themselves more with the urban sprawl flooding the environs of
the old central city nucleus than with the high density formation which
is indeed proper to the city. Some sociologists have even suggested
that the highly agglomerated forms of dense settlement which used to
characterize urban life in the past were in the process of being dissolved by the trend of sprawl, so that relatively average and not very
high densities were to spread all over the countryside, dissolving, for all
practical purposes, the city into a much larger region and perhaps altogether into the nation.

This writer's work on Megalopolis has been sometimes described as
a demonstration of such a trend. Such interpretations are erroneous
and confusing; they do not correspond either to the study of Megalopolis or to the actual trends in the redistribution of population, as they
can be observed in the field. While it is true that the growing central city
is sprawling over the surrounding countryside, bringing about in many
cases a lower average density for the whole urbanized area (although

Reprinted from *Ekistics,* February 1966, 141–45.

this is not necessarily so everywhere), it is just as true that Megalopolis, as defined by this writer, on the northeastern seaboard of the United States from greater Boston to greater Washington, concentrated 20 percent of the American nation—that is, some 37 million people in 1960—over 1.8 percent of the land area of the conterminous United States. The average density for this huge area stood at 688 per square mile (or 275 per sq. kilometer) in 1960. Almost half of the total area, however, was wooded, which means that the actually urbanized area in the Megalopolis region had an average density of more than 1,400 per square mile. Such a concentration of one-fifth of a large nation on something like 1 percent of its area seems a huge formation of density, obviously in contrast to what happens over the rest of the territory.

We know that the other four-fifths of the nation is not equally distributed, either, over most of the American land. In fact, a majority of the Americans outside Megalopolis are steadily grouping themselves inside metropolitan areas, the total area of which represents a very small percentage of the vast expanse of the United States. From 1950 to 1960, while the total population of the United States increased by 18.5 percent, its 216 standard metropolitan areas increased in population by 26.5 percent. This trend is expected to continue and accelerate. Recent presidential messages to Congress have stressed that most of the forthcoming growth of the American population is expected to agglomerate in the major metropolitan regions of the country. This does not mean, of course, that every metropolis will grow at a rate proportionate to its size. Cities grow now in a very competitive world, in which a selective process makes some grow much faster than others, and that is independent of size. But it remains that more square miles have their population thinned out even during the present period of rapid numerical growth, while a smaller acreage is the locus of more agglomeration, creating much higher densities on these small areas than over the rest of the country.

The United States is not unique in this respect; in fact, it can almost serve as a model. In almost every well-developed nation in the world, one can show areas (one to three per country, depending on their structure) where 15 percent to 35 percent of the total population lives on less than 5 percent of the land area. Such distribution, involving considerable concentration of a large part of the total population, can be also observed in a good many underdeveloped countries, although not in all of them. The result is that high density grouping for large numbers of people is no longer exceptional but is becoming a rule in the modern distribution of settlement. One may expect this concentration and the consequent rise of density in the living conditions to accelerate when the more numerous generation born since 1945 comes of age.

It seems, therefore, highly probable that the next twenty-five years are going to see a considerable increase in the density formation in which most of mankind is going to live and work. This unavoidable trend has been deplored too often by public opinion. One hears the rise of density in the settlement of people bemoaned as if it ought to lead to a general worsening of living conditions.

The first point to be made is that such a result would be contrary to past experience as demonstrated in history. It is somewhat hard to accept the idea that the present and future generations will be less able to provide for their material well-being than has been the case for our ancestors. Not that a steep rise of population density did not cause difficulties and problems in the past. But these have always been solved, and the succession of these solutions is nothing else than the progress of civilization as usually described in history.

Archaeologists have abundantly demonstrated in their analyses of antiquity that civilization arose and recorded history began when large crowds of people, previously scattered, congregated at a few selected spots, forming high density and crowding. The most famous cases were the gathering of dense populations along the remaining sources of water in the valley of the Nile, in Mesopotamia, and along the Indus River, for example, at the time when the Middle East became desiccated. The necessity of crowding along the narrow ribbons of land where water was available created the need of regulation of the use of the water, of the irrigable land, and of all the usages of neighborhood. This meant order according to law, a hierarchy to supervise the enforcement of regulations, and a political process to select and control the hierarchy.

Somewhat later in history the rise of the Greek *polis* also came with some formation of density between associates who were close neighbors. The role of the larger cities of Europe during the Middle Ages and the Renaissance as centers of culture, of technological and social progress, as cradles of our modern civic rights and political freedoms, has been well studied and is generally accepted by historians of these periods.

Since the beginning of the Industrial Revolution in the eighteenth century, the process of urban growth was accelerated and generalized, and the political process did not always catch up with the trend of urbanization. Violence and revolution became more frequent occurrences. And then the ideal arose of founding the political stability of democratic regimes on the dominant role in politics of the small and medium farmer. In the cities, meanwhile, where industry too often exploited the workers crowded in slums and blight, arose the revolutionary ideals of the nineteenth century socialists, some leading to utopia and others leading to violence. On the whole, the experience of the twentieth century has been as yet that the industrialized countries have been able to weather their political storms with less internal damage and violence than the predominantly rural and agricultural countries in search of better material conditions of living. There are today two great areas of densely agglomerated people: one of them is highly urbanized on the two sides of the North Atlantic, in North America and Western Europe, and it enjoys the highest level of average economic prosperity, and the prestige and affluence of being the rich nations of the world. The other area of dense settlement is still predominantly rural, and inhabited by the poorer half of mankind with the greatest economic problems, in the South and East of Asia.

The lesson of history seems fairly simple and clear: high density creates a challenge to improve, through better organization and fairer distribution, the lot of the people. In many cases in the past, though not in all, high density formation has led to economic, social, and political development, yielding benefits later enjoyed by mankind as a whole. However, such a constructive evolution is determined by a steep rise of density in communities that face the problem with an understanding of its ethics. The psychological logic may be outlined in the following sequence: a much higher density creates locally a much higher pressure on existing resources within the area concerned; the demand threatens to go far above the supply; a new way of sharing the available supply has to be evolved; either a few people are put in a privileged position to enjoy abundance while the majority are kept down to small and perhaps diminishing shares, or a fairer and therefore more equal system of distribution is established; as density keeps rising with population growth, a steady increase of the supplies must be provided for, to meet the demand. The successful dense settlements have always found the means to produce an abundant enough supply or to procure it from the outside in exchange for the services they offered. Density has been often the mother of greater resourcefulness. While expending the supply, it has often led to the accumulation of surpluses. One of the major functions of the city as a market has been the redistribution of surpluses made available by the citizens' endeavor.

To achieve an economic expansion capable of better supplying a rising demand, some ethical concern must be constantly present in the plans formulated by a community. Conditions of thick density tighten the relations of neighborhood and call for avoiding too sharp contrasts in the conditions of living. Still, in the past men have accepted more easily than they do today great differences in standards of material living. While the ethics of days of yore may have been adequate with a great amplitude along the social scale, modern society calls for a different hierarchy, with lesser differences of material consumption. The increase in the number of consumers and in the tightness of the settlement calls for a greater stress on the ethics of planning.

While this general evolution has been recognized by many analysts of modern society, a rather pessimistic approach to the solution expresses the fear of quantitative expansion. This approach assumes the inability of society to provide in affluent fashion for the needs of the gathering crowds, especially when this gathering occurs over small areas in very high densities. It therefore advocates that the only ethical solution would consist in limiting the amount of space, food, service, and so on that can be made available to each individual in high density conditions. Thus housing is planned according to minimum biological requirements of the human body; water supply is calculated for a city also according to a minimum of needs; and, of course, the lack of many desirable services is explained by the costs and technical difficulties of providing for more. Such an approach is not only pessimistic as to the capability of our society and of our resourcefulness; it is also by modern standards unethical and unrealistic.

Aristotle said in a famous passage of his *Politics* that people gathered in cities first to achieve security, but that they remained in the cities to achieve "a good life." As the Renaissance began to take shape in Italy, Alberti formulated the basic principle of city planning by saying that it had to provide for both "*commoditas et voluptas.*" *Commoditas* has been translated as "functionalism" and *voluptas* as "aesthetics," but perhaps we ought to revise the translation of the latter, which was precisely the new dimension the new times were bringing to Alberti's city: in the Renaissance it had already become obvious that the people gathering in the large cities required more than just security and basic material commodity; *voluptas* goes beyond the welfare city stage and asks for the provision of amenities making life happier and more beautiful for all the inhabitants of the crowded place. If it seemed advisable to plan for it in Alberti's time, with the scanty technological and economic means of his century, such thinking ought to be much easier to do nowadays. *Voluptas* is what the average citizen of the crowded metropolitan areas of today is asking for. Like Oliver Twist, he is asking for more. Only a minority of the citizens of the large cities in the affluent countries of the West are still asking for more in terms of food, clothing, and other basic necessities of material life. But a large majority of these same city dwellers are asking for better services in the city, more beautiful surroundings, and in general more *voluptas*.

In some cases society has steadily provided the environment of a good life; let us take the case of city parks. Since the Renaissance large European cities have provided some park space to their inhabitants for daily use. From the sixteenth to the eighteenth centuries the rich and wealthy had beautiful gardens designed around their mansions in the heart of the cities. The custom was that, with a few exceptions, these gardens were open in the daytime for the dwellers of the neighborhood to stroll in and to enjoy. They added considerably to the enjoyment of city life. We have documents showing that the people of the city often forced the owners of such gardens, who tried to keep the people out, to renounce such exclusive measures. In the same period it was customary for the parks around the castles in rural areas to be fenced off and kept private. Farmers and villagers living in the midst of nature could not have the same claims to share in the use of parks as was the case for the more crowded city people. The difference there is one of ethics. Similarly, as in the nineteenth century the larger cities reached the size of half a million inhabitants and more, the neighborhood gardens of the rich no longer offered an adequate amount of green and open space for all to enjoy. Then the cities had to provide public parks on the larger scale, first in the heart of the city and then around it. The movement developed around 1860, about simultaneously, in the Paris reshaped by Haussmann, and in the city of New York with Olmsted. Since that time the public has been provided with suburban parks, beaches, golf courses, and other open space to be used for recreation and a good life. Even the policy of national parks stems from the existence in a nation of a large number of people who live most of the time in the artificial conditions required by high density and who appreciate particularly the preservation of natural beauty and wildlife.

The particular case of the parks demonstrates that a community can find the results when it wants to, to grace the life of its members; the parks also illustrate a positive aspect of the kind of regulation that high density brings about within a community. For greater density imposing regulation of so many uses and activities, such regulation must have both restrictive and constructive meaning. The restrictive aspects of regulation are of course necessary because of tighter neighborhoods: policing has to be done by public authority according to strict rules in a dense settlement; a series of public health rules must restrict some of the freedom of action of the individual inhabitants, for instance, to avoid the danger of contamination; the owner of a piece of land cannot be as free with the use of his land in the dense neighborhood of a city as he could otherwise be if his land were located in rural territory with scattered population. The restrictions necessitated by density may perhaps be best understood by the famous rule of "no smoking" appearing in the elevators. An elevator is an area subject to crowding at times of heavy traffic inside the building it serves. A cigarette lit in such crowding may burn the clothes of another user or inconvenience another one in some way. To avoid such trouble in conditions of crowding, smoking must be prohibited in elevators. On the scale of the city, density obviously causes a variety of restrictive regulations to alleviate trouble that might arise from the consequences of density. These restrictions are inspired by ethical considerations. But the ethics of density require also regulations of a more constructive nature. For instance, a city may require the owner of any building rising above a certain height to install and maintain an elevator to serve it. Such a requirement may be termed restrictive of the freedom of the owner, but it is obviously constructive in terms of service to the user. When the density of traffic in the streets requires restrictive measures such as red and green lights at intersections, for example, a constructive aspect of regulation comes with the provision of public transportation (to avoid the multiplication of individual means of transportation) and the construction of more thoroughfares, freeways, underpasses, and so on.

All such aspects of restrictive and constructive regulations are well-accepted duties of the community in a densely settled area. They are not enough, however, for modern needs. Only recently has official planning gone into the field of providing adequate housing conditions for all levels of the community. Directly or indirectly the resources of the community are being tapped to improve housing and ensure conditions of better living to those who are underprivileged. But this policy is only in the category of *commoditas*. Public policy helps some sections of the city to build high-rise apartment buildings for a certain category of customers, and in some other sections it fosters one-family detached structures, usually for another level of income users. In both cases planning aims at satisfying the existing demands; the supply of housing as a whole and in most of its types (except for the most expensive) remains below the demand. In such conditions the customer has little freedom of choice as to the type of housing, of location, that he or she may prefer. The possibility of choice is in fact restricted to a small number of privileged persons. We are told that such are the laws of economics. It is, however, obvious that such planning is not ethical, particularly in areas of dense settlement.

Ethics are seldom satisfied when the individual has no freedom of choice for such essentials as the kind of home, work, or leisure he or she may choose. Choice, on the other hand, is only possible when there is no scarcity of supply, that is, when the supply is constantly and systematically kept above the level of known demand. In other words, the planning must aim at surpluses of such goods as housing of various types and in several categories of locations. Unless such surpluses are declared necessary, they could hardly be provided at other than speculative prices.

The economic objection to such basic ethical requirements is hardly realistic. Several sectors of the economy of affluent countries thrive owing to the systematic production of surpluses planned in careful fashion and with the full knowledge and approval of the public. Agricultural surpluses are a well-known, outstanding example. A less well-known example is the picture offered by such a thriving industry as the automobile industry in the United States: one has seldom heard, outside of war years, of a long list of customers for new cars waiting for their wishes to be fulfilled. Conversely, at the end of a season, when new models come on the market, it is usual to see the prices dropping of the previous year's models which remained unsold; the industry's planning was not afraid to provide for a certain surplus. In some European countries, during the postwar years of austerity the automobile industry got used to long waiting lists of orders ensuring consumption of all their production, sometimes a year ahead. The times have greatly changed, and the same European manufacturers are much happier and enjoy a greater profit margin now that they can produce yearly some surpluses of cars. An affluent society is characterized by its capacity to produce and resorb some amount of surpluses. Dense population creating agglomerated markets with great dynamism helps in the production and resorption of such surpluses.

We have come to a stage in civilization when we can have economic surpluses of labor, not only in the form of unemployment, but in the form of work-hours which we transform into leisure in a process creating new resources. It is amazing to notice that people do not detest crowding when it is endowed with some quality of *voluptas*. When most of the people from the great cities leave on vacation, if they go away from home, they do not look for isolation, but gather once more in very crowded spots which happen to be in fashion for vacations either on the seashore or in the mountains, or in some other big city that offers exciting recreation. A large capital and large amounts of well-equipped structures of all kinds have been devoted to such leisure time or vacation use. Much of this investment could be termed "surplus" but in our time and for our level of living it is one of the necessities of life.

The ethics of living at high density require planning for a great many surpluses of various kinds and with some imagination. The biological requirements of the human body are completely irrelevant to the social minimum of our day, a minimum which is quantitatively high and qualitatively not too low. The possibility of achieving such conditions in practice may still seem a faraway dream in the developing countries, whatever their density of population. The capacity of contemporary society to achieve such aims in the well-developed countries, and particularly in their metropolitan areas with high densities, should not be doubted. Such capacity should be carefully planned. A recent master plan for the metropolitan district of Paris opens with a quotation from Seneca: "It is not because things are difficult that we do not dare; it is because we do not dare that they are difficult." One wishes that this axiom were accepted as a prerequisite for any urban planning. As we shall have to deal increasingly with high densities, we should plan for them increasingly with ethical considerations in mind to achieve the good life for all in a better city. This can be done.

Fourteen

Urbanization and Employment: Towards a General Theory

Urbanization and employment have been two major concerns of this century and they are likely to remain so for quite some time to come. It is my purpose to elaborate a relationship between the two phenomena and to show that the *terms* of employment, the conditions regulating the contract of employment, have been essential determinants of urban form and urban life. Changes in the terms of employment have modified the structure and the perception of the city.

This broad, general statement may appear at first to emphasize once again a well-known trend. It has long been accepted that urbanization attracted people to towns and cities because those were the places where jobs could be found. The "pull of the city" resulted from the expansion of the urban labor markets. The "push from the land," that is, from the rural areas, resulted from the shrinkage of the labor required for agricultural production and for servicing the farms. Both trends concurred to accelerate urbanization and both were explained by the advances of technology. The debate whether "pull" or "push" was more decisive appeared largely academic, even immaterial.

Reprinted from *Town Planning Review*, July 1978, 201–8.

There has thus been a stage in the analysis of urbanization that emphasized the process concentrating employment in cities. I do not think this approach has given its true dimension to the impact that conditions prevailing on labor markets have had, and still have today, and will have tomorrow on the shaping of human settlements, on the ways in which mankind organizes and uses its habitat. To begin making my point, I must define what is meant by "terms of employment." Employment is agreed between employer and employee on certain conditions that have greatly evolved through time and still differ greatly in space. These specify the time spent at work during the day, the week, the year, the place of work, the nature of the services, the duration of the arrangement, the remuneration and benefits received by the employee. These are minimum specifications: obligations undertaken by both employer and employee are often much more elaborate. They may determine the place of residence and this obviously affects urban patterns. In fact, they always determine much more.

The Uses of Time and Patterns of Settlement

A general evolution through the ages has gradually restricted the power and privileges of the employer and increased the freedom of the individual employee. The employee's freedom was broadened in terms of work time and workplace, in terms of the options left to his choice of the ways in which he used both the time not owed to the employer and the benefits derived from employment. The gradual shortening of working hours during the day, their distribution over the week, and the increase in the length of paid vacations allowed during the year have been fundamental trends in labor contracts in the twentieth century. These trends have been rapid in the developed countries and their impact on the patterns of settlement has been considerable.

When the terms of employment imposed ten to fourteen hours of work a day, six days of every week, except for religious or national holidays, it was necessary for the workers to reside close to the place of work. Free time was too scarce and precious to be spent on travel between home and work. Few could afford trips away from their place of residence unless they changed employment or engaged on a pilgrimage or some other collectively organized ritual.

The forty-hour and five-day week is a very recent achievement of the laboring masses and is still not fully generalized. In many countries it has made possible massive suburbanization and widespread commuting. Of course, the dispersal of both residences and places of work would not have developed to the extent recently witnessed without modern means of transport and communications. But automobiles, buses, and suburban trains could not have been used on the scale now observed if leisure time during the week had remained as scanty as it used to be.

The hours and days freed from work, at least by the terms of the main employment, created new opportunities and problems for the individuals who had to decide how to use them. Commuting from a distant home to work was one way to use some free time, which then became less free unless one considered those daily periods as free not only from the routine and pressures of work but also from the obligations and pressures of the family at home. Generally it could be counted as an extension of the time reserved for the duties of employment. But willingness to reside at a distance broadens the choice of the size, location, environment, and cost of the home. The choice is, of course, influenced by many factors, some of them economic (such as cost of housing and transport, system of taxation, etc.), others of a social nature (such as status, quality of schools for children, social level of neighbors, etc.).

For certain categories of managerial and professional personnel the desire to be close to colleagues and to belong to an extended community relating to employment or occupation seems to play a part in the selection of residential location. The equation of the choice of location is always complex; the factors in it will vary greatly according to country, to cultural background of the people making the choice, to social and ethnic mix in the community, to economic circumstances, and so forth. The important fact is the newly acquired capacity of the vast majority of the working class in many countries to exercise their judgment in choosing their place of residence and the use of their free time. In a large part of the world this freedom of choice remains quite limited, but it is gradually increasing.

The availability of free time during the day and on weekends made it possible for large crowds to develop active interests in public parks, sports, performing arts, and at a higher level of education in museums, exhibitions, and libraries. The new needs of the masses led to the proliferation of buildings and institutions created to satisfy them. Urban land uses and landscapes have been modified thereby: sports stadia, gymnasia, civic centers, cinemas, theaters, museums have sprung up to assume a spectacular role in urban centers. Such a role of recreational or ritualistic institutions in the urban landscape is not entirely new: it seems to have existed in major cities of the ancient Greco-Roman world. Some of the ancient stadia, arenas, and theaters have been preserved and may even be occasionally in use: thus the arenas in Arles or the theater at Delos. In the Middle Ages, however, these civic-center types of buildings were generally superseded in the Christian and

Moslem countries by monumental temples: basilicas, cathedrals, and mosques. The period of the Industrial Revolution, at least in the West, appeared to ignore these needs of the people; some urban planners of the nineteenth century compensated with public parks for the recreation of the people, chiefly on holidays.[1] But it was only in the twentieth century, with the rapid change in the terms of employment, that recreational institutions, parks, and buildings began to proliferate.

The time is past of company towns and other regulatory powers of employers enabling them to control the life of the employees during non-working hours. At least such has been the trend in most industrialized democracies. Regulation of individual locational decisions by employers or public authority is still enforced in diverse ways in many countries: by large companies in Japan, by local government in the Netherlands, by central and local government agencies in the communist countries. There are special cases: the University of Oxford requires its professors to reside seven months of the year within ten miles of Carfax, the central crossroads of the city of Oxford. The worker's free time may be more or less preempted by the community to which he or she belongs, according to the strength of local pressures exerted either by density of population, or by scarcity of resources, or by collectivistic traditions and legislation. But there again, the freedom the worker has is on the increase.

The length and distribution of vacation time within the year has also affected patterns of settlement. First, the generalization of weekends has increased the number of those for whom it was worthwhile to have a secondary residence, that is, a second place of abode besides the main domicile, which was normally closer to the place of work. That possibility, of owning or having the use of a secondary residence, did not necessarily involve considerable investment by recently urbanized people, many of whom moved to cities from rural areas in which they had roots and where they had inherited houses. France is a case in point; the French Census of 1975 counted 1.8 million secondary residences for seventeen million households. The weekend, however, requires a not-too-distant location of the secondary residence. The latter becomes much more worthwhile if the worker and/or the worker's family can also enjoy it during more prolonged periods of vacation during the year.

Most countries have preserved traditions of several successive days of vacation for most of the labor force around major religious holidays. But Western Europe started to grant periods of paid vacations to employees in summertime or at any time of their choice. Here again France is a case in point, where, in 1936, the Popular Front government began obliging all employers to grant two weeks of paid vacation per year in addition to national holidays. Since then this general rule in France has been extended by law to four weeks a year at least. It has resulted in a large part of French industries closing down during the whole month of August, during which a huge migration develops in that country, seasonally displacing tens of millions of people.

In other developed nations annual vacations may be less prolonged and more diffuse throughout the year, but they exist and have become an essential ritual. Four weeks of paid vacation annually is now common practice in Europe and urban land uses have evolved to fit the new demand. Partly, this was answered by providing more green spaces around homes, and around towns, with more suburban and urban sprawl. But the impact of prolonged vacations for all has gone far beyond local and regional repercussions; it has caused changes across the nations and beyond. More new towns and expanded cities have probably arisen around the world to satisfy seasonal tourism than to decentralize the congested metropolis. The legislation on social security, pensions, and retirement age has widened leisure in the lifetime of large numbers of persons, and expanded the demand for tourism.

Marion Clawson and his associates at Resources for the Future have done much interesting work in assessing recreational land needs.[2] Professor Allan Patmore, in his book *Land and Leisure in England and Wales* has described how the extension of leisure to more time and more people has affected English landscapes since Victorian times.[3] H. G. Wells prophesied in the 1890s, in his novel *When the Sleeper Awakes,* that "pleasure cities" would develop on Mediterranean shores in the twenty-second century for the recreation of the upper classes of an overgrown London.[4] As he wrote, in fact, urban growth due to seasonal tourism was already noticeable in various areas, for instance on the French and Italian Rivieras or the coast of New Jersey. These were the times of the emergence of the leisure class. Since then the tides of recreational travel by well-organized, classless masses have brought about the urbanization of ribbons of coastal territory and mountain valleys in many parts of the world, from Brighton to Miami, via Marbella, Cannes, Corsica, the Alps, the Greek islands, the Crimea, Tahiti, Hawaii, and Aspen, to mention only a few places.[5] Such recreational urban growth often takes the shape of long, thin strip development. This new category in urban morphology deserves to be called *teniapolis* areas.[6] Recreational travel has also brought massive flows of visitors, though usually for shorter sojourns, to older cities of historical or cultural interest, causing them to expand and sometimes to rebuild themselves.

Vacation time allowed by modern terms of employment is thus an important factor in urban morphology and in the urban modes of life which increasingly de-sedentarize people and make them move often during the day, the week, the year. This is so because fewer are satisfied with leisure spent reading, fishing, playing golf or bridge, and watching television at home. The Grand Tour or the athletic club, which were the privileges of a few, are now becoming available to the masses. The evolution of the conditions of employment modifies the form and functions of human settlements.

The Changing Nature of Employment

The terms of employment have also evolved because of the changing nature of the work which employers need to be done. The central functions of the city are being modified to adapt the patterns of settlement to the emerging new socioeconomic structures; this renewal of urban centrality reflects fundamental changes in society which are still little understood. Gradual replacement of hard, constraining physical human labor to produce agricultural and industrial goods by mechanization, automation, and other advances of science and technology, is leading the majority of the labor force into nonmanual and white-collar occupations. It was a great date in history when, by 1955, the number of white-collar workers surpassed that of blue-collar workers in the United States, then the largest producer of agricultural and industrial goods among the nations. Now similar trends have been observed in many other countries. There is no doubt that despite the rising costs of energy and the stricter regulation of polluting processes, which must both exercise some braking action on these trends, mankind will continue saving physical labor, avoiding compulsory muscular effort.[7]

The ancient principle that man shall earn his living "by the sweat of his brow" is being superseded. The leadership of workers' organizations is now aware of this fact. More than ever people will live by their wits. This does not mean at all the return to a Garden of Eden. Rather, it hints at replacing the "hot sweat" of constant muscular exertion by the "cold sweat" of nervous tension in exerting one's brain, nerves, and stamina in transactional work, and probably experiencing the anguish of crisis much more frequently. The nature of work in these nonmanual occupations, which are rapidly becoming the more numerous, is very different from the old style of labor; and the terms of employment are different.

First, it appears that a large and increasing proportion of the white-collar workers are able to discharge their duties better if they do not remain in one single place to perform their work. This is an extremely important and rather new aspect of employment which has been little clarified and analyzed as yet. In the past the production of goods and most services required that labor be attached to the spot where the object was produced; the peasantry, miners, manufacturing workers, and domestic servants were locked into place by the nature of the work and the terms of employment. In past centuries slavery, serfdom, indenture, and other legal devices controlled the freedom of workers partly to give greater power to employers to exploit them, but also to ensure their staying where work had to be delivered, a place chosen entirely by the employer or his agent. There were a few exceptions to this rule: itinerant workers, messengers, shepherds, certain categories of tradesmen, and, of course, those in the professions, many of whom were in practice self-employed. How different is now the structure of society!

The modern organization of the world produces an enormous volume of information. To make the complex mechanisms of that organization run smoothly, more knowledge, more information are needed, and more and more people are employed to gather, correlate, and process the data, then make the decisions using it. In the past information was scarce, hard to come by. The world seemed to change slowly, if at all, and the various parts of it could carry on with little knowledge of or dependence on other parts. These static conditions have yielded to unprecedented dynamism. Present survival requires close contacts with a vast world, expanding in internal complexity and producing as a result an immense, overwhelming quantity and variety of bits of information.

Concluding the meetings at the Massachusetts Institute of Technology, celebrating the first centennial of telephone communication in March 1976, Arthur C. Clarke remarked: "The real value of all the devices we have been discussing is that they have the potential for immensely enriching and enlarging life, by giving us more information to process—up to the maximum number of bits per second that the human brain can absorb." And he went on to suggest the slogan: "The purpose of life is information processing."[8]

It has been accepted for some time that the division of labor increases with the size of the market (Adam Smith) and with the advancement of civilization (Emile Durkheim). This self-refining subdivision of the occupational structure of society has deepened and accelerated in recent times; it is unlikely to be stopped or reversed unless all the economic and technological systems by which we live break down. This growing specialization requires more communication, exchange, and teamwork between specialists.[9] No government agency or corporation headquarters, no laboratory or even university could expect to find on its own staff all the specialists, and in its files all the data, it may need for urgent business at some time. The modern world is too varied and is changing too fast. The division of labor and of knowledge among white-collar personnel is subdividing and self-refining also too fast. Those employed in the upper-level services, which I like to call the quaternary occupations—the managerial, research, and professional personnel—need frequent consultation of data and with specialists that are not within their daily reach.

Hence the growing importance nowadays of information and communications in theory and in practice. Employers are concerned with communications in several respects. Labor relations call for good communication between management and employees to avoid conflicts within firms or institutions and consequent disruption of work; this is the result of the evolution of legislation about terms of employment which has granted more freedom of action to the workers in most so-called capitalist countries. Marketing requiring application of an art of communicating with customers has brought about the rise of new industries and occupations, to be found in the mass media, advertising, and public relations. Finally, the need to process information in the various stages of decision making for administration, research, development, and other transactions determines a constant flow of communications between specialized elements of the labor force. Management is concerned with the quality of communications achieved and of information obtained by their personnel, because in white-collar transactional activities the quality of communication and information is a decisive determinant of the final product's value and of employees' performance.

The role of communications in the structure of the city has been much studied by geographers and planners. As modern trends began to be felt they caused strong centripetal forces to develop; offices and other places of white-collar work congregated in the central business districts of some cities more than others. The daily gathering in these districts of large numbers of relatively well-paid workers in the upper brackets of the white-collar scale, and of visitors coming to transact business at these places, attracted a variety of services ranging from department and speciality stores to fashionable clubs, theaters, and night clubs to the vicinity of city centers.

The growth of the central areas in most cities endowed with some functions of centrality has been spectacular. It emphasizes in the modern urban landscape and land use the complementarity and interdependence of the proliferating specializations, and the general need of all the personnel working in them to know one another, in order to exchange information, and discuss its processing and interpretation. The nature of urban centrality has changed with this evolution of the nature of work and of the consequent employment policies.[10]

A variety of factors—the congestion and cost of this concentration, the pressures felt in some overgrown skylines, the insecurity caused by

criminality attracted by the congregation of wealth, the political rivalry—
has caused centrifugal forces to develop, particularly in American cities
and in major European capitals, decentralizing or at least deconcentrat-
ing the central districts. However, the more places of specialized quaternary employment scatter, the more employers and workers alike feel the
need for communication, consultation, and discussion between those
dispersed. Places of gatherings and formal meetings have been provided, through which flow crowds of participants in seminars, symposia,
conferences, conventions, and so forth. Expenses for these meetings
are provided in some cases by employers or by professional agencies;
in other cases they are tax deductible.

   In the teaching professions there has long been a tradition of recurring
periods to enable teachers to recycle their knowledge and methods, to
take part in courses and conferences in other institutions than their
own. Sabbatical leave was intended for such purposes. Recycling and
updating for specialists in many occupations are now common prac-
tices. The time spent away from the main place of work is readily
accepted by employers as part of the working input by the employee to
improve his or her competence and performance. Certain professional
organizations (and I understand that the American Medical Association,
for instance, is one of them) have come close to requiring their members to attend yearly one or two professional conferences in the field of
their specialization. Among the rapidly changing trends and forces dyn-
amizing the contemporary professional environment such systematic
endeavors to improve competence are indeed desirable and considered normal.

   These new features of employment have generated new categories
of institutions, buildings, and traffic flows. The central districts have not
borne their imprint alone. New decentralized districts, especially outfit-
ted for the purposes of these gatherings, have also mushroomed in
selected categories of location: for instance, in the vicinity of major airports or on the contrary, in secluded quiet resorts such as certain Riviera towns or the Village of Barbizon, long a picturesque retreat for
painters and writers on the edge of the forest of Fontainebleau.

   Architecture has taken notice of the needs of the transactional, communication work and learned to provide the facilities which the gatherings require: convention hotels, conference centers, galleries, libraries,
even hospitals. Twenty years ago, Houston, Texas, had few high-rise towers. Besides a large hotel and the Veteran's Hospital, I noticed then
along the main axis of that spreading city only two high towers, small
skyscrapers, which were doctors' office buildings. To congregate at the
same location, private medical offices were using the vertical pattern for
complementary specialists' offices and some of the technical and labor-

atory services they often needed. Harley Street specialists in London have traditionally congregated in the same vicinity, along one axis, as has the advertising industry along Madison Avenue in Manhattan. Many more examples of this sort could be cited. The most impressive conglomeration of interdependent urban activities is probably now found in the vast and sprawling conurbation of Tokyo-Yokohama, though another, more compact system exists in Manhattan along Wall Street, Broadway, Rockefeller Center, Madison Avenue, Park Avenue, Fifth Avenue, Times Square, Madison Square Garden, and now also on the East River. These are products of another civilization than the traditional Main Street or High Street. Their giant size and complex systems are not simply facts of concentration; they are the outcome of the dynamics of modern labor markets, the occupational structure of which requires so much communication. These centers constantly receive large numbers of visitors coming from afar on business.

Technological devices have greatly improved the means of communication in the last hundred years. Telecommunications are credited by many with obviating the need for dense concentrations of quaternary types of work. Despite a century of rapid progress, this technology has, in fact, favored both concentration and scatter, depending on the particular activities concerned and the circumstances involved. Geographers have researched these matters at length and in depth in several countries, and under diverse regulation. Even under legislation favoring dispersal, the role of the communications factor in office location and decentralization has been found to be multiple and complex. The office has not yet become predominantly a dispersed "cottage industry" as was forecast in the 1960s. A vast and scholarly literature on office location and scatteration of office work has shown that, despite considerable pressure, even by legislation in favor of dispersal, white-collar transactional work continues to agglomerate in selected locations and to need face-to-face meetings. Such were also the conclusions of several symposia on the social impact of telecommunication technology held at the Massachusetts Institute of Technology in 1975–76.[11]

The evolution of the work performed by a large and growing sector of the labor force towards information processing, requiring more and more communication, determines several trends within urban structures. It reinforces the centrality of certain cities which are nodes of transactional networks. It develops the physical and social importance of institutions that provide the facilities and the personnel to service, on the one hand, the meetings that multiply, and on the other, the training, updating, and recycling of those who process information and make decisions. Hence the physical expansion not only of convention and conference centers but also of universities, scientific institutes, laboratories, and libraries. Hence also the growing role of networks of such centers and cities and the intense traffic between them.

The employment of quaternary personnel is nowadays adapted to the geographical fluidity of places of work and to the frequent traveling of employees. Perhaps some employees would prefer a more settled life to the rather nomadic schedule which the nature of their work and the instructions of their employers foster for them. The consequences of these trends create for many workers a pluralistic geography of their way of life. Added to the choices of the places where the worker spends his or her free time, the various locations to which work takes the quaternary employee result in great spatial fluidity. The urbanites used to be classified as sedentary population. I am not sure this classification still applies. We ought to recognize among ways of life a new category of *transhumant bourgeois*.

Grasping the Fluidity of Urban Life

Changes in the terms of employment have many more aspects which can be mentioned only briefly here. The higher levels of pay helping to improve the average income of employed personnel, the pensions, insurance, and social security schemes improving the means of the aged and unemployed citizens—all concur to increase the individual's relative freedom of choice as to the location of residence, recreation, and other activities. In the modern world the individual also obtains the opportunity of changing his or her employment with much greater ease than was ever possible before, not by long-range migration, but by moving from one part to another of the same city or region. In fact, the shortage of housing in certain areas frequently makes it difficult to find adequate lodgings close to a new place of work. It may well be erroneous to suppose that, if the number of commuters still increases, this is mainly because people prefer to live farther away from places of employment.

The shortage of housing in major transactional cities, especially close to the business centers, is often caused by the multiplication of part-time residential units provided in these cities for transients who are neither domiciled nor employed there, but required by the nature of their work to transact business in those places recurrently. Thus the number of housing units in the city of Paris proper has been increasing in the recent twenty years, while the figure of the resident population has been decreasing, to be compensated for by rapid suburban sprawl.[12] These trends are not measured as they ought to be by census data which record every person at the place declared to be the major residence. The snowballing volume of statistical information now provided on urban areas does not always help to measure the increasing fluidity of urban life in realistic terms. The categories and definitions used often need revision and innovation.

The major obstacle to our better understanding of modern urbanization may perhaps be rooted in the scatteration of concerns and methods of approach resulting from the specialization of those who analyze this fluid and multifaceted phenomenon. Surely most of the trends caused by changes in the terms of employment have been studied separately. Recreational land use, length of working hours, commuting, tourist travel patterns, office location, occupational structure, labor relations, labor market areas, benefits in employment, and other social trends which I have alluded to, have all been studied, each by another profession, by another set of agencies. But employment and urbanization are closely related phenomena. The total impact of the terms of employment and of their evolution on urbanization could provide us with a much-needed general theory which may not be all-encompassing but which will offer a useful tool of analysis, correlation, and comparison, even on an international scale.

We have recently lived through an era of great unsettlement in urban places. Our perception of this revolution in the world around us has been blurred by the too diverse, specialized, and in some respects old-fashioned information provided about it. That perception may perhaps be clarified and improved if we recognized that urbanization has been deeply affected by a gradual liberation of the individual occurring on a massive scale. That liberation can be surveyed and perhaps measured through the process that has loosened the old shackles binding the individual in use of time and location in space. These bonds and their evolution are best expressed, I submit, in the rapidly changing terms of employment.

Notes

1. See especially August Heckscher, *Open Spaces: The Life of American Cities* (A Twentieth Century Fund Study), New York, 1977; also, for the case of Japan, see Japan Center for Area Development Research, *The Fourth International Symposium on Regional Development, Tokyo, 1972:* the symposium's theme was "A Design for Japan in the 21st Century." Also J. Fourastié, *Des Loisirs pour quoi Faire?*, Paris, 1970.

2. Marion Clawson, R. B. Held, and D. H. Stoddard, *Land for the Future*, Baltimore, 1960, especially chapter three, "Land for Recreation."

3. J. A. Patmore, *Land and Leisure in England and Wales,*1970.

4. H. G. Wells, *When the Sleeper Wakes*, London and New York, 1899. In the volume "A Design for Japan in the 21st Century," the distinguished architect

Kenzo Tange outlined "free-time cities" for his country (see note 1, above, 53–55). 5. In France the impact of leisure and employment on land use has been noted and occasionally elaborated by such scholars as Georges Freidmann and Jean Fourastié. G. Coronio and J. P. Muret have prepared an overview, *Loisir du Mythe aux Réalites*, Paris, 1973; and see J. Dumazedier, M. Ibert et al., *Espace et Loisir dans la Société Française d'Hier et de Demain*, Paris, 1967; see also, Prudenski, *Problemy rabochevo i vnerabochevo vremeny*, Moscow, 1972, especially 236–80.

6. The term *teniapolis* had been suggested to me years ago by Professor Homer Thompson, of the Institute for Advanced Study at Princeton, to describe a narrow, tenuous but continuous ribbon of urban development. We used it first in print in a paper published in the volume *Megalopoli Mediterraneo*, edited by Professor Calogero Muscara, Venice, 1978.

7. The French geographer André Siegfried emphasized this trend as a major American contribution to contemporary times in his book *Les Etats Unis d'Aujourd'hui*, published in English as *The United States Comes of Age*, 1927. In his conclusion he suggested that our era could be a debate between Henry Ford and Mahatma Gandhi.

8. Arthur C. Clarke, "Communications in the Second Century of the Telephone" in *The Telephone's First Century and Beyond* (New York, 1977), 110.

9. See Jean Gottmann, *Megalopolis: The Urbanized North Eastern Seaboard of the United States* (New York, 1961), especially chapter eleven, "The White-Collar Revolution."

10. See Jean Gottmann, "The Evolution of Urban Centrality" in *Ekistics* 39, 233 (April 1975): 220–228; Susanne R. Walker, "Linkage Structure in an Urban Economy" in *Regional Studies* 11, no. 4 (1977): 263–273; and Georges Freidman, *Le Travail en Miettes* (Paris, 1964).

11. See P. W. Daniels, *Office Location* (London, 1975); Ithiel de Sola Pool, *The Social Impact of the Telephone* (Cambridge, Mass., 1977); *The Telephone's First Century and Beyond*; and J. B. Goddard and D. Morris, *The Communication Factor in Office Decentralization* (*Progress in Planning* 6, Part 1) (Oxford, 1976).

12. See Jean Gottmann, "Paris Transformed" in *Geographical Journal* 142, no. 1 (March 1976): 132–135.

Fifteen

The Metamorphosis of the Modern Metropolis

Geographers have long been concerned with the form, the functions, and the ways of life of the metropolis. These have been changing very fast in the twentieth century, so fast that I shall dare say it has not been simply growth, or evolution: it has been a metamorphosis, meaning a very deep change not only in the appearance (the material shape), not only in the flows of transport, but in so many important facets of the functioning and the contents, material, and even more the human contents—that is, the types of population, of movements, of activities, of community relations—of all that makes the nature of the metropolis, that I can speak of a mutation in the nature of these large cities and their surroundings. Hence the metamorphosis.

What has caused this extraordinary change? The very size of the impact and the all-embracing range of the metropolitan metamorphosis suggest that the change has had many causes largely due to technological change: all the stages and the infinite number of innovations of the Industrial Revolution, of mechanization, of automation, of managerial rationalization and organization. It is also due to socioeconomic forces

Reprinted from *Ekistics*, 292, January/February 1982, 7–10.

and trends, such as changes in the use of human labor, the division of labor, the evolution of the terms of employment, the considerable increase in the volume of money and credit available to larger numbers and greater proportions of the population in most nations. Thus, I maintain that a higher proportion of individuals and families have benefited from the urban growth and economic expansion of the last fifty years than was the case in the past. This can be shown not only for highly developed economies but also for Third World countries except, perhaps, those that have experienced a very rapid demographic increase with limited urbanization.

Thus, economic, social, political, and technological forces have been at work, interweaving in different patterns according to countries, cultures, and political systems, and producing a variety of urban patterns. The important point is that the metamorphosis of the metropolis reflected a deep and extensive restructuring of society, resulting from choices made amidst all the opportunity offered by the forces at play in the world. The choices were, are, and will be made partly by the leadership, the political and economic authorities, and partly by the mass of the population, which does not always follow blindly the directions it receives from above. The freedom of choice offered to the mass of individuals in a population is greater when change develops faster and when the directions given are therefore many, and often self-contradicting and canceling one another.

The deep metamorphosis of the metropolis is, in fact, the product of endeavors to solve two great problems: first, a human problem; second, a geographical problem (i.e., a problem in the organization of space by people). The two are related and intertwined.

The Human Problem

First, the human problem. It is the outcome of the interplay of the diverse forces we have outlined. It may be said that technological opportunity has been used in a diverse manner by different metropolises and nations according to their cultures and to the economic interests and tastes inherited from their respective pasts. The choices they have made and the impact of these choices on the habitat and ways of life are best understood, I submit, by examining, analyzing, and comparing the various ways in which human labor is used and allowed to evolve. This is illustrated by the trends (easy to survey and partly measurable) of the division of labor, of the resulting occupational structure, and of the concomitant evolution in the terms of employment.

May I briefly remind you of this well-known past and present trend.

As agricultural practice improved and production expanded, fewer hands were needed to produce the agricultural goods needed by the people to survive. As commerce and manufacture expanded, people flocked to metropolises. The latter grew in all directions and multiplied around the world. Meanwhile, the human endeavor to save physical work for the production and distribution of goods continued: the white-collar revolution set in. Fewer workers became needed to produce goods, but more were required in the white-collar occupations and qualified services to manage, govern, and supervise people, machines, and related processes, including the biological and biochemical processes of agriculture and industry. More people were needed to be employed in research, development, education, medical care, public health, and so on. From manufacturing plants, manpower shifted to offices, laboratories, schools, hospitals, libraries, computer centers, even museums and art galleries.

We know all that now; however, one still occasionally finds persons (even writers) surprised at their discovery that white-collar work replaces blue-collar work, services employ more people than production, and offices supplant factories and warehouses in the heart of the metropolis. Whether realized or not, these changes go on. But what does this evolution do to the population and to the ways of life? Or perhaps we should ask what does the population of metropolitan regions do and want to do with all these changes and the opportunities they open? There should be no doubt about one thing: the great majority of the individuals prefer white-collar work and the terms of employment of a researcher, a manager, or even a teacher, to those of a peasant or of a worker at the blast furnace or in a spinning factory. The migration to cities and especially to larger metropolitan urban centers results from the hope that fills the hearts of the migrants: that migration to the great cities will open the road to a better life, and greater opportunity either for the migrants or at least for their children. The Japanese are very conscious of all this. It is not a random occurrence that almost half the university students in Japan study at higher education institutions in the Tokyo area. And it is because higher education offers the indispensable training for the quaternary services developed by the "information society," which is replacing the industrial society, that universities, colleges, and technological institutes have acquired such physical, economic, and political influence in the national systems and in the cities.

If one wishes for a practical illustration of these trends, one may look at what has happened in the city of Seville (Spain), a great metropolis for many centuries. In the center of the city, close to the cathedral where Christopher Columbus is buried, and to the Alcazar, the royal palace, a large and monumental set of buildings is the Manufactura de Tabaccos, the old factory of tobacco products, in which worked women, such as Carmen, the heroine of the famous opera by Bizet. Today, the Manufactura de Tabaccos, well preserved, has been turned into the university central buildings. The young women who now study there look towards a better sort of work and life than Carmen's co-workers!

The ways of life of the information society are somewhat different from those of the industrial society. The main difference is undoubtedly that they form another step towards the liberation for most of the individuals in the mass of the population from the old shackles imposed on them for ages in the past. The ancient servitudes had to be imposed by society in order to secure the conditions in which the goods would be produced and the services performed that were necessary to the functioning, indeed to the survival, of that society. The local or regional environment had to be cultivated in a rather self-sufficient manner by the local population. Most people were locked into place, in terms of employment and of location, by very strict rules which, in most civilizations, included conditions such as slavery, serfdom, indenture, severe tribal customs, or strict discipline in certain occupations, such as seamen and the police.

As human physical labor became less necessary for the production of goods and basic services, greater freedom of individuals was allowed. As resources for survival were increasingly supplied by long-distance commerce, taking advantage of an increasing spatial division of labor between countries and regions, the local population of large urban concentrations became less dependent on local resources, and more dependent on the adequate functioning of trade and transport transactions. These trends contributed further to unlock the individuals from their enforced rooting in a given place. The liberation broadened. Employers were seeking workers who would be competent and give them a quality service of their own volition. This was partly due to the evolution in the occupational picture, in the nature of work required. Partly it was due to the delocalization of the geography of supplies. Many writers have remarked, even in past centuries, on the links between the importance of commerce for a nation and a greater freedom granted by its system of laws: such remarks are found in Montesquieu (1750) and Tocqueville (1835) among others.

The Spatial Problem

From what has been said we may infer the existence of certain linkages between the organization of space and the limits of freedom. Four points must be made in this connection, which may help clarify these interesting and far-reaching linkages.

1. As individuals are given more freedom, they must be allowed more movement. Unlocked from their position in geographical space, they will be much more on the move and that space will need to be better organized to sustain increasing flows of traffic and even migration. The attraction of a large metropolis will be able to exercise itself more freely, and we have seen the results in terms of urban growth. But the freer movement has also resulted from changes in the terms of employment. Traditionally, employers assigned to the workers they employed a place of residence close to the place of work. Some of these spatial linkages still subsist in many countries. Even the University of Oxford requires its professors to reside within ten miles of Carfax, the central crossroads of the city; sixty years ago this limitation said one mile from Carfax! But such servitudes are gradually being relaxed, as they are less necessary for the performance of work, because of the improvements in the means of transport and because of the changes in the nature and hours of the work. So residences scatter, and suburbs and commuting develop and may cause terrible nuisances in the larger metropolises, especially when land speculation has spurred on a vast suburban sprawl.

2. The evolution of the terms of employment has substantially reduced the time due by workers to the employer. Individuals are, therefore, free in their choice of their use of a larger proportion of their time during the working day (due to shorter work hours); during the week (due to longer weekends, which in some countries frequently extend to three days); during the year (owing to entitlement to paid annual vacation); during their lifetime (as they usually enter the labor force at a later age and retire earlier). This shortening of working time provides the mass of the population with increasing leisure. How to occupy it remains the individual's choice, often restricted in some respects, such as by cost (not everyone who wishes to have a yacht can afford it), but the choices made have considerably affected modes of life and land use, particularly in and around large urban agglomerations. Thus, all the equipment required for indoor and outdoor sports and other forms of recreation has become an important component of the modern metropolis. The range of this equipment is impressive and it extends from libraries and concert halls to football stadiums and marinas. It occupies much ground, marks in various ways the cityscape, and employs numerous personnel. A large part of the uses of leisure time involves collective activities, and what used to be the privilege of a few now tends to be normal routine activities for the millions.

3. The evolution of an increasing sector of the work force towards the quaternary occupations, engaged in transactional activities, causes other forms of uprooting and movement which modify even more dras-

tically the life of the metropolis. In a way, this trend and its consequences should also be considered as a further liberation of individuals
from old shackles. It results from the nature of quaternary work, which
requires constant processing and interpreting of information. The mass
of bits of information available nowadays, on most questions, is enormous and is snowballing. Nothing of the kind had been available in the
past to those discussing policies, making decisions, or pursuing
research.

The data are also changing faster because the various processes in
human affairs move faster. Situations are influenced by more factors
and a greater diversity of considerations. It is absolutely untrue that the
world is shrinking, getting smaller. It may be so in terms of the time it
takes to overcome distance for transport and communication, so that
sheer physical distance is less important. But for the individual involved
in the information society and the managerial era, the world is continuously expanding in terms of the knowledge available and the numbers
of people with whom to keep in touch. The results of these trends can
be measured through the number and frequency of meetings, consultations, committees, symposia, conferences, conventions, and so on. All
these meetings handle a variety of transactions, including exchange of
information, collective analytical work, ironing out of agreements, and
many other decisions.

4. White-collar work has become more collective than individual, as
recreation has also grown more collective. All this leads to crowds moving about within a metropolis and between several metropolises, sometimes according to regular, recurrent patterns, at other times in a more
irregular fashion. In the past, this sort of life was a privilege, or perhaps
a servitude, of a few people: a top managerial layer, the "jet set,"
famous artists. Now it has become a duty for millions of people who
have to travel frequently to many selected places for work, for recreation, or for social obligations. The modern metropolis functions in a moving, commuting, transhumant, rushing around environment. All this
rushing around may be hard on the individual's physiology, but it is stimulating and exciting for the mind, and sometimes rewarding for the soul.
It is a new mode of life for very many who tend to adopt it for their vacations, and go "touring" and visiting, even if they do not have to do it for
their work. An immediate consequence for the metropolis is that its centrality is based less on its surrounding region and more on its status in
a large, far-flung network of transactional cities. The geography of the
metropolis is thus deregionalized as the region around it, what some
have called its hinterland, recedes as a primary interest and the role of
a network of outside relations on a much bigger geographical scale
comes to the fore.

Conclusions

The multifaceted evolution which I have sketched in some of its major human aspects explains, in my opinion, many puzzles and contradictions in North America and parts of Western Europe. A diagnosis of predominating trends formerly expressed as "metropolitanization" has been replaced by such formulas as "counterurbanization." While until recently town planning was proclaimed indispensable, it is now often declared failing, superfluous, even undesirable. While concentration in large urban systems was said to be the predominating trend, such systems are now proclaimed unmanageable and, in certain countries, dissolving. Theories of urban growth have indeed been inconsistent and insecure.

Certainly in a time of metamorphosis, all the phenomena related to the modern metropolis are in flux and difficult to predict. Changes in trends have to be expected and their effects should be carefully and cautiously interpreted. From the deeper social evolution that I have tried to describe here, several consequences follow, which I would like to evoke briefly in conclusion.

The modern trends of change develop differently in different categories of cities which were in recent centuries great metropolises. Some of these, which were lively centers for large surrounding regions and, as seaports or inland market centers, articulated the life of their hinterland with outside systems of relations, are now losing much of their activity and centrality. This is because the networks have shifted and large-scale transactional activities have migrated to other cities. These now usually concentrate in a smaller number of selected large metropolises which are specially well fitted for transactions and quaternary occupations. Manufacturing and warehousing functions, including handling of cargoes, may continue in the metropolitan region, but these functions have often separated from the business center and moved to peripheral locations. With automation and mechanization, the blue-collar population has shrunk. More often than not, a gradual divorce is separating city and industry, and therefore, city and harbor equipment.

The growth of white-collar personnel and quaternary activities can be observed in those metropolises, not necessarily the larger, which are traditionally equipped for transactions. These also usually develop a variety of recreational, civic, and academic functions. This concentration is not entirely a blessing, as it calls for much restructuring, renewal, displacement of people, and general turmoil. But these selected centers fare well, even though their central districts often lose residential population and, in a few cases, even some jobs. The transactional activity, as a hinge in a network of cities, replaces steady work in inner areas by the servicing of transients who come and go, some for recreation, and some for work, but of a sort which is not recorded in any of our traditional measurements of a city's features and role. The metropolis must service all the daytime activities and crowds, and the volume and diversity of services the metropolis must deliver are not accounted for by our normal analysis of its functioning. Hence, the endless misunderstandings and worsening conditions in budgetary and governmental affairs.

This can be helped by renouncing our old-standing measurement of city size by its "nighttime population," as the censuses count it. Payroll figures of employment are more significant and accurate, especially in countries where the employer deducts "pay as you earn" tax, or social security contributions. Still, to account fully for all the daytime population serviced in a transactional and/or recreational center, statistics of local employment must be complemented with other counts of transients and visitors, about which we have few data. Geographers could do a great deal to educate the authorities responsible for all the statistical data which badly need to be reformed and improved.

Some studies are already available that provide hints in the direction I have stressed. The Conservation of Human Resources Project, of Columbia University in New York, an interdisciplinary research team, has made an extremely interesting study of the corporation headquarters complex in New York City. They demonstrated the extraordinary growth of a whole world of advanced services to business, serving the whole American nation, plus the expansion of offices of non-American firms with North American interests. Then the study extended a comparative analysis of the location of advanced services to business in other large metropolises in the United States. One consequence is quite clear: the relationship between nighttime population in a city and its daytime transactional activity is often inverse, because the expanding transactions concentrating in choice sectors chase ordinary residences out to peripheral areas.

A fascinating corollary of this American study has been a report on the contribution of the Japanese business community to the economy of the city of New York. It is considerable and could have served as the basis for a substantial city's survival. Another report has now extended the study of Japanese firms in other large American metropolises. But what about the contribution to those metropolitan economies of business conducted in America by the British, French, German, Dutch, Italian, Swiss, Brazilian, Mexican, and other business communities? This is, undoubtedly, also substantial. And what about the Japanese, American, and German business activities in London, in Paris, in Brussels, in Zurich, or Milan? Another fascinating study and atlas directed by Professor Jean Bastié, of the University of Paris, has shown what changes in land use and floor space use occurred in the central city of Paris (Ville de Paris) between 1954 and 1975: manufacturers went out, offices expanded, and residences expanded. The census showed a drop of 600,000 residents in that period while the number of housing units increased by 210,000. How do you reconcile these two figures? Any visit to Paris will convince the observer that the transactional activity of that city is booming.

The ways of life and the community structure in the modern metropolis undergo such metamorphosis as to transform the nature of the processes at work. The emerging pattern must be understood as less localized, more pluralistic, and more transactional than productive of material goods, and more dependent on far-flung urban networks.

New methods of measuring and analyzing need to be elaborated; old confusing standards must be eliminated. The metropolis changes with the structure of society. The trend of central cities to become largely crossroads, hubs, and hinges in complex networks has already modified the long-standing relationship between residents, transients, local employment, and local activities within the urban structure. One consequence has been that censuses of population are now taken according to outdated formulae. The statistics they yield do not give a true picture of the reality. It is essential to reform the censuses. This will be a difficult reform. Until it is achieved, new methods, less dependent on census statistics, should be applied to measure the present trends and needs. These may be assessed, in temporary, more correct fashion, through the occupational structure, the terms of employment, and the relationships between the various individuals in modern society. A constructive approach to the analysis of the metamorphosis and of its consequences for the future should pay attention to the potential implied in the process of the individual's complex, gradual liberation from old shackles. It calls for the acceptance of new, readapted sets of values which may well vary from one culture to another. It is an exciting field and it involves many aspects of geography, of planning, and of the other social sciences.

Part Seven   **Implications**

Recently this writer has travelled widely through North America, western Europe and some Mediterranean countries. Everywhere he found cities expanding. The larger metropolitan areas are attracting the larger part of population growth. Cities are expanding one toward the other. The nebulous structure of urbanized regions is becoming frequent and hints at a new redistribution of functions within such regions. Residential land use is gaining in all directions around the congested older nuclei. The more densely agglomerated nuclei no longer specialize in manufacturing and administration as they used to. Production industries often move out to the periphery of the city and beyond into spaces that were until recently considered rural or interurban. The functions that continue to gather in what may be called central districts or hubs of the urban nebulae are offices, laboratories, and all the activities related to the various forms of entertainment. As in Roman times, the arena and the forum, in their modern versions, occupy an increasing share of the hubs. Entertainment and offices are related to one another, thriving on proximity. They create a large market for white-collar labor. All these trends started at an earlier time and they have already developed on a great scale in Megalopolis. The forces bringing about this evolution are rooted in a deep transformation of modern modes of life and habitat. They are not determined in other areas just by an imitation of Megalopolis, and yet the element of imitation spurs the evolution on.

These trends bestow a heavy responsibility upon the present inhabitants and leadership of Megalopolis. In many ways they may be rightly proud of serving as a model. They must, however, be mindful of the long-range consequences of these trends. People imitate those wealthier, more powerful, more successful than they are, in the hope of achieving through such imitation a better and perhaps an equal status. Mahatma Ghandi told how in his youth he tried to eat beef, despite deep repugnance, in hope that it would make him intellectually and politically equal to the beef-eating British who then dominated India. He soon understood that that was not the way to solve his problem. Megalopolis may feel some concern at the thought that similarly unreasonable but instinctive imitation may and will develop; but in the field of urban and metropolitan problems one cannot prevent such undesirable imitations. Nevertheless, there remains some responsibility in the very fact of leadership, for the behavior of the followers is under the leader's influence.

Megalopolis,
"Novus Ordo Seclorum"

Sixteen

Transatlantic Orbits:
The Interplay in the
Evolution of Cities

"Orbits" has become a commonly used term since satellites, space shuttles, and other artifacts have been orbiting around the Earth. Used in astronomy to describe the trajectory of celestial bodies that gravitate along more or less regular routes, "orbit" also designates the cavity that contains and protects the eye, within which the eyeball rotates and moves. In the latter sense orbit defines a frame delimiting the field of an individual's vision.

The Evolution of Cities

Cities evolve constantly. The constant change going on inside a large urban community seems to be a basic characteristic of the concept of the city. The dynamic change is what really makes the difference between a town and a city. A dynamic town, unless it fades away, usually rises to city rank. In a real city things are constantly brewing;

Reprinted from *World Patterns of Modern Urban Change,* ed. M. P. Conzen (Chicago, 1986), 457–72.

change may be gradual, in some periods more accelerated than others, but it develops constantly, more substantially than local people perceive it. Buildings change more slowly than the population and lifestyles they contain. However, the pace of change has greatly accelerated throughout the world since the middle of the nineteenth century, and increasingly so since 1920. These changes, both in the built environment and in the socioeconomic circumstances of the city, are generally resented by the local leadership. I have often found that, unless it displaced them, the first instinctive reaction of the rank and file of the city people, especially of those who feel underprivileged, is to welcome changes in the built environment. New buildings and new activities at first often arouse new hopes for improvement of everybody's condition. Moreover, "modernization" is generally taken as a sign of progress and of enhancing the status of the place.

The "established" leadership stratum looks at change differently. It usually distrusts large-scale innovation that may herald or even implement modifications in the established structures, or unsettle social hierarchies and political processes. Also, most people's tastes are formed early in life, and adapting to new landscapes and styles takes time and tolerance. Baudelaire, who lived through the beginnings of the renewal of Paris in the 1840s and 1850s, expressed this resistance well in a verse: "The lively city changes faster than a mortal's heart." What would he have said had he witnessed the rise of the Eiffel Tower? Still, Baudelaire, while a good analyst of it, was surely not a spokesman for the Parisian establishment. A later and more conservative poet, Theophile Gautier, took long detours around Paris to avoid the sight of the Eiffel Tower. Similar attitudes could be observed among good Parisians in recent years towards the Centre Pompidou! The latter is, however, a loved attraction for large crowds of youngsters.

The twentieth century has seen forests of skyscrapers, large and high blocks of apartments, and a frequent use of glass and metal structures arise in many cities in various countries. In the past, it took at least a century for a new architectural style to be accepted for a few monumental buildings. Then, it may have spread, but only within a restricted geographical compass reflecting a certain cultural zone. The speed of the diffusion of the new styles has been such both in time and in space, particularly since 1920 and even more since 1950, that the evolution of cities in the twentieth century took on a completely different allure and significance from what these may have been in past ages.

I was born in 1915, the year when Patrick Geddes published his famous book entitled *Cities in Evolution*,[1] a milestone in the history of planning. I read it when I was twenty-five years old and found it very interesting, its historical and analytical method stimulating, but the basic philosophy in some way hopelessly outdated. Twenty years of inter-wars life in Paris and a little traveling to some other places had created the feeling of a too rapidly moving present, of processes in which the mortals' hearts will bleed but cities will overcome it all.

Since then, some forty years of transhumance over the North Atlantic has also taught me to beware of projections in time and generalizations in space. Surely some processes repeat themselves through history and in different countries; certain diffusion or evolution patterns are repeated for different innovations. But the city is far too complex an entity, made of too many human beings, groups, and shifting interests; it has so many diverse characteristics, many of them unstable, and is submitted to the influence of so many outside factors, that it could not be easily predictable.

In the spring of 1953, while touring the large crystalline plateau of the Ardennes, which extends from northeastern France into Belgium and Luxembourg, I visited Rocroi, a French frontier stronghold town designed in the sixteenth century in the shape of a pentagonal wheel, with radio-concentric streets, probably by Italian military engineers. In the seventeenth century, its ramparts were reinforced by Vauban. A market town in a poor rural depopulating region, Rocroi seemed fossilized; some empty houses were badly in need of repairs; only two notable structures stood outside the walls—the railway station and the gas service station. Means of transportation had improved but seemed to have taken more life out of Rocroi than contributed to it. A few hours earlier, I had visited across the border the city of Luxembourg. The capital of the grand duchy was another strong, small city, a castle town, dating back to the Middle Ages. Its population around 1700 must hardly have been larger than Rocroi's. But in 1953, although still a small city by European standards, it looked thriving, a capital and an international crossroads. Some of the contrast in the evolution of these two places may be explained by physical circumstances. Luxembourg stood in a *Gutland* on the periphery of the Ardennes, iron ore mines were discovered and worked, and so forth. Still, there is no doubt that the political function of the capital city has been essential to differentiate the evolution of Luxembourg from other nearby towns, despite the small size of the city (only 75,000 in 1983) and of the state.

The striking contrast between these two neighboring towns may serve to illustrate, first, the way in which a city reflects the economy and society of the region around it, and second, the importance of the function it has in relating that region to the outside world. The role of cities must be to serve as *hinges* between the region (or country) within their immediate orbit and the wider orbit in which each city's life revolves in the world at large. That role also used to be rather stable, only seldom changing, due to great events in the past. In this century, both kinds of orbits are being modified constantly by rapid shifts of local or worldwide portent. The evolution of the grand duchy of Luxembourg, which by its size could well be assimilated nowadays to a metropolitan region, has led it in the last 150 years from the status of a feudal land reputed for its forests and wolves, to that of a center of European Community politics and of international offshore banking. Its present prosperity and functions have neither been planned nor even expected.

I went to look at the Ardennes in 1953 mainly because a few months earlier, starting my study of the state of Virginia,[2] I was impressed and puzzled by the differences I observed in the settlement and economy of the Piedmont regions in Virginia, on the one hand, and in North Carolina or Pennsylvania, on the other. A large natural region, divided into political segments which correspond to somewhat different cultural elements and traditions, produces different types of urban life and of networks of cities. This was obvious comparing Virginia to North Carolina. The differences between the cities of their Piedmonts, or their Tidewaters, appeared much greater than the differences between their land uses and types of rural settlement. Cities, that is, urban places of substantial size and diversified activities, became far more independent from their natural regional environments than rural countrysides. This is no novelty, but it takes on special significance when related to the historical past and cultural background. The determinism in a city's evolution is at least of a triple nature: there are the elements of *location* (which encompasses the natural and human regional environment), the *inner economic organization,* proper to the city and rather fluid nowadays, and the *external orbit,* in which the city's life revolves, dynamic network certainly related to location and inner structure but governed by external forces resulting from what happens in distant places.

Modern evolution has enormously increased the radius, scope, and complexity of most cities' external orbits, and has made their inner structures more dependent on external forces. Geographers have been aware of this essential trend for a long time. Statements to this effect may be found repeatedly since the 1880s in the works of Mackinder, Ratzel, and Vidal de la Blache. Still, the majority of the scholars in the generations that followed continued to emphasize the impact of the local or regional circumstances. These have certainly remained influential to this day but mainly in building up cultural variation and political differentiation, and in resisting the full impact of the momentous changes in the modern world as a whole. One could see in the vogue, in the mid-twentieth century, of quantitative models such as the rank-size rules and the hierarchies implied in central place theories derived from Christaller, devices to regionalize the external orbits and simplify the growing complexity of their dynamics. Chauncy Harris was first to apply such quantitative analysis to the Soviet Union network of cities.[3]

Two broader theoretical approaches have been applied to the study of modern urban evolution in more fecund manner: the technoeconomic and the sociocultural. The former emphasizes the economic forces shaping and modifying urban form and society, especially as determined by the advances of technology and the techniques of management. The latter focuses on the interplay between the established social system and local cultures, on the one hand, and the momentum of change caused by demographic, ethnic, and ideological kinetics of the time and country, on the other hand. The conflicts and problems generated mainly by this sociocultural momentum have greatly broadened the field of urban studies, attracting to it many more social scientists and creating new fields of research, such as "social geography," and "urban sociology." To compare how these various approaches and factors interacted on the two sides of the North Atlantic, it has seemed necessary to consider separately the technoeconomic dynamics first and then the sociocultural kinetics.

The Search for the Good Life

Artistotle said that groups of people gathered to form cities in search of security and that they remained in cities for the sake of a good life. For some time this explanation of urban settlement has been disputed. A vast literature and a long history of troubles and of legislation to quell them has claimed that, to the contrary, life in cities is hard and bad, that the good life is to be found outside, in the countryside where the patricians' villas, the old manors, and castles were. As this debate went on for millennia urbanization proceeded and cities grew, multiplied, and expanded. In the second half of the twentieth century, the condemnation of city living reached a quasi-hysterical pitch. Simultaneously, urbanization generalized and accelerated. In the more advanced economies, which, even in periods of depression, enjoyed a higher level of living and a more generous welfare state, the proportion of agricultural and mining workers dropped to one-tenth or less of the total labor force, so that 90 percent of the population lived from urban pursuits, whether in dense or scattered settlements.

Cities were in crisis in many cases but they grew, either in residential population or in the extent of suburban and metropolitan territory. One could tinker with the precise definition and meaning of the terms "city" and "urban," and with the statistics of inward and outward city migration. But it remains that, on the whole, throughout the world, higher standards of health, national wealth, and greater consumption of goods and services have been related to higher levels of urbanization. Between the facts observed *in vivo*, or on the maps, and the clamor against cities, especially large cities, one could not help recognizing a clear contrast and contradiction. Critics of the cities have often answered with the argument that people were still gathering in or around cities, because they were compelled to do so by economic and technocratic forces, and the results were not a good life but an evil situation.

It is usually agreed, however, by both sides of this momentous debate, which seems to involve a great deal of mankind's future, that cities do not *have* to dissolve; they could be made much better. Furthermore, there is seldom heard a call for the sacrifice of all modern technology, a return to medieval, if not prehistoric, methods of tilling the land, of hauling loads, of using masses of controlled (or enslaved?) human labor. On the contrary, we hear that modern techniques and adequate economic planning could more than ever bring about a new golden age, the really good life. It was only a matter of reforming the laws, of adopting and implementing the right kind of planning.

My experience after almost half a century of observations on both sides of the Atlantic does not confirm such a simplistic view of the enormously complex process of modern urbanization. In the ideas, methods, and legislation concerning cities and urban planning there has been a great deal of transatlantic interplay and, indeed, of interaction in the twentieth century. I shall not go so far as to suggest that North America and Western Europe formed a sort of common market for urban technology and ideology; such a formula would not be correct, as will soon be shown. But there exists one vast transatlantic orbit in which all the main planning policies, technological innovations, and methods of management are exchanged, attempted, at least debated. The outcome, however, does not provide a straight, generally applicable solution.

Let us first consider approaches to urban *design*. All those who took part in the designing—architects, planners, administrators, geographers, politicians, and businessmen—moved freely around within the transatlantic orbit. They used a *common lore* of ideas and techniques. It may take several volumes to demonstrate in detail this interplay. Certainly the North Atlantic has been and remains the large portion of space on this planet most intensely crisscrossed by ships and airplanes, telephone connections and other telecommunications, people, goods, and messages. The results in terms of evolution of cities are nevertheless strikingly at variance, not only between Anglo-America on the one hand and continental Europe on other, but even on the two sides of the Channel between England and France, or between Switzerland and Belgium.

First of all, the same ideas are not understood and accepted in the same way. In the 1960s, the Urban Design Committee of the American Institute of Architects tried to assess, and reassess, the situation in American cities. A large project, involving many experts, was undertaken. The four articles published as a result in 1962–63 in the *Journal of the American Institute of Architects* are well worth rereading.[4] The same names of master-designers, the same famous models repeatedly recur on these pages: the ancient monuments of Greece and Italy, the masters of the Italian Renaissance and the modern giants: Fourier, L'Enfant, Haussmann, Ebenezer Howard, Frank Lloyd Wright, Le Corbusier, Burnham, Raymond Unwin, Patrick Geddes, Abercrombie, the team of the Bauhaus, and so on. The committee discussed the historic precedents, the roots, and the modern concepts of urban design, guidelines for the visual survey, basic principles in the practice of urban design. . . . It was magnificent, dedicated soul-searching by the leaders of American town planning, all architects, of course, at a time when American models, though largely inspired by European thought, immediately found powerful resonance in Europe.

The master-designers were architects, that is, both artists and technocrats. They believed that, as Matthew A. Rockwell put it when introducing the project,

Throughout history man has sought to gain greater control over his physical environment, according to the needs and preferences of his times. His attention has been largely focused on the shaping of his cities. His successes, while sporadic, are marked by magnificent levels of achievement and artistry . . . As Carl Feiss has recently written: "A major conversion of architectural practice is now taking place: the comprehensive architecture of whole communities." This task is as difficult as it is necessary. Healthy cities are fundamental to healthy societies.[5]

The pages that follow in that series do not quite support the main points of this statement. Historic precedents of fully planned communities abound, such as the ancient Greek town of Miletus, the medieval *bastides* of Languedoc, Rocroi, and Versailles, as well as Philadelphia and Washington, D.C., to mention only a few. But did the architects actually structure the whole community? Or did they only design the built environment amid which the community adapted, evolved, and pursued a more or less healthy existence? A certain confusion may be detected in the four articles of this report between the city's infrastructure (that is, buildings, streets, open spaces) and the life of the people that formed the local community. Certainly, both are closely related. The interaction between the two has always been much more effective and involved than that between container and contained. But what this relationship actually is has never been clearly brought out.

The designers seem to believe that what they design, if actually built, determines to a great extent the sort of community that live there. Still, it is obvious that the form of the city is often modified against the will of its inhabitants. And it is just as true that, in dynamic periods of history, such as the last 500 years for the transatlantic orbit, tastes and socio-economic structures change faster than the buildings they use. Traditionally in Europe the built environment lags behind the people's needs. That lag may be explained by the impulses provided by technological innovation and the ensuing economic evolution. Thus, the Industrial Revolution attracted crowds of workers into towns before proper housing, schools, and parks were provided for them. Recent urban growth failed to develop adequate means of traffic and transportation throughout urbanized areas, leading to congestion in the buildings and on the streets, as well as in the trains, buses, and other channels of traffic. Altogether, modern urban change brought a double onset of contrasting worries in both Europe and North America, on one hand, the size and congestion of the rapidly developing cities, mainly the larger ones, and on the other, the blight and plight of the declining towns, especially those of smaller size. In France, Paris has been a classical example of the former category, and Rocroi has been typical of the latter.

Similar trends could be observed in the other countries within the orbit under consideration here. In the Canadian Prairie or even in Illinois, one could see many examples of these trends in the twentieth century, and in the 1960s one felt sorry for many small towns of Saskatchewan or southern Illinois. Only a few of them blessed with some special function or industry were holding their own. The state of Illinois created in a half dozen smallish towns, small university campuses which revived those places, such as Carbondale, Edwardsville, and Charleston, but others nearby were sad sights, despite resounding names like West Frankfurt, Venice, and even Cairo. Shawneetown, on the mighty Ohio River, long ago an important business center, is just a ghost town visited by tourists, who wonder at the urban fossil.

There are many "ghost towns" in the American West, chiefly on abandoned mining sites. But that sort of fate has befallen also deserted towns along the rivers that used to be the essential arteries of trade and transportation in the eastern United States, and also along railway lines in the Canadian Prairie. Economic activities on a local or regional scale needed local market towns, transactional and servicing centers in past centuries. In the twentieth century, with larger-scale operations and easy means to overcome distance, transactions and services concentrated in a smaller number of selected locations. These were not always the larger metropolises, as Detroit and St. Louis have discovered, but in places endowed with proper *hosting environments* for transactions on a large geographical scale and with a great diversity of ancillary services.

Historians quote the episode of the Bank of Shawneetown refusing, around 1830, credit to help develop a place called Chicago in northern Illinois; it was too far from Shawneetown![6] The thinning out of agricultural populations and, for a time, the concentration of manufactures may be cited as an illustration of the power of technological and economic forces. Europe did not quite have ghost towns, but concentration factors worked efficiently to empty the countryside.

Concentration led to congestion and social conflict in the larger and more successful metropolitan areas. The European cities lost much of their quality of life in the nineteenth century as a result of the growth of manufactures and of wealth, due to economic and imperial expansion. Decentralization, or at least deconcentration, became the essential worry of London and Paris then and, even more, during the twentieth century. North America came to the same concerns after 1920 and more acutely after 1950. Urban designers of different origins offered a recipe for the good life in an urbanized and industrialized country, to cure the ills of over-concentration and congestion, which has been very popular for a century: surplus growth was to be resettled in well-planned new towns. The *new towns* were to be small, rather self-contained, preferably *garden cities*. While the creation of new urban places, many of which became cities, has been a normal occurrence in the process of land settlement for ages, few of these were originally and systematically planned, except perhaps by colonial powers (for example, Spain in the Americas). Each of these towns established a center amid unstructured territory. The new towns, advocated in the nineteenth century and often implemented in the twentieth, proceeded from a special philosophy of decentralization of congested large cities not only to relieve the pressures within them but even more to provide an urban environment conducive to a good life. The French dreamers Ledoux and Fourier started the concept (especially the *phalanstere*). Ebenezer Howard really formulated both the theory and plan of modern new towns in his *Garden Cities of To-morrow*, first published in 1898.[7] All the nineteenth century new town proposals were offered as expressions of social reforms, to achieve, with the good life, a better society. Howard offered the most reasonable design, and he was considered the real father of the new town theory.

What developed under the "new town" label varied greatly from one country to another and evolved fast. Books have been written repeatedly on this theme and I shall not attempt to summarize the ideas, the implementation, and the debates that arose. It is, however, relevant to make two points at this juncture. First, while the same ideas and technical means were available and well known throughout the whole transatlantic orbit, the implementation or lack of it varied with national and regional cultures and politics. Second, planners used the new town ideas more to decentralize large cities than to achieve social reform. In France, after 1960, new towns, particularly around Paris, were aimed at a better structure of sweeping suburban sprawl. Once again, a type of built environment became the aim, the purpose, and the ingredients for a good urban life. It was expected to determine human mood and behavior. When one considers the diversity of towns and experiments that ensued in a dozen countries, one realizes that the population in fact determined the outcome locally, especially the use of what was built.

New towns helped to decentralize. In a few cases they did not alleviate the pressures in the neighboring central city. In other cases they sucked out so much of the growth from the central city, when the latter was not booming, that only more decline and greater problems ensued for the central old nucleus, modifying the sort of crisis that developed but also deepening or accelerating it. Liverpool and Newcastle-upon-Tyne may be cases in point. The basic facts that I have observed in my own urban transhumance indicate that the evolution of society and regional cultural diversity have been essential factors in determining both the forms and the conflicts in the evolution of cities. In brief, the people have used cities and suburbs for their purposes and ideas; they have not obeyed or even respected what the planners and architects have tried to impose on the city attempting to control the population and the quality of life.

The City Is the People

Under that title, the American architect Henry Churchill published in 1940 a thoughtful and stimulating book.[8] He thought the population, with its tastes, moods, and diverse trends, should be given more attention by architects and city planners, because that was the most determinant factor in urban evolution. I remember vividly a long conversation once with Henry Churchill in Rittenhouse Square in Philadelphia, while I was working on my book, *Megalopolis*.[9] He had been traveling recently in France. He spoke of the gradual change he observed, visiting churches in the South of France, in the expression of the Madonnas, from the soft and benevolent expression of the ones of Provence to the severe and rigorous of those near the Spanish Pyrenees. He also referred to the symbolism of monuments in Paris, that the Arc de Triomphe signaled the end of a long period opened by Greco-Roman architects, while the Eiffel Tower heralded the new era of history opening up in our century with skyscraping, liberation from old molds, and new engineering taking over the design of the environment. Gifted artists just express the trends and traditions in the local people's spirit.

In 1966, the Council of the World Society for Ekistics, founded a year earlier at meetings in London, met in Paris to elaborate the statutes of the association. We sat in the gold and purple splendor of one of the most decorated rooms of the Palais-Royal. Constantinos Doxiadis spoke on the definition of ekistics, a new "science of human settlements." Listening to him, Buckminster Fuller registered disapproval by saying, "I do not think we should emphasize 'settlements.' I see much of the young all around the world; they are not interested in settlement." Asked by the chairman, Lord Llewellyn-Davies, what the youth was then interested in, Bucky answered: "Unsettlement." Since 1967, he was many times proven right on both sides of the Atlantic. That our time is one of unsettlement in all the meanings of the word is not the result of urbanization, and the consequent problems could not be solved just by urban policy and design. Rather, modern cities and urban change are a product of the unsettlement. They should be managed by taking into account these kinetics decided upon by the people.

Concluding its report, the A.I.A. Urban Design Committee had taken into consideration human scale and human vision, popular needs and traditions. It still emphasized form as a determinant:

Form is the idea; design, its fulfilment. As the scale of design increases in a city, as the participations multiply, we have what David Crane calls the city of a thousand designers. They are the many people who act on the basis of the form concept which is furnished in an urban design plan. The thousand designers fulfill the promise of the initial form.[10]

Architects are not alone in being preoccupied with form. So are also the geographers, as form delineates sections of space and provides some geometrical frame and appearance of stability. In our time, however, these approaches seem outdated. Moreover, the purely morphological approach is constricting for the understanding of the dynamic phenomena developing in modern urban space.

Let us return to what has happened since Ebenezer Howard to the new towns concept. The garden city Howard offered for tomorrow by 1900 would have been excellent for the nineteenth century. Welwyn Garden City has been a success, but this was because it evolved very fast after the 1930s into a satellite in the regional orbit of London, taking on a character which would have greatly surprised Howard, if he could have looked at it in 1985. It influenced the thinking of Rexford Tugwell, director of the U.S. Resettlement Administration in 1935–36, when he proposed a Greenbelt Town Program. The program was defeated, for it seemed too disturbing to those already established in the areas concerned, and too "socialist" to the consensus of powerful private interests working on urbanization. Some new towns were nevertheless established in the United States after careful planning: first, to answer wartime urgent needs, such as Levittown, New York, and Oak Ridge, Tennessee; later, in congested interurban locations and by private rather than government initiative, such as Levittown, Pennsylvania, Reston, Virginia, and Columbia, Maryland.

In France new towns succeeded on the contrary as governmental foundations on public land. The decisive step there was the first master plan for the Region of Paris, prepared and applied by Paul Delouvrier. He visualized a half-dozen new towns with populations of 2–400,000 each to deconcentrate and structure the growth of central Paris from 1967 on. Some of these foundations have taken on substantial size and are achieving success. But they were, in 1985, just better planned suburbs of a large, still expanding metropolis with a good deal of green space within and around them.

Paris is still extending tentacles beyond what is officially recognized as its region. In Rouen, the old capital of Normandy, new residential neighborhoods have recently arisen next to the railroad station to house families, one member of which works in the heart of Paris. A good electrified rail service makes the arrangement attractive and benefits the "inner cities" of both Paris and Rouen. A comparable relationship shapes up between Paris and Orleans to the south.

Indeed, the attitudes towards the central city and the suburban periphery differ greatly on the continents of Europe and North America. In the United States the middle class has always preferred to live *uptown* while working *downtown*. Not so in Europe. As a gradual gentrification of society occurs, due to the shift of the majority of the labor force to qualified services (better paid, more specialized, and requiring higher education), large masses acquire, therefore, new lifestyles, generally of higher standing and status, despite the aberrant vogue of blue jeans. This effect of technoeconomic progress has met with different reactions on the two sides of the ocean.

In France, the people with status prefer to stay close to the business center, whether they work there or not. The uptown is a belt immediately surrounding the downtown. The former may expand farther away from the original kernel but only following an expansion of the downtown and in the same direction. Thus the best sections of Paris are in the Ville de Paris or along the main axes of historical royal moves to suburban castles: St. Germain-en-Laye, Versailles, and, to some extent, Fontainebleau. The best suburbs like Neuilly or Rueil-Malmaison line the road (and the new R.E.R. line) to St. Germain. When Haussmann rebuilt Paris between 1850 and 1868, he "cleaned up" the central district and pushed the poorer working masses out to the suburbs. This has not been forgotten. The French move to the suburban periphery only if and to the extent that they cannot do otherwise.

In American cities the tradition was opposite: status came with uptown residence. With the gentrification of society, an immense suburban and metropolitan sprawl developed, taking urbanization out of bounds. The emptying central districts of cities were taken over partly by the expansion of offices and other institutional uses of the land, and partly by the poor migrants flowing into the cities in the hope of a better life, that is, better jobs, better schools for their children, and more welfare from richer communities. The result has been often an active and expanding central business district surrounded by a belt of "refugee camps" housing the newcomers who hope to fit themselves first into the lower occupations abandoned by established groups and later to benefit by the process of general gentrification.

Social conflicts between the wealthy and the poor have always been a standing feature of city life and growth. My contemporaries complain bitterly nowadays about the insecurity, criminality, and hostility they feel in modern cities. I am not sure at all that moaning is not basically caused by short memories. Today, even wealthy people dare to go about their business in cities without being guarded by armed escort, which was a necessity, generally accepted, in the cities and towns of days of yore. Let us turn to the medieval history of Florence, or the normal atmosphere of seventeenth century Paris or Amsterdam—all very civilized places—to realize that there was *less* security there then than what we now enjoy. Statistics of criminality are now better made, urban populations and the middle classes amidst them are much more numerous, and the carrying and use of arms is not as readily accepted.

Orbits and Diversity

Such historical comparisons do not mean, of course, that the unsettlement of our time is not disturbing and troublesome. Cities have immense problems. Adapting to the speed and complexity of modern change is not easy. It is undoubtedly a good thing that we have now realized to what extent the city is the people and how necessary it is to study and improve the condition of the people in those gigantic artifacts that are the urbanized areas of the late twentieth century.

Each country, each region, must be allowed to search for its own solutions, its own style of life. No stereotyped recipe will do for a diversity of communities. Perhaps those who concern themselves with the interplay of forces, factors, and places within urban orbits of large and small scale should ponder an idea offered by various modern scholars in different fields. As evolution of living beings proceeds, the major change is not only size but much more the functional alteration, or *mutation*, which restructures the organization in some of their organs. The brain does not produce higher quality of thought by growing bigger, but it may achieve such progress by changes within its organization, the way it functions. The same can be said of society. In 1776, Adam Smith observed that the division of labor in a community increases with the size of the market, and he gave large cities as examples. But the size of a market may increase or decrease independently of the number of the potential consumers, as we have experienced in recent years of depression. It is a function of the organization of the market.

Anthropology and history have shown evolution that accompanied the march of civilization has led to increasing human diversity. British, Italian, or French settlements scattered around the planet have produced a constantly growing variety of communities, of groups at variance from the original kernel. The concentration of population in large metropolitan agglomerations may very well increase this diversifying process around the world. The "melting pot" idea is far too simple for human behavior. Human diversity is just beginning to be studied. It holds enormous promise for the students and cultural leaders of cities, and of the orbits each of the cities construct for themselves, to achieve in an interdependent world the role which they think fits them best.

Notes

1. Patrick Geddes, *Cities in Evolution: An Introduction to the Town Planning Movement and to the Study of Civics*, reprint of 1915 ed. with new introduction by Percy Johnson-Marshall (New York: H. Fertig, 1968).

2. Eventually published as Jean Gottmann, *Virginia at Mid-Century* (New York, 1955).

3. Chauncy D. Harris, *Cities of the Soviet Union* (Chicago, 1970).

4. *Journal of the American Institute of Architects* 38 (December 1962); 39 (February 1963); 39 (April 1963); 39 (June 1963).

5. Matthew A. Rockwell, "Introduction" to series on the architecture of towns and cities, *Journal of the American Institute of Architects* 38 (December 1962): 43.

6. *The WPA Guide to Illinois: The Federal Writer's Project Guide to 1930s Illinois*, with a new introduction by Neil Harris and Michael Cinzen (New York, 1983), 436.

7. See Ebenezer Howard, *Garden Cities of To-Morrow*, with an introduction by Lewis Mumford (Cambridge, Mass., 1965).

8. Henry Stern Churchill, *The City Is the People*, 2d ed. (New York, 1962).

9. Jean Gottmann, *Megalopolis: The Urbanized Northeastern Seaboard of the United States* (New York, 1961).

10. *Journal of the American Institute of Architects* 39 (June 1963): 74.

Urban
Publications
by Jean Gottmann

1949

"Baltimore: Un grand port industriel." *Revue de "La Porte Océane"* 5, nos. 52–53 (1949):11–16, 5–8.

1955

"La ville américaine." *Geographia,* no. 48 (1955):9–14.

1957

"Expansion urbaine et mouvements de population." *R.E.M.P. Bulletin* (The Hague) 5, no. 2 (1957):53–61.
"Locale and Architecture." *Landscape* 7, no. 1 (1957):17–26.
"Megalopolis; or, The Urbanization of the Northeastern Seaboard." *Economic Geography* 33, no. 3 (1957):189–200.

1958

"Megalopolis: Some Lessons from a Study of the Urbanization of the Northeastern Seaboard." *Annual Report, 1957,* Twentieth Century Fund. New York, 1958.

1959

"Plans de villes des deux côtés de l'Atlantique." *Cahiers de Géographie de Québec* 3, no. 6 (1959):237–42.

1960

"The Impact of Urbanization." In *The Nation's Children,* edited by Eli Ginzburg. Vol 1, *The Family and Social Change,* 180–208. Golden Anniversary White House Conference on Children and Youth. New York: Columbia University Press, 1960.
"L'urbanisation dans le monde contemporain et ses conséquences politiques." *Politique Etrangére,* no. 6 (1960): 557–71.

1961

De Dynamiek der Grondstofmarkten. Translated by John J. Hanrath. Amsterdam: Antwerpen, Wereland-Bibliothek, 1961.
Megalopolis: The Urbanized Northeastern Seaboard of the United States. New York: Twentieth Century Fund, 1961.
Review of *Niveaux optimas des villes, Champagnole,* and *Lyon: Ville industrielle. Economic Geography* 37, no. 4 (1961):371–73.

1962

Economics, Esthetics, and Ethics in Modern Urbanization. New York: Twentieth Century Fund, 1962. Pamphlet.
"Mégalopolis: Région laboratoire de l'urbanisation moderne." *Cahiers de la République* 7, no. 46 (1962):590–97.

Review of *New York Metropolitan Region Survey,* by Raymond Vernon et al. *Geographical Review* 42, no. 2 (1962):312–14.

1963

"Economics, Esthetics, and Ethics in Modern Urbanization." *Ekistics* (Athens) 15, no. 89 (1963):197–204. (Summarized from the 1962 pamphlet.)

"Megalopolis." In *The Book of Knowledge Annual, 1963,* 144–53. New York: Grolier, 1963.

"Urban Growth and Planning in Europe." *Newsletter,* The Twentieth Century Fund, no. 46 (1963):4.

"L'urbanisation en Amérique du Nord et en Europe occidentale: Notes comparatives." In *Information sur les Sciences Sociales.* Mouton pour le Conseil International des Sciences Sociales, Paris. 2, no. 3 (1963): 33–52. (Translated into Italian in *Nord e Sud,* Naples, March 1964.)

1964

"Civilisation des Etats-Unis." In *Encyclopédie Visuelle.* Paris: Armand Colin-Verenèse, 1964.

"De la ville d'aujourd'hui à la ville de demain: La transition vers la cité nouvelle." *Prospective,* no. 11, *L'Urbanization,* 171–80. Paris: Presses Universitaires de France, 1964.

"Destin de Paris: Remarques de conclusion." *Urbanisme* 33, no. 84 (1964):66–68.

"Great Capitals in Evolution." *Geographical Review* 54, no. 1 (1964): 124–27.

"Mankind Is Reshaping Its Habitat." In *Metropolis: Values in Conflict,* edited by C. E. Elias, Jr., James Gillies, and Vend Riemer, 3–8. Belmont, Calif.: Wadsworth Publishing, 1964.

"Problemi e promesse dell'urbanizazione." *Mercurio* 7, no. 10 (1964): 41–45.

1965

"The Future by Design of New York City: An Interpretive Summary." In *The Future by Design.* Transcript, New York City Planning Commission, October 14–16, 1964 (published 1965), pp. 156–63.
"Grandeur et misères de l'urbanisation moderne." *Urbanisme,* no. 88 (1965):40–50.

1966

"The Corrupt and Creative City." *Center Diary,* 14, Center for the Study of Democratic Institutions, Santa Barbara, September–October, 1966, 34–37.
"La création de villes neuves." *Revue Economique et Sociale* (Lausanne) 24, no. 2 (1966):111–23.
"Emerging Problems of Growth and Development." *International Conference on Regional Development and Economic Change,* Toronto, 1965. Mimeograph, 1966, pp. 186–94.
"Environment and Ways of Life in the Modern Metropolis." In *North Geographical Essays in Honour of G. H. J. Daysh,* edited by J. W. House, 3–13. Newcastle upon Tyne: Department of Geography, The University, 1966.
"The Ethics of Living at High Densities." *Ekistics* 21, no. 123 (1966): 141–45.
"Megalopolis: The Main Street of the Nation" (reprinted from the 1961 book). In *Perspectives on the American Community: A Book of Readings,* edited by Roland L. Warren, 117–29. Chicago: Rand McNally, 1966.
"Morphologie et modes de vie des villes de demain." *Commerce et Urbanisme: Rapports Introductifs,* part 4, chapter 1. Brussels, Fédération belge pour l'urbanisme et l'habitation, le développement et l'aménagement du territoire, 1966.
"The Rising Demand for Urban Amenities." In *Planning for a Nation of Cities,* edited by Sam B. Warner, Jr., 163–78. Cambridge, Mass.: M.I.T. Press, 1966.
"Why the Skyscraper?" *Geographical Review* 56, no. 2 (1966):109–212.

1967

Review of *The American City: An Urban Geography,* by Raymond Murphy. *Geographical Review* 57, no. 4 (1967):588–89.

Metropolis on the Move (coedited with Robert Harper). New York: John Wiley, 1967.

"Que seront les villes de demain?" *Revue Générale Belge* (January 1967):11–25.

"Urbanization and the American Landscape: The Concept of Megalopolis." In *Problems and Trends in American Geography,* edited by Saul B. Cohen, 37–46. New York: Basic Books, 1967.

"Warum Wolkenkratzer?" *Der Monat* (Berlin) 223 (April 1967):55–65. (Translation of "Why the Skyscraper?")

1968

"The Growing City as a Social and Political Process," *Transactions of the Bartlett Sociey* (London) 5 (1968):11–46.

"A Vision of the Future of the Urban Environment." *The Papers and Proceedings of the International Symposium on Regional Development,* Japan Center for Area Development Research, Tokyo, 1967–68, pp. 49–64. (Summarized in *Ekistics,* May 1968).

1969

"Environment and Ways of Life in the Modern Metropolis." *Urban Affairs Annual Reviews* 3, *The Quality of Urban Life,* 61–94. Beverly Hills, Calif.: Sage Publications, 1969. (Reprint of 1966 article, with addition of discussion with editors Warner Bloomberg and Henry J. Schmandt.)

"Evolution des villes et avenir de la civilisation urbaine." *Revue Générale Belge* (January 1969):161–77.

"The Growing City as a Political Process." *Southeastern Geographer* 9, no. 2 (1969):4–16.

"Prospecting Future Trends of Human Settlements." *Ekistics* 28, no. 167 (1969):281–82.

Virginia in Our Century. Charlottesville: University Press of Virginia, 1969.

1970

"Expanding Metropolis." Review of *Chicago: Growth of a Metropolis,* by Harold M. Mayer and Richard C. Wade. *Geographical Journal* (London) 136, no. 4 (1970):600–602.

"The Green Areas of Megalopolis." In *Challenge for Survival: Land, Air, and Water for Man in Megalopolis,* edited by Pierre Dansereau, 61–65. New York: Columbia University Press, 1970.

Megalopoli, funzioni, et relazioni di una pluri-città, edited by Lucio-Gambi. 2 vols. Turin: Guido Einaudi, 1970.

"Urban Centrality and the Interweaving of Quaternary Activities." *Ekistics* 29 (1970):322–31.

1971

"Forme, funzioni, e composizioni della città contemporanea." In *Enciclopedia de la Scienza e della Tecnica, Annuario dell a EST 71,* 457–68. Milan: Mondadori, 1971.

"Grandeur et misères de l'urbanisation aux Etats-Unis." *K.N.A.G. Geografish Tidjschrift* (Nieuwe Reeks, Groningen, The Netherlands) 5, no. 4 (1971):511–16.

"Office Growth and Decentralization: The Case of London." *Geographical Review* 61, no. 1 (1971):136–38.

"Pour une geographie des centres transactionnels." *Bulletin de l'Association Geographes Français,* nos. 385–86 (1971):41–49.

"The Urbanization Phenomenon and Its Implications." *Plan,* Town Planning Institute of Canada, Toronto, special issue (1971):15–24.

"Urbanization: Planning Human Environment in Europe." In *Citizen and City in the Year 2000,* 82–84. European Cultural Foundation. Deventer, The Netherlands: Kluwer, 1971.

1972

"The City is a Crossroads." *Ekistics* 34, no. 204 (1972):308–9.

"Comments on a Design for Japan in the Twenty-first Century." *The Fourth International Symposium on Regional Development,* Japan Center for Area Development Research, Tokyo, 1972.

Review of *Milan,* by Dalmasso, *Geographical Journal* (London) 138, part 1 (1972):78–79.

"Nuevo caracter de las centralizacion urbana." *EIDOS* (Madrid) no. 35 (1971):61–84.

"L'utilisation de l'espace européen." In *L'Europe en l'an 2000,* Fondation Européene de la Culture, 139–67. Paris: Fayard, 1972.

1973

"The Hong Kong Experiment." *Ecology Poster Exhibition.* Hong Kong Arts Centre, Hong Kong, 1973, pp. 4–5. Pamphlet.

Papers at Seminar on the International Comparative Study of Megalopolises, Japan Center for Area Development Research, Tokyo, June 25–28, 1973.

Review of *Suburban Land Conversion in the United States,* by Marion Clawson. *Economic Geography* (1973):86–88.

1974

"Apollonion: Its Significance for Ekistics." In *D. A. Review* (Athens) 10, no. 87 (1974):18–20. (Also published as "Plato, Aristotle, and Alexander." *Ekistics* 37, no. 219 [1974]:146–48.)

"The Dynamics of Large Cities." *Geographical Journal* (London) 140, (June 1974):254–61.

"Dynamics of Large Cities and Planning Policies." Symposium on Urban Development, B.N.H., Rio de Janeiro, 1974, pp. 125–28.

"The Evolution of Urban Centrality: Orientations for Research." *Research Papers* (School of Geography, University of Oxford), no. 8 (February 1974).

Foreword to *Population and Urbanized Area Growth in Megalopolis,* edited by Clyde E. Browning. Studies in Geography, no. 7, 1–11. Department of Geography, University of North Carolina, Chapel Hill, 1974.

1975

"The Agglomerations of the East." *Times Literary Supplement,* no. 3802, January 17, 1975, p. 58.

"The Centrality of Oxford." In *Oxford and Its Region: Geographical Essays,* edited by C. G. Smith and D. I. Scargill, 44–47. New York: Oxford University Press, 1975.

"The Evolution of the Concept of Territory." *Social Science Information* (Paris) 14, no. 3/4 (1975):29–47.

"The Evolution of Urban Centrality." *Ekistics,* no. 233 (1975):220–28.

"When in Milwaukee . . . ." *New York Times,* June 2, 1975, p. 25.

1976

"The Ekistic Philosophy of C. A. Doxiadis." *Ekistics* 41, no. 247 (1976): 383–85.

"Megalopolitan Systems around the World." *Ekistics* 41, no. 243 (1976):109–13.

"Megalopolitan Systems around the World." *Geografski Glasnik* (Zagreb) no. 38 (1976):103–11.

"Paris Transformed: A Review." *Geographical Journal* (London) 142, part 1 (March 1976):132–35.

"Les poussées mégalopolitaines dans le monde." In *2000* (D.A.T.A.R.) no. 35 (1976):3–6.

"The Present Renewal of Mankind's Habitat: An Overview of Present Trends of Urbanization around the World." *Towards a Better Habitat for the Twenty-first Century.* Report of Nagoya Habitat Conference, Chubu Region Development Research Center, Nagoya, Japan, March 1976, pp. 42–49.

"Urban Geography and the Human Condition." *Man in Urban Environments,* edited by G. A. Harrison and J. B. Gibson, 6–24. New York: Oxford University Press, 1976.

"The Urban Quest for a Better Life." *Improving Urban Settlements,* edited by H. P. Oberlander, 1–16. Vancouver: University of British Columbia Press, 1976.

1977

"The American Quest for a New World." In *Three Europeans Look at America* (with Wilhelm Nolling and Oliver Franks). Institute of Governmental Studies, University of California, Berkeley, 1977, pp. 21–36.

Various entries in *The Fontana Dictionary of Modern Thought*, edited by A. Bullock and O. Stallybrass. London: Fontana, Collins, 1977.

"I limiti dello sviluppo urbano." *Scienza e Tecnica* (Milan) 77, Annuario della EST (1977):265–78.

"Megalopolis and Antipolis: The Telephone and the Structure of the City." In *The Social Impact of the Telephone*, edited by Ithiel de Sola Poole, 303–17. Cambridge, Mass.: M.I.T. Press, 1977.

"The Role of Capital Cities." *Ekistics* 44, no. 264 (1977):240–43.

1978

"The Child in a Moving, Quaternary-Oriented Society." *Ekistics* 45, no. 272 (1978):348–50.

"Forces Shaping Cities", Fiftieth Anniversary Jubilee Lecture, Department of Geography, University of Newcastle-upon-Tyne, 1978.

"How the Central City Works: The Case of New York." *Geographical Journal* (London) 144, part 2 (1978):301–04.

"How Large Can Cities Grow?" *Revista da Universidade de Coimbra* (Coimbra) 26 (1978):3–14.

"The Mutation of the American City: A Review of the Comparative Metropolitan Analysis Project." *Geographical Review* 68, no. 2 (1978):201–8.

"New Avenues for Urban Geography." *Herbo News* (School of Geography, University of Oxford) no. 20 (November 1978):2–6.

"Terms of Employment and Urban Concentration." *Isveimer Bulletin* (Naples) no. 7 (May 1978):15–30, 51–58.

"Urbanization and Employment: Towards a General Theory." *Town Planning Review* (Liverpool) 49, no. 3 (1978):393–401.

"Verso una megalopoli della Pianura Padana?" In *Megalopoli Mediterranea*, edited by C. Muscara, 19–31. Milan: Franco Angeli, 1978.

1979

"Office Work and the Evolution of Cities." *Ekistics* 46, no. 274 (1979):4–7.

"The Recent Evolution of Oxford." *Ekistics*, ibid., 33–36.

"World Cities and Their Present Problems." In *Survival Strategies: Paris and New York*, edited by George G. Wynne, 75–80. The French-American Foundation and the Council for International Urban Liaison. New York: Transaction Books, 1979.

1980

Centre and Periphery: Spatial Variation in Politics (editor). Beverly Hills: Sage Publications, 1980.

"The City and the University in the 1980s." *Selected Papers from the 1980 Annual Meeting of the Council of University Institutes for Urban Affairs. Washington, D.C., March 1980,* edited by Harvey K. Newman. Atlanta, 1980, pp. 3–17.

"Organiser l'espace japonais pour l'avenir." *L'Espace Geographique* 9, no. 2 (1980):162–64.

"Planning and Metamorphosis in Japan: A Note." *Town Planning Review* 51, no. 2 (1980):171–76.

1981

"Japan's Organization of Space: Fluidity and Stability in a Changing Habitat." *Ekistics* 48, no. 289 (1981):258–65.

"Managing Megalopolis in Europe." *Geographical Journal* 147, part 1 (March 1981):85–87.

Review of *Planning Smaller Cities,* by H. J. Bryce. *Town Planning Review* 52, no. 4, (1981):480–81.

Book notes on *Villes françaises, L'espace urbain, Le grand Paris,* and *L'hôpital et la ville. Town Planning Review* (Liverpool) 52, no. 3 (1981): 260–61.

1982

Review of *L'espace urbain,* by J. Bastié and B. Dézert. *Geographical Journal* ibid. 104–5.

Review of *Le grand Paris,* by Michel Carmona. *Geographical Journal* (London) 148, part 1 (March 1982):80–82.

"The Metamorphosis of the Modern Metropolis." *Ekistics,* no. 292 (January-February 1982):7–11. (Italian translation: "Le metamorfosi della megalopoli moderna." *Nord e Sud* [Naples] 29, no. 19–20 [1982]: 45–56.)

1983

"The Bounty of the Tropics." Review of *Terres de bonne espérance*, by P. Gourou. *Times Literary Supplement*, no. 4163, January 14, 1983, p. 41.

"Capital Cities." *Ekistics* 50, no. 299 (1983):88–93.

La città invincibile: Una confutazione dell'urbanistica negativa. Milan: Franco Angeli, 1983.

"The Coming of the Transactional City." Institute for Urban Studies, monograph no. 2. University of Maryland, College Park, 1983.

"Conclusion sur l'informatique et la ville." *Cahiers du CREPIF*, no. 2 (September 1983):226–227.

"Third World Cities in Perspective." *Area*. 15, no. 4 (1983):311–13.

1984

Review of *New York: The Politics of Urban Regional Development*, by Danielson and Doig. *Town Planning Review* 55, no. 3 (1984):376–77.

"Orbits: The Ancient Mediterranean Tradition of Urban Networks" (Twelfth Myres Memorial Lecture, Oxford) London: Leopard Head Press, 1984.

1985

"The Study of Former Capitals." *Ekistics* 52, no. 314/315 (1985):541–46.

1986

"La profezia di Venezia." *Ateneo Veneto* (Venice) 172, vol. 23, no. 1–2, 1984–85 (1986): 5–13.

"The Role of the University in Modern Urban Development." *Policy Studies Journal* (March 1986):429–36.

"Transatlantic Orbits: The Interplay in the Evolution of Cities." In *World Patterns of Modern Urban Change*, edited by M. P. Conzen, research paper no. 217–18, pp. 457–72. Department of Geography, University of Chicago, 1986.

1987

"Megalopolis Revisited: Twenty-five Years Later." Institute for Urban Studies, monograph no. 6. University of Maryland, College Park, 1987. Review of "Urban Policies in Japan." *Town Planning Review* 58, no. 2 (1987):220–22.

Interviews with Jean Gottmann

"Megalopolis: The Super City." *Challenge* 5, nos. 11–12 (1957):54–59.
"Megalopolis Revisited." *Railway Age* (November 6, 1967):18–23.
"Pogovori z delosovei: Dialogues with the Delians," by Milos R. Perovic. *Sinteza* (Ljubljana) nos. 36–37 (June 1976):57–77. (In English and Slovenian.)
By S. Kiuchi. *Chiri* (Tokyo) 25, no. 1 (1980):58–71. (In Japanese.)
"Une città museo? Perché no!" by Luca Muscara. *Marco Polo* (Venice) (1985):76–81.

Index

Library of Congress Cataloging-in-Publication
Data

Gottmann, Jean.
  Since Megalopolis : the urban writings of
Jean Gottmann / edited by Jean Gottmann
and Robert A. Harper.
      p. cm.
  Contains excerpts from author's Megalopo-
lis originally published by the Twentieth Cen-
tury Fund in 1961.
  Bibliography: p.
  Includes index.
  ISBN 0-8108-3812-6 (alk. paper).—ISBN
0-8018-3927-0 (pbk. : alk. paper)
    1. Cities and towns.   2. Cities and towns—
Growth. 3. Metropolitan areas. I. Harper,
Robert Alexander. II. Gottmann, Jean.
Megalopolis. Selections. 1989. III. Title.
HT155.G68   1990
307.76'0974—dc20   89-45484
                                              CIP

Lightning Source UK Ltd.
Milton Keynes UK
UKOW02f2130270317
297630UK00001B/29/P